The hijacking of the Enigma machine and its dramatic return to the glare of the *Newsnight* programme certainly brought Bletchley Park to the public's attention in a way that the villain who perpetrated the crime had probably never intended. There are many excellent books and articles and a website covering the various aspects of Bletchley Park's codebreaking activities and the uses made of its secret intelligence in helping to win the war. Christine Large has now cleverly succeeded in bringing the story up-to-date in *Hijacking Enigma* by linking codebreaking and the successful police work in recovering Bletchley's jewel in the crown, the German Secret Service, Abwehr machine. The skills are remarkably similar; determination to crack the problem whatever the odds, lateral thinking and connecting seemingly unrelated evidence, exploiting the psychology of the quarry and waiting for him to make the fatal careless mistake that allows a 'way in', the art of double cross and above all total commitment to the job and keeping your mouth shut in the knowledge that men's lives depend on it. Christine Large, the Director of the Bletchley Park Trust, who has herself demonstrated a remarkable commitment to the job and resourcefulness, says that she hopes that the wartime Bletchley ethos might inspire a 'new generation of pathfinders'. The Trust's efforts and aspirations deserve all the support the public can give and it is to be hoped that the heritage bodies will come together to ensure the long-term future for Bletchley Park that it deserves; this book cannot but help the cause.

Mavis Batey, World War II codebreaker at Bletchley Park.

A mystery worthy of the codebreakers of Bletchley Park.
Robert Harris, best-selling author of _Enigma_, _Pompeii_ and _Selling Hitler_.

An intriguing book – two intertwined tales of mystery and intrigue.
Adam Hart-Davis, TV presenter and best-selling author of _What the Romans Did for Us_.

An astonishing tale of mystery with more twists than a Jeffrey Archer novel.
Michael Smith, best-selling author of _Station X: The Codebreakers of Bletchley Park_ and other works.

With delightful irony, this book combines the fascinating history of Enigma with a modern detective story. _Hijacking Enigma_ gets right under the skin of the investigation, in which the famous Enigma machine was instrumental in its own recovery. I have heard it said many times that 'you don't get many of these in your career!', meaning this type of extraordinary, high-profile case, where an intelligent criminal plays a cat-and-mouse game with his prey. The full essence of the police work is vividly captured in the story, which features many unusual characters and events.
Sir Charles Pollard, Chairman of the Justice Research Consortium, and former Chief Constable of Thames Valley Police.

The Insider's Tale

Christine Large

WILEY

Published in the UK in 2003 by John Wiley & Sons Ltd, The Atrium, Southern Gate,
Chichester, West Sussex PO19 8SQ, England
Telephone   (+44) 1243 779777

Email (for orders and customer service enquiries): cs-books@wiley.co.uk
Visit our Home Page on www.wileyeurope.com or www.wiley.com

Other Wiley Editorial Offices

John Wiley & Sons Inc., 111 River Street, Hoboken, NJ 07030, USA

Jossey-Bass, 989 Market Street, San Francisco, CA 94103–1741, USA

Wiley-VCH Verlag GmbH, Boschstr. 12, D-69469 Weinheim, Germany

John Wiley & Sons Australia Ltd, 33 Park Road, Milton, Queensland 4064, Australia

John Wiley & Sons (Asia) Pte Ltd, 2 Clementi Loop #02-01, Jin Xing Distripark, Singapore
129809

John Wiley & Sons Canada Ltd, 22 Worcester Road, Etobicoke, Ontario, Canada M9W 1L1

Wiley also publishes its books in a variety of electronic formats. Some content that appears
in print may not be available in electronic books.

British Library Cataloguing in Publication Data

A catalogue record for this book is available from the British Library

ISBN 0-470-86346-3

Typeset in $10\frac{1}{2}/13\frac{1}{2}$ Photina by Mathematical Composition Setters Ltd, Salisbury,
Wiltshire.
Printed and bound in Great Britain by Biddles Ltd, Guildford and King's Lynn.
This book is printed on acid-free paper responsibly manufactured from sustainable
forestry in which at least two trees are planted for each one used for paper production.

Contents

CONTENTS

About the author

Christine Large continues a line of individualistic Bletchley Park directors. Her career began with a law degree and includes private sector business roles and voluntary work. She has been employed by the National Federation of Women's Institutes, has been a university lecturer in business studies, a CBI London council member, chaired the governing body of London's largest state primary school and chaired a national charity.

She helped Bletchley Park as a volunteer for eighteen months before being appointed its director in 1998. Christine's mother-in-law worked at Bletchley Park during the war and her father-in-law retrieved Allied spies from overseas for Special Operations Executive. Her mission is to build on the codebreaking pioneers' work, transforming the site into a heritage park famed for education and technology innovation.

Christine lives in London and is married with two daughters. Her hobbies include playing the cello and learning Russian.

Dedication

This book is dedicated to three people:

To the memory of Paul Allen, a policeman who died unexpectedly during the Enigma theft investigation. Paul was a family man and one of the team that recovered the stolen machine. He is remembered with pride by his widow, two sons and the colleagues who turned out in force to salute his quiet professionalism.

To Sir Edward Tomkins, once a trustee and afterwards a patron of the Bletchley Park Trust. Edward has been my mentor and friend, above all sustaining the idea of Bletchley that has fortified me in difficult times.

To Brigadier Tim Pulverman. When I was unaccountably and unceremoniously sacked by the former Trust Board, Tim immediately protested and resigned as Bletchley Park's operations director. It is rare to meet a person with the courage of their moral convictions and I would like to thank Tim publicly.

Acknowledgements

I don't deserve to have such a supportive and affectionate family. Sophie (or 'Sofy' as she likes to be described), elder of two daughters and eighteen in 2003, says her early memory is sitting on my office floor playing with Lego (in a little red bucket with a yellow handle). Imogen, who turned a teenager the year this book was published, draws witty cartoons that restore my sense of humour. I hate losing arguments with Eric, who has a mathematician's intellectual rigour and studied architecture to improve his general education, but he has tolerated my idiosyncrasies for nearly a quarter of a century.

Mavis Batey, Bletchley codebreaker, architectural historian, Lewis Carroll aficionado, crossword wizard, is an inspiration. She is mentioned as Mavis Lever, her maiden name, when appropriate. With kindly erudition, she and Keith Batey improved the book's first draft. Sofy, who reads at the speed of light, told me exactly what she thought of my efforts and Eric tactfully flagged the inconsistencies. Sally Smith at John Wiley & Sons taught me that a good editor is a word doctor, not a scythe-wielding censor.

Simon Chesterman helped a great deal by checking for factual errors, arranging access to people and records. Trevor Fulton tutored my detective work.

I could add a whole chapter of thanks but will conclude by warm ones to the Bletchley trustees, staff and volunteers who have and who are keeping the Park in good spirits and good hands.

Introduction

It is Christmas, 2001. In the heart of London's theatre land, a family entertainer is struggling to answer a riddle without whose solution the handsome prince will be denied his princess. 'Oooh,' he said, 'this puzzle is so difficult. It's just like the Enigma code.' The audience understands the allusion and giggles sympathetically.

The November before, I had attended a Royal British Legion act of remembrance for Second World War heroes. The event consisted of a series of tableaux and songs performed in the presence of the Legion's royal patron, Her Majesty the Queen. There were many moving depictions of Second World War history, often portrayed by young people and relatives or descendants. As is customary, the audience stood to show respect for Her Majesty and the UK's national anthem. The New York Fire Brigade were the year's special guests. In a gesture of solidarity that acknowledged the Anglo-American bond in post-11 September 2001 military and intelligence operations, the audience also rose for them. Then came a tableau on Bletchley Park. It dramatised how codebreakers at the secret wartime establishment in the heart of England's countryside would receive an Enigma message, break its code, translate, extract the intelligence and transmit it for use in planning key operations, ultimately shortening the Second World War by two years. The story ended and the motorcycle despatch rider roared off with his mission-critical information. There was a moment's complete silence. Unprompted, the audience stood to pay tribute, swelling in a wave from the stalls to the top of the auditorium.

This book is a detective story about Enigma. It brings together historians' interpretation of 'Ultra' and the codebreakers' actual story, relating how the Enigma machine began life as a commercial

project until it was eventually 'hijacked' by the German military for wartime use. Ronald Lewin's *Ultra Goes to War: The Secret Story* was the first comprehensive history and the author, who went to see Bletchley codebreakers Mavis and Keith Batey in 1977, admitted in his letter of thanks how difficult it had been to gather the material,

> So far as the rest of the war goes, if I am feeling a bit at sea, I can usually fix my position by taking a bearing on some known point, but when I am writing about Bletchley I feel as if I was constructing a map of a remote and abandoned territory from the disconnected evidence of survivors none of whom, in any case, knew much more than their own patch of ground.

Enigma's technical side had not been written up until Gordon Welchman's book in 1982 (*The Hut Six Story: Breaking the Enigma Codes*). Even to this day, new information is coming to light, often through veterans who provide evidence that deepens our knowledge and affects our overall understanding of the subject. 'I know I have thought a great deal more about Dilly and the breaking of Abwehr of late!' wrote Mavis Batey after she and Keith had worked with Bletchley Park Trust to prepare an exhibition in 2002.

An experienced war historian writing twenty-five years ago faced great difficulties in piecing together a coherent account, much more so than nowadays, when a body of scholarly texts exists (including the excellent *Action This Day*) and much, though not all, the detail of Bletchley's and British Allies' wartime codebreaking establishments has been released from secret realms. Of Lewin's 'remote and abandoned territory', Mavis Batey wrote to me in 2002,

> thanks to Bletchley Park Trust it isn't quite such a remote and abandoned territory and I do think you have been able to encourage a lot of veterans to dig deep and remember their 'own patch of ground'.

Hijacking Enigma interweaves the history of Enigma as a whole with the story of a particular Enigma machine, 'G312', describing the crucial roles played by the Poles, the French, the British and the Americans, who all, in their own ways, captured Enigma to help win the Second World War for the Allies. Winston Churchill was Britain's prime minister for much of the war and he rarely missed an opportunity to stress the strategic necessity of winning battles where breaking Enigma messages would determine victory or defeat. Speaking of the Battle of the Atlantic, he said,

> We never have less than two thousand ships afloat and two or three hundred in the danger zone ... it is the Battle of the Atlantic which holds the first place in the thoughts of those upon whom rests the responsibility for procuring the victory.

After the Second World War, orders were given to destroy Bletchley Park and all its secrets, including the means to break Enigma. It was not until the 1970s that the first inklings about Bletchley Park's work began to reach the public domain, eventually giving rise, in 1991, to a movement to save the wartime site and make its achievements known to the wider world. At the same time, the door was opened to people who would again attempt to use Enigma for their own devices, culminating in the spectacular theft of a priceless Enigma machine from Bletchley Park's museum on 1 April 2000.

My own involvement in the Enigma saga was, almost, an accident. Mary Large, my mother-in-law, had been sent to Bletchley, 'for wartime secret work, which sounded thrilling to a somewhat naïve and inexperienced country girl', along with flocks of other young Wrens (WRNS – Women's Royal Naval Service) recruits. Bletchley was reputed to be the country's best Wrennery! She arrived in 1943, spent her time in Hut 8 and didn't say a word about it afterwards, not even to her husband Bob (one of the few wartime survivors of Special Operations Executive's secret missions to retrieve Allied agents from enemy territory). However, Bob did know where she worked because, as the family discovered over fifty years after the event, he and Mary concluded their trysts by saying 'goodbye' at Bletchley Park's forbidding military-style gates.

So the phrase, 'Bletchley Park', was an unexplained mystery whose significance only began to dawn on me when I attended an unrelated exhibition there in 1996, went on a historical tour of the crumbling and sparsely populated estate and subsequently volunteered to play a part in helping Bletchley out of its troubles. 'BP', one of its shorthand descriptions, had been almost stifled by the secrecy that was once its strength. It was shabby and, day-to-day, rudderless. I had no aspiration to become the Park's next director. Indeed, when the question arose, some good friends in academia and business warned me 'not to touch the place with a bargepole', saying that it would be a career graveyard and that Bletchley Park was regarded as a 'basket case' by most sane people in the heritage field. Now, had I been able to foretell the further controversy and difficulties in which Bletchley would become embroiled before beginning its recovery, either I would have pursued other more genteel hobbies or, I suspect, my family would have divorced me. When I wrote this book's first draft, I did not appear in it personally till the end; I was a somewhat distant public figure, 'the director'. My family was written out of the action, not to subvert history, but because I wanted to protect them from the remembered pain. I could not bear to look at some of the Bletchley files (and others I have locked away for a few years' hence), the vitriol directed against me made me feel sick. As time passed, distance made the memory more manageable and I could confront Enigma's theft as a — very — personal experience. With hindsight, my friends were amply correct about the problems, but they had overlooked the critical factor. Breaking the Enigma code was fundamentally important between 1939 and 1945, but the influence and the practical effect of that outstanding human endeavour and intellectual achievement touches our culture now. I was, and am, hooked.

The real-life narrative that follows features many of the dramatic episodes in Enigma's history. Enigma machine G312 was hijacked in 2000 from Bletchley Park's exhibition, and the violation sparked off a worldwide wave of interest and support that contributed to bringing one offender to justice. Reaction to the theft and the requests for money, the fact they occurred at all, attest to Enigma's potency and romance. I have allowed myself a very little poetic licence in order better to tell the tale. For the first time, I can reveal exactly how the middleman was caught. I have concealed the identity of certain police and intelligence operatives in order not to compromise their future operational status. In some cases, the exact technicalities of surveillance and detection are fudged, I admit, for I think it far more important to preserve their potential for use against serious criminals than to flaunt my inside knowledge by unmasking them. The ramifications of September 11 should give us all pause for thought about 'the need to know'. The high-profile intelligence collaboration between Britain and America after the World Trade Center's destruction in 2001 had its origins in Bletchley Park, whose wartime intelligence feats were protected by Ultra secrecy.

Inevitably, as myth transcends reality, Hollywood has taken a hand, with films such as U571 and *Enigma*, based on the best-selling novel by Robert Harris. Robert, who was appointed a Bletchley Park Trust patron in 2001, inaugurated our first Enigma Festival in September 2000. Marie Bennett, who for many years organised the Enigma reunion around which the (now annual) festival is run, afterwards wrote that, 'The only complaint was that our coaches left too early – a mistake I will not make next year!'

Despite its significance, Bletchley Park does not receive any public funding and its future is not guaranteed. Every penny so far has come from belief, commitment and toil. The Trust's mission is to celebrate and build on the work of the wartime pioneers but it needs capital funds in order to bring the wartime archaeology alive, save the famous codebreaking huts and become financially self-sustaining. A debt that all free people in the Western world owe to the Allied wartime codebreakers is still unpaid.

There are some outstanding books and documentaries on Bletchley Park and Enigma. These have undoubtedly increased interest in the whole subject and Enigma in particular. Conversely, there are occasions on which the truth may have been hijacked for the sake of convenience or profit. How misconceived and wasteful; only go to the source and you will certainly find that the real story is more incredible, more full of daring, more human and more inspiring than anything imagined. The Enigma legend lives once more and Bletchley Park is its umbilical cord.

CHAPTER ONE

Alice digs in

The surveillance officer's identity has been protected for security reasons

The sun split the black horizon, casting shards of copper light across flat, khaki fields. From the hollow tree beyond the wide clearing encircling the graveyard, officer Sandy McGovern had a rare vantage point. He trained his infrared binoculars on the craggy shadows that cloaked the somnolent tombs. Still no movement.

Last night, the church ringers, practising English hymnal music, had broken the tedium. The original bells at St Chad's, Longford, were mentioned in a parish record of 1650 but had presumably been recast when the church was restored. Across the level, open countryside, the sound had chimed true. Officer McGovern imagined large mugs of steaming hot tea and freshly baked home-made cakes. The local clergyman, the Reverend Michael Bishop, ran a spotless parish and he and his trustees had been very understanding about McGovern's operation, once the circumstances had been explained. Consecrated ground would not be affected by the incursion, which was a matter of national security, McGovern had said. He couldn't tell them what the local connection was, of course, but it was left in the air that drugs might be involved.

The brief was engraved in the minds of McGovern and his team. On 1 April 2000, an extremely rare and valuable Enigma machine had disappeared from Bletchley Park in

Buckinghamshire, England, right from under the noses of the museum's staff. An unprecedented police and special services exercise had been mounted to track down the stolen property, but the trail had set as cold as leftover porridge. Then, the menacing letters and phone calls had started coming. With great patience and skill, the police had led the perpetrator into a trap, which it was McGovern's job to spring. So now, on a dank October morning he was waiting, interminably waiting, for the guilty man to turn up and collect the £25 000 ransom he had instructed Bletchley Park's director to bury at the graveside of a certain Alice Fletcher. 'Oh yes,' the officer thought, 'he'll certainly collect his dues. When he shows up. If.'

McGovern eased into a familiar exercise routine designed to keep his constricted limbs ready for action and his brain alert. 'Seventy-nine, eighty, eighty-one …' as he pumped the blood through his weary calf muscles, next the thighs and so on. An almost weightless silvery suit, designed for Arctic conditions, insulated him from the freezing nights, three of them, while he had kept watch over the collection point. Underneath the sci-fi material were layers of standard-issue police clothing, tested by special operations units on North Sea oil rigs and stakeouts in Highland winters. Thin, flexible attire, so he could move swiftly when the moment came.

The pale sunlight was too weak to warm the night-chilled earth and wisps of mist banded together, snaking across the plain, wreathing the graves in melancholy drapes. Friday, 27 October stretched out impassively. McGovern drew a long draught from the water reservoir taped to the inside of his suit and he chewed resignedly on the compact, high-protein rations that were part of the sophisticated survival kit. Despite the training, he was weary, very weary. Two bitter nights with scant rest and the prospect of another day holed up in the meticulously appointed hollow tree. His son's birthday was on Saturday and, with the best will in the world, he wanted to be home with the little feller, not awaiting the pleasure of the suspect's company. 06.59. He clicked on a miniature radio to file his hourly report, so far, entirely uneventful.

At 15.00 the same day, there was life in the graveyard. McGovern shielded his eyes against the late afternoon's glare and spotted a tall, soberly dressed man, whose face he could not clearly see, making his way towards the worn wooden archway with rickety palings, which were age-bleached and stained green, as if colour had crept from the short weeds curling under the stakes. Either side, thinning trees swayed like ageing dancers, ushering the visitor through the entrance. He ducked under the crossbeam inscribed in capitals, 'In Memoriam 1914–18.' Left and right of the centre, two short beams curved up to the roof and between them was a straight strut aligned with the undecorated, weathered, wooden cross atop the apex. The man crunched up the pebble aisle, though McGovern could not hear him, and stopped by a gap in the left-hand row of head-high, conically obese bushes. He looked up to the sparsely populated crows' nests teetering in denuded poplars opposite the entrance, and then scanned the black tombstones, whose faces were made up with gold. More recent residents wore flower garlands, so it was to the older, church-window-shaped memorials by the hawthorn hedge at the back that he turned his attention. Through two yellowing bushes the man saw the appointed destination, 'Chez Alice,' registered McGovern.

Except for the fact that it was a Friday, the lone figure was indistinguishable in appearance from the general run of Sunday afternoon visitors come to pay their respects to the dear departed, with a peaceful demeanour and measured gait. Yet he carried no flowers and tucked under his armpit was a spade. The man was obviously not a cleric or a church worker – he looked too young and prosperous for that – and when he took off his quality dark blue overcoat to hang it neatly over an adjacent gravestone, McGovern could see the glint of a substantial watch around his wrist.

Apparently unconcerned by any prospect of discovery, the man kicked away walnut-toned leaves that had curled up in tubes as they dried, and drove the blade of the spade into the ground behind the grave. 'No qualms about disturbing Alice, then,' was the idea that momentarily interrupted McGovern's watchfulness. The arched stone adjoined a simple rectangular plinth in the same material. There was scant decoration but for the tracery of pilasters at the side and under the apex, a celestial frieze that acid rain and winds had buffed away. Mouldy pockmarks stretched up towards the commemoration, 'In Loving Memory, Alice Fletcher, Longford who died October 14 1923 aged 54 years. "Peace, Perfect Peace."' McGovern's subject cut out a neat square of turf, laid it to one side and pressed on, digging purposefully. Suddenly, he stopped, cast away the spade and dropped to his knees, plunging both hands into the hole. Soft, fecund earth piled up haphazardly around the grave. Animated, he crouched right over the dig, his arms no longer visible above the surface. Out came a bulky package. The man held the find above his head, as if in unacknowledged triumph. Right by the graveside, he removed the oilcloth wrapping and tore through the waterproof layers of insulated plastic and heavy-duty tape that had deterred rodent predators. Then he tidied up the evidence, put on his police cap and went back to the waiting patrol car.

McGovern's radio crackled into life. 'We're pulling out. Get moving.' The stakeout operation was officially over, called off by the chief. Inside the package there was videotape, with a message recorded by the police for the *de facto* owner's representative, the middleman, but he had chosen not to take the bait. The tape had been recovered by one of McGovern's colleagues. 16.00. 'Screw *you*. Mission aborted. Thank God it's Friday!' and McGovern went home, exhausted, stiff, boiling with frustration, to buy his son a birthday present.

Two hours later, the middleman turned up.

His protruding pale blue eyes had surveyed the scene from afar and concluded that his instructions had been carried out. He and his partners in crime had led the police, the media and the Bletchley Park Trust, which operated the famous wartime codebreaking site, by the nose so far. Why should anything change? The middleman had carefully selected St Chad's, which he knew, as a local, because it was in an exposed position, isolated in the Derbyshire countryside in the middle of a triangle between Derby, Church Broughton and Ashbourne. Any police surveillance would be obvious from a long way off. Oh yes, he was a careful man, nobody's fool and now he was about to collect the cash that would pay off the thieves who had stolen the machine and fulfil his client's objective. He himself was mainly interested in the money, though the assignment had been more amusing and challenging than many of his projects.

It was early evening, with dusk beginning to seep through the far-off foliage and darken the already obscure churchyard. He padded towards Alice Fletcher's tomb. Satisfied that the ground had been disturbed and that his reward was close at hand, he pulled on a pair of gloves, standard precaution; glanced around again, constantly vigilant; saw no lights or sign of human activity and started to dig. He was working quickly, couldn't rule out being interrupted; today wasn't a music rehearsal day but you could never be quite sure; had to get clear in case some dutiful relative or unfortunate historian should visit at the weekend; dug deeper, still nothing; empty? There must be some mistake. Empty! Had someone beaten him to it? Inconceivable, he ran a very tight ship. Could his client have double-crossed him? Even if his client had wanted to intervene, the fear of being found out would have kept him at a distance. Had there been a mistake over the grave? No chance, not remotely possible. Well, no chance now for his adversaries. He flung the spade angrily aside and it sparked in the gloom as it hit a chunk of flinty rubble. Breathing heavily from the effort, he drew himself up to his full height. Tall and lean, he tensed his cheekbones, narrowing his cold, angry eyes. He crisped long, hostile fingers under their covering and slowly, deliberately retrieved the spade, made good the disruption. Alice Fletcher could resume her slumber but he planned to make sure that I, the Bletchley Park Trust's director, would be punished with some sleepless nights. Furious, he slid away from the scene in his nearby, well-honed Jaguar.

Next day, I received a message. The speaker felt that he had been betrayed. The Enigma machine would be destroyed. The hijacker was about to exact revenge.

Although the modern-day hijack dates back to 1 April 2000, it was by no means the first time that Enigma had been stolen to order. It could well be the most hijacked machine in history, a history of obsession, compulsion and impossible odds.

CHAPTER TWO

The vanishing

The odds of winning the jackpot in the UK's national lottery are calculated to be fourteen million to one. The odds against cracking the Enigma code make that look like a safe bet. In simple terms, the dice are loaded 150 million million million against.

For the purist, Enigma is not a code but a cipher; for a code works by replacing a whole word or phrase with letters, numbers or symbols whereas a cipher substitutes individual letters in a word. The approach to solving them can be very different, but the terms are often used interchangeably and making the messages themselves secret goes back as far as language existed. Mesopotamian peoples in around 3300 BC developed a universal picture code – pictograms – to describe the world around them, as had the cave painters before them who left messages in paintings and simple symbols. Central American Mayans in 300 BC combined whole ideas and sounds into what we call 'glyphs', representing numbers with dots and bars. Their meaning was undiscovered till 1980. The Aztecs who ruled what has become Mexico from the 1200s also used complex pictures and symbols to record time's passage. Experts have still not discerned the meaning of one 4000-year-old, sophisticated Indian script.

Hieroglyphs were an Egyptian system in use between 3100 BC and AD 600, but it was not till centuries later that the ancient language revealed its secrets. At the very end of the eighteenth century, the Rosetta Stone was discovered in the Nile delta. Weighing three-quarters of a tonne, the black slab was chiselled with text in hieroglyphs; demotics, the business language of Ancient Egypt's scribes; and in Greek – which was to provide the crucial 'crib' or way in to the message. Champollion, a Frenchman who had been a child prodigy, had prepared himself for the attempt by learning twelve ancient languages. Eventually, by studying sets of inscriptions in different languages, he found one common letter, deduced that vowels had been omitted and found that the hieroglyphs, representing sometimes whole words, sometimes letters, started to make sense to him. His mental abilities foreshadowed those of Dillwyn Knox, a prominent Enigma codebreaker.

With written language, we can all remember how, if you write in lemon juice on paper the page appears to be blank. Hold that page over a source of heat and the concealed message gradually appears in parchment shades. One of the earliest accounts of secret writing comes from the historian Herodotus, who chronicled the long-running feud between Greece and Persia in the fifth century BC. Herodotus describes how a loyal Greek expatriate concealed military information for the Spartans by scraping the wax off writing tablets, inscribing on the wood below and then recovering the tablets. Spartans also used *scyltale*, or 'secret stick,' a multi-sided device, around which they wrapped strips of leather, then wrote a message. Unwound, it made no sense. Another innovative method of secret communications, according to Herodotus, had been to shave a messenger's head, write the message on the head and dispatch the messenger once the hair had grown back. This is a branch of secret communications called steganography, which translates as 'covered writing'. Alongside steganography, a form of message protection called cryptography (from the Greek for 'hidden') evolved, whose intention was to conceal the meaning of the message, not just the message itself.

Humans are not the only messengers to carry secrets. From Egyptian times, carrier pigeons have been used to transport information. Early Greek Olympians despatched pigeons from the Games with news of athletic victories. The Roman Emperor Nero sent sporting bulletins to his friends via pigeon post. During the Siege of Paris in the Franco-Prussian War, 1870–71, the birds were intelligence conduits. Pigeons travel one way, flying back to their loft from the place they are released. In the First World War, Germany operated a network of secret pigeon lofts throughout England, discovered only when a passenger aroused suspicion by releasing a bird from a railway carriage. The truth was learned by tracking the winged messenger home. In the Second World War, 200 000 pigeons served Britain, dropping to their destinations variously in canisters attached to parachutes and with other hosts such as parachutists, aircraft and ships. Around 16 500 birds worked in continental Europe, coming back with information from Allied agents in enemy territory. Microphotography was employed to condense up to a million words in dots on a message. At the Allied codebreaking centre – Bletchley Park, in Buckinghamshire – a cohort of forty pigeons carried top-secret Second World War intelligence. To this day, the Indian and Swiss armies deploy carrier pigeons.

One of the world's greatest generals, Caesar, was using ciphers regularly in the first century BC, as revealed in his chronicles of the Gallic Wars. The occasional delivery method, such as attaching the message to a spear, might be unconventional, but he was a classic cryptographer, substituting letters in a text according to a system that allowed the recipient to decipher the message without the enemy being able to read it. Julius Caesar invented his own cipher, substituting one letter for another – a technique that Enigma was to take to unprecedented lengths many centuries later.

Arab cryptographers between AD 800 and 1200 used secure communications to protect sensitive affairs of state, following complex rules set out in *Abdab al-Kuttabb*, or *The Secretaries' Manual*, a tenth-century book with instructions on cryptography (secret message-making). More routinely, Arabs utilised cryptography to protect tax records. Yet their greater achievement was to develop techniques for cryptanalysis, the reading of secret messages without having the way in, or 'key'.

In Europe, it was not until the thirteenth century that the first stirrings of cryptography were documented by the polymath Franciscan monk Roger Bacon. Geoffrey Chaucer, the fourteenth-century writer best known for his *Canterbury Tales* was also an astronomer and cryptographer. The Renaissance of arts and sciences in fifteenth-century Europe was fertile ground for the development of cryptography and cryptanalysis, which found new uses in diplomacy.

There are many reasons why the need for secrecy has caused message senders to conceal their intent, and message recipients or interceptors to wish to reveal what is concealed. Kings, queens, the military, security forces, politicians and businesses had discovered the advantages of systematically keeping messages and information secret but without doubt, the prime motivation for doing so was the presence or threat of an enemy.

In the sixteenth century, a legendary spymaster and a father of modern cryptography served Her Majesty Queen Elizabeth I. Sir Francis Walsingham was in the first rank of Elizabeth's ministers. He was ferociously bright and ruthless, which he needed to be in order to protect the queen's security. Arguably the forerunner of MI6, the UK's overseas intelligence agency, Walsingham had established a network of foreign agents to send him information from enemy territories abroad, where anti-royalist conspiracies often originated. He operated from over thirty locations in continental Europe, as well as Constantinople, Algiers and Tripoli.

Queen Elizabeth I presided over a strongly anti-Catholic regime and her Catholic cousin, Mary, Queen of Scots, had long been under a form of house arrest for fear of her ability to unify and motivate a Catholic uprising. In 1586, Anthony Babington, an intelligent bon viveur with a hidden, political agenda of revenge for Catholic persecution, conspired against Elizabeth. Members of the Babington plot used a cipher and code alphabet to communicate with Mary and took the added precaution of concealing their letters, on several occasions, in the bung of a beer barrel. They were no match for Walsingham, who recruited a double agent to provide the messages ('traffic') and established a cipher school in London to analyse the material. Walsingham's cipher secretary was a fine linguist and outstanding cryptographer, whose work rapidly revealed that Babington had proposed Elizabeth's assassination to Mary. Walsingham bided his time until Mary had confirmed her collusion and Babington had been manoeuvered into naming the co-conspirators. Elizabeth's justice was brutal, swift and final.

New generations of codemakers and codebreakers devised ever more complex means of concealing messages, among which Blaise de Vignère's (1523–96) 'square' is remembered as a huge advance, being a twenty-six cipher code arranged in a square that, effectively, puts twenty-six alphabets at the cryptographer's disposal. Europe's Black Chambers of the 1700s, the most powerful of which resided in Hapsburg Vienna, were code-breaking hubs designed to intercept and lay bare the secrets from diplomatic 'traffic' – usually sealed letters that were artfully opened, copied and put back into the system apparently intact.

Occasionally, steganography and cryptography combined, as in the Second World War when German agents scrambled messages, condensed them to the size of a dot and hid the information in regular text. Recently, details have come to light about terrorist groups using the Internet, an 'open' medium, to conceal secret coded information in familiar places such as digital paintings. The enemies may have mutated and changed their ground, but the need to preserve and uncover secrets is very much alive in our society today, whether for military reasons, or in daily situations that affect us all, such as ensuring the integrity of financial transactions.

It was in the financial sector that Enigma started its commercial life, far from the battlefields of Western Europe that would be Enigma's eventual arena. Arthur Scherbius, an electrical engineer, was trying to sell his wares. He had intended his version of Enigma for the banks, for which transaction security and retaining the lead in security issues are abiding issues and business drivers. In April 1918, Scherbius wrote to the Imperial German Navy saying he had applied for a patent for a cipher machine. Scherbius claimed he had invented a wholly new system of cryptography, embodied in his electrical Enigma machine.

However, the prototype rotor machine was devised as early as 1915. Its Dutch inventors, the naval officers Spengler and Hengel, were prevented by the Navy from patenting the machine though the Navy decided not to adopt the device. A patent attorney whose firm supported the inventors' abortive application was Scherbius's brother-in-law and Scherbius later worked with a Dutchman, Koch, which may explain later, successful patent filings.

The Enigma machine was based on rotors, wired codewheels made of nonconducting material. Evenly spaced around the circumference of the disk on both sides were flat, shiny electrical contacts, usually twenty-six, usually made of brass. The contacts on one side were connected to those on the other side by wires through the body of the rotor in a random arrangement. Each contact represented a letter, so the rotor was a 'coded' alphabet. To encipher a letter the operator pressed the appropriate key on the typewriter-like keyboard, thus completing an electrical circuit into the rotor at the corresponding input contact. The circuit continued through other rotors to a different output and on to a light bulb, which showed the letter as the enciphered version.

Electrical encipherment was not in itself revolutionary. In 1917, an American building contractor, Edward Hugh Hebern, had invented a rotating device for multi-alphabetic substitution using independent alphabets. Scherbius has filed the rotor-principle patent in 1918, Dutchman Hugo Alexander Koch 'reinvented' the rotor concept in 1919, when it had also been invented independently in Sweden. Much later, in 1927, Scherbius bought Koch's patents. These machines all had the rotor in common. Scherbius's innovation lay in the machine's wiring and the ability of its wheels to rotate. Imagine a type of infinite electronic pinball, where the ball is a current whizzing unpredictably along tracks and it eventually pops up in a random pocket.

Batteries provided the current in Scherbius's machine. The operator pressed a typewriter key that completed an electrical circuit through the input plate into the machine. The impulse was twisted and turned through the rotor wiring. The electrical circuit went from the output plate to a bulb. Instead of type appearing on a page, what the operator saw was a letter lighting up on a flat, horizontal glass panel behind the keyboard.

The genius of the rotors was that when a rotor reached a certain position, the rotors on its left would be turned, individually or in groups, thereby altering the routes through which the electrical impulses would pass from the key before arriving at a bulb and dramatically increasing the encipherment options. Therefore, the machine's most important characteristic was that, if the operator pressed the same key on the keyboard over and over again, a random series of letters lit up on the glass panel. The original letter was randomly scrambled through the internal wiring, making it almost impossible to predict what the enciphered letter would be, or to work backwards from an enciphered message to the original text. After one analysis of Enigma's defences, a German cryptographer wrote,

> due to the special procedures performed by the Enigma machine, the solvability is so far removed from practical possibility that the cipher system of the machine, when the distribution of keys is correctly handled, must be regarded as virtually incapable of solution.

The incredible number of ways to set the keys and the machines convinced the Germans who used it in the Second World War that Enigma was invincible.

However, in the First World War, the Germans were comparatively cavalier about codebreaking and they neglected it, unlike the British, who read most of the German codes throughout. Germany was shocked and horrified when Winston Churchill's bestseller, *The World Crisis*, published in 1923, revealed the extent to which German security had been compromised. The British had been reading coded German naval messages for much of the war. A first inkling had come from a memoir published by retired First Sea Lord, Admiral of the Fleet Sir John Fisher. Unfortunately, this publication and other revelations prompted the Germans to reinvent the way they communicated in wartime.

Churchill had become enamoured of codebreaking during the First World War, ironically, due to Germany's coding activities. German battle cruisers were targeting the Russian fleet in the Baltic from the outset of war. About four months into the action, the Russians found a German warship called *The Magdeburg*, carrying material on German codes. Russia, being an ally at that stage, arranged for British naval officers to go to St Petersburg to collect their find, which was handed to Churchill, then First Lord of the Admiralty, in October 1914. Churchill was cock-a-hoop. He immediately realised the strategic advantage of being able to read the enemy's plans, in this case the German navy and the lesson remained with him, to be applied later on in even more challenging circumstances.

Meanwhile, the British Admiralty had been running a deeply secret codebreaking agency whose staff increased as the First World War followed its course. 'Room 40', where the codebreakers worked in what was known as the Old Building, had become the agency's unofficial name. Recruits had come from Cambridge, with classicists and linguists in the majority. They included the frequently startling and highly unorthodox papyrologist, Dillwyn (known as 'Dilly') Knox.

Dillwyn was the second of four sons of Manchester's Anglican bishop. While at Eton, he became friendly with John Maynard Keynes, who later said that Dillwyn had a powerfully confused brain. The lanky Dillwyn also had grace, charm and wit, an aphrodisiac to the writer Lytton Strachey, who fell in love with him at King's College, Cambridge. Knox had a powerful and intuitive intelligence. After the First World War, he spent eight years translating 700 verses of Herodas, a third century poet, from the original papyri. This cryptanalytic feat was typical of the gifted mind that would serve the nation well at a critical time in the Second World War.

Germany in the First World War saw no reason to believe that its codes had been jeopardised, lacking sufficient, as they saw it, anecdotal information or compelling facts. The effect of admitting that the enemy might have broken German codes would have been to compound the military's sense of inertia and unwillingness to face reality, for it would have required battle plans to be changed and a complete overhaul of codes, planning, administration, security and personnel. It was not a prospect that the Germans seriously contemplated and it was an arrogant mistake that would be repeated in the Second World War, with devastating consequences. Nevertheless, the Germans' eventual solution to protecting their messages in the Second World War did give them a formidable basis for confidence. It was the undeniably brilliant and wonderfully complex Enigma machine.

CHAPTER THREE

Rules and regulations

To the casual observer, the Enigma machine looked like a quirky typewriter, housed in an oversized, chunky wooden case. Inside the workings, the voyager trying to trace the enciphering process would have found themself in an electric jungle, after dark, without a map. Enigma was not a typewriting device, nor could it transmit or receive.

The German navy had been underwhelmed by the opportunity Scherbius had presented in 1918, concluding that the low volume of naval traffic did not warrant the machine's hefty price tag and eight-week delivery time. Furthermore, the navy would have had to buy typewriters (included in the cost) to print the output. The German Foreign Office was not swayed either and Scherbius deployed all his sales expertise and showmanship to attract potential customers. Having failed to engage the military for the time being, he turned to the commercial market. This sector used the greatest volume of codes. It cost money to send messages by cable and the longer the transmission, the greater the cost. Businessmen turned to codes mainly with a view to saving on communication fees by shortening the messages. Scherbius's machine had been designed with banking security in mind and he moved quickly to impress his target market. In an inspired stroke, he bestowed on the machine the name by which it would become renowned, 'Enigma', from the Greek for 'riddle'.

At the International Postal Union's congress in 1923, Scherbius printed flyers and exhibited Enigma. The German post office was trialling a printing version of Enigma. It weighed in at a monstrous 100 pounds, was about 14 inches high, 18 inches wide, 26 inches long and had knobs and handles on the right-hand side. A version that took its input from punched teletype tape and produced the output to tape had been developed. By the next year, his company had persuaded the German post office to exchange its annual Christmas greetings to the postal congress, enciphered on Enigma. The press latched on to the idea and articles appeared in industry publications at home and overseas.

Scherbius appreciated that Enigma was unwieldy and took steps to streamline it for the mass market. A version called the 'glow lamp' went into production. It weighed less than a fifth of the hefty printing version and was the size and weight of a standard typewriter. Its three rows of typewriter keys were arranged in the conventional German 'QWERTZU' order and behind the keys in the same QWERTZU order were the three rows for enciphered letters, lying flush with the machine body. Underneath each letter was a flat-topped lamp, which would light up whenever the appropriate circuit was completed. To the left, on the top of the machine behind both sets of letters, the rotors were visible above slots on the lid. The lid could be lifted up and the rotors, held by a spring-loaded spindle, lifted out when they were to be changed.

The Enigma family had started to grow and mutate, resulting in a number of refinements to Scherbius's 1918 prototype. Each rotor was enhanced with an interchangeable, movable ring bearing letters. The ring floated round the rotor, was moved to a given position and then locked with a pin on the rotor. Notches that had been used to move (or 'step') the rotors at intervals were transferred to the rings and the rotor to the far left of the operator facing a machine became a non-turning reflector. The reflector had electrical contacts on one face, not both, and its function was to return the current through the three other rotors but with the electrical impulse following a different route, before exiting as usual to an illuminable cipher letter.

The net result of these refinements was to make Enigma more flexible, user-friendly, cost-effective and, especially, more difficult to break.

When Enigma was at last adopted by the German military, various modifications had been engineered in to stiffen the machine's already robust defences. The procedures for enciphering, sending, receiving and deciphering messages were rigorous and subject to change in order to minimise the slight possibility of the enemy reading the messages. To ignore or modify these procedures was to introduce a systemic weakness that could undermine at least a proportion of the codemaking structure. Discipline was imperative.

Scherbius's vision, adaptability and persistence paid off. Before businessmen could take full advantage of Enigma's attributes, the German military recognised its relevance in the coming conflicts and hijacked it back for use in the field. By 1925, the German navy had commissioned Enigma machine production, in yet another variation of the original design. Security was the prime consideration in specifying the changes. The keyboard was alphabetically ordered and three letters added – o, a and u, accented with umlauts (two dots above the letter). The rotors had been wired differently. Although three rotors were used (plus the reflector, which to an unfamiliar eye looks like a fourth rotor), five were supplied to multiply the options for secure keys. The machine variations were complemented with new prescriptions for operating them and for managing the security of keys, all naturally intended to make it impossible for the enemy to understand a message, even if it were intercepted. In due course, a 'plugboard' was added at the front, vertical to the operator. Its wire loops multiplied the routes for enciphering letters.

A message would often start its journey from land and might begin with a senior command officer or close subordinate writing it out. The watch officer took the message to a command transmissions officer, whose job was to stamp it with the time and pass it on to a radioman who began the enciphering process. Radiomen were responsible for enciphering, transmitting, receiving and deciphering radio messages and they commonly had access to a bank of several Enigma machines.

Only officers were allowed to prepare the machine's inner settings, which remained in force for a matter of days or less. Details of the appropriate settings were provided in books of tables. It was customary to leave one Enigma machine set with the previous day's (or period of days') keys (the introductory part of a message) so Enigma messages that arrived late could readily be deciphered. When the officer had established the settings, a radioman plugged in the plugboard jacks – rather like a miniaturised antique telephone exchange. A radioman then took over, turning the rotors to set the message key. Enigma was ready to encipher.

The radioman took the message and pressed it out key by key on the keyboard. A colleague wrote down the enciphered letter that appeared as a different, illuminated letter behind the keyboard. The message was written down in four-letter groups, with two, four letter 'indicator groups' at the beginning that were copied at the end. The message was annotated with a date time number, a number stating how many four-letter groups the message contained (not counting the indicator groups repeated at the end) and it was given a serial number.

An error in the enciphered text would have produced a nonsensical or misleading result when it was deciphered. Another radioman therefore did a dummy run of the procedure that the receiving radioman on a U-boat would follow. If the message did not decipher correctly, it was corrected.

The radioman's next task was to choose the radio network on which to transmit and the frequency that he used within the network, depending on the time of day. There were networks based on geography, on legend and on history. The names were often chosen to inspire a feeling of prowess and good fortune; for example, invoking by implication the powers of Diana, Greek goddess of hunting. The radioman turned his radio to the frequency and tapped out the enciphered message in Morse code, a series of aural dots and dashes. These signals were relayed by wire or pumped through the airwaves by relay stations and could be repeated several times. If the radioman's job seems privileged from the outside, imagine the actual conditions in which he might be operating.

From the comparative comfort of command control, the message sped to a player on the chessboard of war, perhaps a U-boat in the North Atlantic. U-boats could receive messages up to 40 feet down and the receiving radioman would be stationed in his cramped office, in the bowels of the ship cocooned by the inky deep. Of medium height, mentally tough and physically wiry, he had volunteered for submarine service, liking the independence and the responsibility. Hunched at the desk, able to touch all four walls from his seated position, he would be temporarily oblivious to the sounds and scents that infused every aspect of life aboard. Fetid, stale air clung to every surface if the ship had been submerged for some time as it moved towards a target, skirting enemy-occupied sea and avoiding surveillance. Unsleeping engines resonated in the background, a low vibration that set teeth on edge, drilling through the dark Atlantic underbelly.

Yesterday's dinner wafted from the galley, mixing indiscriminately with human sweat, condensation and machine oil odours in the submarine community. Clutching earphones to his head, the radioman blocked it all out, closing his eyes and concentrating on extracting the Morse signal from a mass of white noise hissing through the air. The ship juddered and his books crashed to the damp metal floor. He was hot, exhausted, hadn't eaten because he had been expecting the transmission, always on vigil. Serial numbers told him if he had missed any messages. Negligence was punished, but sometimes a message could not be received because the U-boat was too deeply submerged. The radioman had committed the enciphered message to paper. His Enigma machine had been set up mirroring the procedure at command control, according to the instructions of the day. He set about deciphering it, translating a letter of Morse to the typewriter – it required some pressure to depress the stiff keys – and backwards the signal span through the rotors and plugboard, finding the right exit at the illuminated panel and ending that stage of transit in the original 'plaintext', the unenciphered message that originated at its German author's hand. A convoy contact report; top priority. He pushed himself up from his hard stool, closed the wooden lid of the Enigma machine, switched off the reading light suspended on a cord over the tiny desk, eased stiffly out of the narrow door, which he locked, and hurried to his captain with the deciphered message. It might have been only a routine weather report, another short transmission, headquarters could have been establishing a key, or a rendezvous with a submarine carrying fuel for the boat, the message might not have been for his particular boat, but this time ... they would be seeing action.

The overgrown typewriter with space-age insides had come of age.

CHAPTER FOUR

A mock turtle

With calculated irony, it was a wartime typewriter that the self-nominated 'Master' used first to communicate orders and opinions to me, the director at Bletchley Park. The letters had been preceded by months of earnest but fruitless police searches and enquiry.

On Saturday 1 April 2000, after visiting hours, a four-rotor Enigma cipher machine had been reported missing from the exhibition in the mansion at Bletchley Park, the Buckinghamshire home of the codebreakers whose achievements probably shortened the Second World War by two years and started a revolution in computing and communications.

Merryl Jenkins, Bletchley Park's administration manager, is the site's professional 'earth mother', always on hand with a word of advice or support. Merryl is a tall, comfortable figure. Her garments flow rather than hang, her close-cropped pewter-grey hair and twinkling eyes recall the younger gamine. On Saturday 1 April, she was the duty manager and she had set off home in the early evening having concluded another day full of satisfied visitors. She had barely turned the house key in the latch when the phone started ringing. It was about 7 p.m. Thinking it likely to be one of her family, she hurried to pick up.

Staccato laughter rattled in her ear.

'Is it an April Fool's joke? Where's the Enigma machine?' burbled John Gallehawk, a volunteer in the archives and museum. Merryl didn't understand at first, the man sounded quite hysterical.

'The Abwehr is missing,' said John.

It took a few minutes to calm down Gallehawk and get him to explain that an Enigma machine had disappeared, that it had been prominently on display in a room at the front of the Park's historic mansion, one of three Enigmas in Bletchley's collection. Hoping that the machine had simply been mislaid, Merryl met John Gallehawk and Carol Moon, the retail manager, on site and searched every open room in the mansion, thinking that the Enigma machine might have been put under a chair ...

'As far as I was concerned,' said Merryl, 'it was just an old box.' She couldn't really remember what it looked like. Old box or not, the police were called and two panda cars shortly deposited a couple of local beat officers. After preliminary formalities and checking the search area, they left, but not before dashing hopes that a mistake had been made and the machine had been mislaid.

'It's astonishing what people walk out with, even washing machines.'

Merryl telephoned me at home in London.

Early the next morning, an understated news release from the Trust reached the day shift of leading news agencies.

> The machine, whose value is difficult to assess, appears to have been taken from a display case while the Park was open to visitors. It was used during the war to protect German secret messages. Enigma machines exchange hands for cash values starting at several thousand pounds.

I was quoted as saying,

> This is a selfish act, calculated to deprive the visitors and students of Bletchley Park of the chance to enjoy and appreciate a unique piece of history. The Trust will be deeply grateful for any information that may lead to the return of the machine.

My first call, once sure that the Trust's then chairman, Sir Philip Duncombe, had been put in the picture, was to the security firm that had agreed to sponsor installation and management of a high-tech security system at the Park. How odd that they had been due to begin surveying just one week after the theft took place. The company's managing director did not falter. Within that week, as the press release stated, the first phase of the enhanced security project was underway, ultimately to encompass asset tagging on all sensitive information and equipment, infrared labelling and television monitoring at two control centres.

Back in Bletchley on Sunday morning, a regional radio reporter, Paul Meurice of the BBC was (as often happened) first off the mark and already running stories that set the tone for the following coverage. Sunday afternoon and evening dissolved in a blitz of reporters seeking information. The news was prominently covered in the national press on Monday morning. 'Hitler's secret weapon nicked,' summed it up. The journalists had done their homework and gave full rein to Bletchley Park's historical importance in breaking the code that the German high command thought unbreakable. The police had put out an 'all ports warning', alerting customs officers throughout Britain that the missing machine might be en route for the borders.

By breakfast time Monday it had been confirmed that the stolen Enigma was by no means a standard machine. G312, as it came to be known by the serial number on the back of its case, had been used by the Abwehr, Germany's élite military intelligence force, to communicate top-secret, high-level infor-mation. There was speculation about the number of these particular machines in circulation. There might be three or as few as one other. To a black-market collector – how could such a rare machine be sold on openly? – the Abwehr Enigma might be worth £100 000. The jewel in the crown of Bletchley Park's collection had disappeared, as mysteriously as it came.

The origins of G312 were a puzzle emanating from Government Communications Headquarters (GCHQ), Bletchley Park's direct descendant and post-war successor. GCHQ had removed its last representatives from Bletchley Park, where it had run a training school, in 1987, due to unwelcome media interest. When the Trust was set up to try to save Bletchley Park from developers' bulldozers in 1992, liaison was formally re-established with GCHQ, which gave a number of historically important items on permanent loan to the Trust for display in its exhibitions. Abwehr Enigma G312 later came through that route but no record of its history was provided. As David Hamer, who has studied for more than fifteen years the cipher machines used by the German armed forces in the Second World War remarked,

> Such a lack of background is not uncommon with cipher machines ... given the secrecy under which they were manufactured, distributed and used and also the fact that many records ... were likely to have been destroyed during the defeat of Germany.

Dr Hamer is small, neat, intense punctilious. He runs long distance to keep himself in shape and is not given to exaggeration. He also knew from his own experience in broking deals for bona fide collectors that there are aficionados, who do not care how high a price is asked for an item, '... all that matters is that they must have it!'

Value is a matter of perception and desire. In May 2000, a much more readily available naval Enigma, 'M4', sold for more than one third of G312's value at auction: US$37 374. The very same day, the same model was sold privately for US$17 500, less than half the price extracted in the public bidding race. At auction in September 2000, an identical Enigma M4 brought US$51 000. Given the 'G' model's rarity, £100 000 was probably far too conservative an estimate. Since most of the museum and site staff and volunteers had little or no idea that G312 was special or different from other Enigma or cipher machines at Bletchley Park, the thief was, it seemed, either a lucky opportunist, a prankster or extremely knowledgeable.

GCHQ has its own, private museum for security-cleared staff and visitors only, though in collaboration with Bletchley Park, it has opened a modest public exhibition in the town museum of its home, Cheltenham. GCHQ's US counterpart is called the National Security Agency (NSA), which is based in Fort Meade, Maryland. NSA's National Cryptologic Museum does have an Enigma model G on display to the general public. The machine's number is not known because it is screwed down inside a secure case whose double plate glass is bolted together.

The unit in which the Abwehr Enigma had been on view could neither be locked nor bolted. It was a waist-high, wooden, rectangular plinth with a shallow glass case on the top, lined in pinky-grey velour more suitable for displaying jewellery or leather goods than priceless historical artefacts. The Trust was desperately short of funds and had procured the case from a friendly retailer who judged it out of date. One peculiarity was that the display tray could be accessed only from the back of the plinth and unless the operative knew how to lift and twist the back panels, it would take some jiggling around to work out how to open the case and remove part of the exhibition.

The fingerprint men arrived at the Park on Sunday morning. Before the visitors had started to arrive around 10.30 a.m., David Marriage, known around Bletchley Park as 'Mr Clipboard' because he always carried one, along with Gantt project management charts and well-worn pencils, organised a thorough search of the site. The feeling among staff and volunteers was that the thief might not have realised what an important machine had disappeared and, having heard the morning news, could have dumped it locally or in the twenty-eight acres operated by the Trust. As many volunteers as could be mustered joined the search party.

'I felt for days that we would find it, that somebody had overlooked it and suddenly it would turn up, "goodness me, why didn't we think of looking there?",' said Merryl.

Bletchley Park is a vast site and its buildings were full of neglected nooks and crannies. When Bletchley Park's code-breaking activities were closed down after the Second World War, Morag Beattie (then Maclennan), a bombe technician, was one of the people winding up the operation. She remembers finding 'thousands of secret decrypts stuffed behind pipes and cupboards and propping up furniture ... and we destroyed them all.' Evidence about the hands behind the theft eluded detection – superglue vapour tests on the now-vacant cabinet neither confirmed nor disproved speculation.

Around the site, the universal reaction was disbelief. Quiet staff huddled around radio news bulletins, volunteers scrutinised notice boards, visitors enquired in hushed tones. It was as if there had been a death in the family and, in a sense, there had. Bletchley Park's existence was fragile. With Enigma's disappearance, the patient had taken a severe body blow, a possibly mortal attack on confidence. The site's operations carried on in a dazed semblance of normality, with the volume turned low. There was only one topic of conversation, from Peggy who was furiously polishing the brass door-furniture to Nigel setting up for conferences. Where was the machine? Who had taken it? What lay behind the theft? Would we get it back? News had travelled as far as St Lucia, the island paradise where one leading volunteer, Mac Hobley, who was engaged in mental health charity work at Bletchley Park, was having an extended 'boy's night out'. Mac's usual cheery sarcasm had been mellowed, he admits, in a haze of rum punch and tropical sunshine. News headlines from the beach bar radio warbled across the sparkling sand, 'A priceless Enigma machine has been stolen from Bletchley Park, England.' Mac could have been forgiven for thinking he was hallucinating.

John Gallehawk, a dedicated volunteer, was close to tears. He blamed himself for the machine's disappearance. A retired reactor physicist, John's technical and academic background prepared him to supervise the cherished collections. He was less suited to more ordinary disciplines and his colleagues had observed an aspect of his character like the White Rabbit in Lewis Carroll's *Alice in Wonderland*, permanently distracted and swinging a pocket watch, in search of a meeting held the previous week. John's moon-like face was gaunt, he had forgotten to put on a tie and he twisted his wispy brown hair absent-mindedly. As one of the Bletchley Park Trust's official liaison officers with GCHQ, he felt doubly culpable. Only he and a very few others were allowed to move the machines. To get into the case, you had to put your hand underneath the back and up inside it. How could such a cumbersome machine have been removed from a non-standard case under the noses of 400 visitors, a duty manager in the mansion hallway, the only exit from the room, and a volunteer roster to check key areas regularly? Gallehawk shrugged his narrow shoulders, he pouted his bottom lip, he tilted at theories Don Quixote-style but found no solutions.

Perhaps it was not removed on 1 April. The evening before, Milton Keynes orchestra had celebrated its silver anniversary with a gala dinner at the Park. Later, when the theft had been publicised, one of the attendees phoned up to say that the Abwehr (as he then knew it to be) machine had been out of its case on the Friday and the caller had been talking to a person in the same room. Neither the caller nor the person has been identified.

The Park tried to maintain a 'business as usual' stance, but the story had broken and, acting like relieved relatives at the tea following a funeral, the visitors became more vociferous, jostling to know where the Enigma machine *had* been, straining to photograph its former resting place and, said manager Merryl Jenkins, 'everybody was ooohing and aaahing, where is it, which room was it in?' The home team's prevailing emotions during the day were shock and guilt. No one knew how Bletchley Park's reputation would suffer, whether its relationship with GCHQ would be adversely affected, if there might be copycat theft attempts, what the effect on visitors might be. There was fervent speculation, concern that Bletchley Park minus the Enigma would lose its growing appeal. Gloomily, a volunteer from the early days of Bletchley Park Trust's formation, Bill Boyes, shuffled up to me. Could he have a word?

'You know I don't mean any harm,' Bill said, but his question was, would we have to shut down? 'It's right serious, this, it's a bad omen,' he said.

I put my arm round his shoulders and replied, in the most convincing tone I could muster, that it might take time but it *would* be all right. Really.

By 3 April, media speculation had shifted to the notion of an insider, prompted by comment from the police, who wanted to interview a woman seen in a small red car parked at the back of the mansion around the time of the theft and in an area to which there was no public access. Experts were describing the Enigma hijack as 'a devastating loss' to modern British history and I, Bletchley Park Trust director, had likened the theft to the disappearance of a famous Cézanne from Oxford's Ashmolean Museum. The Ashmolean's director, Dr Christopher Brown, is a friend and neighbour and I had sought his advice on Sunday 2 April, seeing potential parallels in the situation.

Later in the week, I took an unusual phone call.

'Christine, I'm a wanted woman. They tell me there's a nationwide hunt going on. What should I do?'

It was a dear, eighty-year-old supporter who had been involved in Bletchley Park from the outset of the campaign to save it. Ouida Unger had parked her car at the back of the mansion before she went to the garden centre because 'My legs are getting old you know,' she said. 'Will you ban me from parking there, after all this fuss?'

I assured her she would always have a place at the Park, but said that it would be ever so helpful if in future she could 'have a word with one of the staff' before leaving her car in the grounds unannounced. The car had been a bright red herring.

Theories about an insider rumbled on and the *Daily Telegraph* mooted a connection with opposition to 'my' plans for the site. In fact, the plans were not 'mine', they were the Trust's, but they were closely identified with me and had been the subject of a bitter fight the year before, culminating in seven trustees leaving the Trust Board. Most people do not welcome change unless it is aligned with their self-interest or will not affect their personal status quo. I and about half the trustees believed there was a growing threat to Bletchley Park's viability and that a business plan based principally on museum use would neither give the site the best chance of survival, nor immortalise its world-class achievements. Others had disagreed strongly, though not much openly. The Trust appointed in 2000 rejected the idea of mothballing Bletchley Park and chose instead a mission to build on the Second World War codebreakers' work. There would certainly be new exhibitions about wartime Bletchley Park, foundation of the Anglo-American special relationship. The Trust would also explore how those people and events have shaped the technology we take for granted. Education, from young people to lifelong learners, would be at the heart of everything we did. Trustees considered that Bletchley's codebreakers would be let down if their work were not perpetuated by using it to inspire new generations of scientists, mathematicians, engineers, technologists, linguists, historians ... and politicians. Technology innovation and conferencing were to be important features of Bletchley Park's development. The site had been in suspended animation for as long as anyone could remember. It was time to bring it alive again, animated and bustling as it had been sixty years ago. In other words, looking forward.

Back came a cohort of policemen to comb through the grounds with sniffer dogs. In the areas away from public view, disused buildings and unruly scrub could have been honeycombed with hiding places. A team of fourteen police divers caused a stir in the media and in the lake they had come to search at the Park. I had declined their invitation to don the 'gear' and join in, much as it would have delighted staff and tickled the local press. Arm's length apart, sealed in wet suits that would also protect them from the attentions of pond life, they waded through the shallows and hopped, waist-deep, through the sludgy reeds, searching for the machine. On an overgrown miniature island in the centre sat a cantankerous resident, warily referred to as the 'mutant attacking turtle'. He could give vicious bites (his malign preference was snapping off ducklings' feet) and one of the team was delegated to watch his movements. The divers pulled out a ladder, a German radio, a supermarket trolley and a 1950s teapot. I had hoped they would recover coffee cups reputedly cast away by codebreaker Josh Cooper on pensive evening strolls but they were never found, and of the machine, there was no trace.

Reports that a fifty-year-old Bedfordshire man had been arrested precipitated an outbreak of conclusions haring after evidence but the suspect was later released without charges. 'Milton Keynes police disclosed few details of the Bedfordshire man who was arrested in connection with the crime,' reported *Wired News* on the Internet. 'The suspect was not identified and the nature of charges against him were not explained.' Not generally known was the fact that a fifty-year-old Bletchley Park volunteer, a male telephone engineer, had made a hoax call. Although he lacked the necessary expertise to have stolen the machine, he had been apprehended. Suspense and excitement had simply overwhelmed him; he reacted like a silly schoolboy. As the hoaxer had acted out of character, he was let off with a caution. I had told *Wired* that the machine could be damaged if it was indeed somewhere on the trust's grounds. If it had been left outside it could quickly deteriorate in the British weather, 'which is why police are sparing no effort'.

Details of the elusive machine were posted on the Internet and members of the public were very generous indeed with their time and energy. 'The search for Bletchley Park's missing Enigma machine has gone into cyberspace,' wrote the Milton Keynes *Sunday Citizen*. It had. Emails flooded in from around the world with details of forthcoming specialist equipment auctions, sale catalogues containing versions of Enigma machines, information on dealers and offers of support. Some callers and emailers offered money, mainly in small amounts, but always with heartfelt interest in the subject and ready to do whatever they could, within their means, to get G312 back to Bletchley Park. There was occasional mischief-making. For instance when I got a mildly offensive email whose main point was, 'You (the British) stole the machine ... this was revenge for 1938.' The implication was never quite understood but as with every lead, even the tenuous ones were checked out to the police's best ability. 'And while the hunt continues on the ground in England,' reported *Wired*,

> cryptographers worldwide have offered to help in the search by spreading the word of its disappearance, making it difficult for a thief to resell the machine.
>
> Frode Weierud, a historian and crypto simulation group member from Geneva, Switzerland, said he has studied the Enigma for years and takes its loss personally. 'I hate seeing one of the very rare Abwehr enigma machines disappear,' he said. 'We feel that in helping Bletchley Park solve the case of the stolen Enigma, we can help recover a priceless historical artefact and at the same time give Bletchley Park and historical cryptography some well-needed publicity,' said Weierud.

Bill Glauber, a member of the *Baltimore Sun*'s foreign staff, reported me as being hopeful that the wider community in the USA could help the museum retrieve the machine. Do you think you'll ever see the Enigma again? asked the newspaper.

'I believe we will get it back,' I had said. 'Somehow.' I was not feeling as confident as I had sounded.

Special Branch officers were reported to be investigating whether neo-Nazi sympathisers might be behind the Enigma machine theft and Interpol had been notified. At a later stage, well-known historian David Irving telephoned Bletchley Park and wrote to me offering information on the market for Enigma machines. The police and I considered his invitation, which I declined. A German news programme wanted to interview me, to which I agreed after some reflection. Enigma had been a brilliant German invention and breaking the ciphers saved lives of Germans as well as Allies, so any sting in the interview could be counteracted. I need not have worried about Bletchley Park being pilloried. The crew was young, bouncy and uncomplicated. In the shadow of the guns outside London's Imperial War Museum, the first question was framed, 'Well, we think that the Enigma must have been stolen to order for a group of neo-Nazi sympathisers in Germany. There's a big black market there. Do you expect to see the machine again?'

A dowser was put in touch with the Trust. Rather like diviners who locate water sources by following a forked willow twig, dowsers are supposed to be able, through undefined powers, to find missing people and items. While the police could have nothing to do with the matter officially, they did not discourage any reasonable effort to augment the shreds of hard evidence. Over a period of about ten days, the dowser gave several very specific map references. One identified a location in St Albans, down the motorway towards London, where I had given a talk on Enigma the day before to a branch of the British Computer Society. The room had been full to bursting and the attendees, hungry for a crumb of news about the missing machine.

A second dowser reading identified a house not far from Bletchley. It turned out to be owned by the Trust's chairman. Sir Philip Duncombe's military bearing gave him an added advantage when firing off graphic one-line quips, which peppered his conversation. The police had asked Merryl Jenkins, who had become pivotal in day-to-day liaison on the investigation, to stress that Sir Philip should stay away from the house in Great Brickhill until the police had searched it and ruled him out of any involvement. Sir Philip's sense of humour temporarily deserted him. 'I'm not having the police telling me not to go to my own property,' he bellowed, brandishing his country walking stick. Before the police got near the cottage, Sir Philip had conducted the equivalent of a strip search, from rafters to potting shed. No one at the Park was surprised and no one had truly expected a 'find'.

Staff and volunteers were 'running a book' on likely suspects. John Gallehawk was in second place, preceded by me in the top slot. Everyone on the home team was trying to keep cheerful after an orgy of fruitless fingerprinting and interviews. A great effort had been made to contact all visitors and personnel on site over the weekend of 1 April, as the police had explained that fingerprints were needed to eliminate the innocent as well as to identify potential suspects. Had there been a result, or even a hopeful glimmer, it would have boosted morale. The police drew a blank and we began to feel quite dejected. Public interest in Bletchley Park was welcome, but my colleagues and I were concerned that once the novelty wore off, recrimination might set in. Security was paramount, but so were health and safety, directional signs to the Park and new toilets for visitors. There was so much to put right operationally, so little cash and so few qualified staff to do it. Good volunteers were treasured but they had their own lives to lead and the pressure on staff was visible. Answers to the usual 'missing Enigma' questions became robotic.

'Police fail to crack the Enigma theft mystery,' trumpeted the coverage in early summer. An appeal had gone out to all traceable visitors at Bletchley Park on Saturday 1 April. Hundreds of do-it-yourself fingerprint kits had been sent out to visitors and volunteers and hundreds came back, without producing any new insights. Detective Constable (DC) Dave Barker teased me by insisting on messy, eight fingers and two thumbs' autographs, then palm prints and whole hand sets. It was like being interviewed for a pen at London Zoo. It was entertaining. It hadn't dawned on me that I too, was a prime suspect. Police spokesman Jon Brett told the media, 'The investigation is still active but so far we have no new leads on the theft, nor any new leads on where the machine may have been taken. We will soon have eliminated all the visitors we have traced on that day.' The Abwehr Enigma might have been in Germany or California; both are active markets for electronic antiques. In truth, the enquiry was torpid. After the initial furore, there was silence, a silence that was to last until September 2000, when the first letter arrived.

CHAPTER FIVE

The alphabet cipher

Perhaps more than anything, codebreakers dread silence, the absence of comprehensible communications when they cannot tell if reinforcements lie 100 miles away, or the troops are a step from the deepest abyss. Often, that silence is broken by intuition and luck as much as by intellectual prowess. The *Magdeburg* capture that sparked Churchill's lifelong passion for codebreaking was a good example.

Poland was one nation that could not afford an intelligence blackout, for Germany was a river's width away, poised aggressively on the border. With self-interested foresight, the Poles founded a cipher bureau in 1918 and started to monitor Germany's activity through its coded messages, which they were able to read from the outset until 1926. In that year, the Poles noticed a change in German cryptograms that they deduced to be attributable to the introduction of machines.

There was a curious incident in Warsaw's customs office around the end of 1927 when a package labelled 'radio equipment' turned up, due to what the sender's German representative described as a 'shipping mistake'. The German insisted that the package be returned without being opened, but not before the cipher bureau had identified it as a potentially interesting cipher machine – not a transmitter/receiver – and temporarily hijacked the parcel. An eager Pole who purchased a commercial Enigma for the Polish cipher bureau must have been among Enigma inventor Scherbius's first customers, maybe not realising that it could not decipher military messages. The analysis of mechanised codes after the First World War could not depend on word- and code-based linguistic techniques. New thinking was required to deal with the ciphers being generated by Germany's secret servant. The first machine-enciphered military messages were intercepted in July 1928.

German-speaking mathematics students were sought to demystify the machine and one of their number was Marian Rejewski, a promising young man aged twenty-three. Rejewski had attended a cryptology course run by the cipher bureau at Poznan University. He was deputed to work alone on breaking the Enigma cipher. He devised a set of equations to try to understand the significance of the six letters, the 'key' that appeared at the outset of an enciphered message, but it was a struggle to make the mathematics sufficiently simple to solve. For good measure, not wishing to overlook any clues to the fiendishly difficult puzzle before them, the Poles also called in a clairvoyant. The breakthrough, for which they searched, eluded the mysterious arts, just as it was to do in the Enigma case some seventy years later.

The Polish entrepreneurs did not depend on external stimulus – none was needed – or support but, unbeknown to them, the French were working on parallel tracks. Before the First World War, the French had been relatively successful at cracking German military messages, but their codebreaking strength and effectiveness had atrophied by the late 1920s. Gustave Bertrand, a trained cryptologist posted after the First World War to the French forces' cipher section in Constantinople, decided that the tough new strain of ciphers warranted a strong, surprise attack. Bertrand proposed to solve them by having the message keys hijacked.

In summer 1931, before Bertrand could implement his proposal, fate played into his hands. Over in Berlin, a German who had seized instructions on the army's Enigma machine and its key settings had covertly approached the French embassy. Through their intermediary, codenamed 'Rex', a handover was arranged. The material was disappointingly general but Bertrand showed it to the British and later to the Poles, who pointed out that to arrive at the rotor positions for each message, the rotor wiring, alphabet ring positions and plugboard connections would be necessary.

Rex had only begun to explore his duplicitous protégé's potential. The informant, codenamed 'Asché', exploited the opportunity in order to indulge a taste for fantasy and the high life. Had a camera captured Hans-Thilo Schmidt, his real name, over a series of more than twenty meetings, he could have been pictured in Tyrolean finery with a knapsack on his back; concealing Enigma cipher keys in a pack of chilled food entrusted to a railway conductor, or celebrating bohemian delights in Paris's saucy Moulin Rouge. Schmidt had no compunction in indulging his louche and luxurious tastes, which merely compensated for betraying his own brother, on whose recommendation the German army had deployed Enigma.

The keys for 31 December's daily settings were delivered; more meetings followed. Key lists bought from Schmidt were valuable, but Rejewski was to discover that Enigma's Achilles heel was its opening three-letter message key, which was enciphered twice. Rejewski designed a grille to test which rotor was in use and what its starting position was, moving on to discover where the alphabet rings had been set on the rotors. The plugboard settings were largely irrelevant and the Poles' attack on Enigma started to yield results. Some messages could be read on the same day and the Polish unit was geared up to deal with the increase in volume. Enigma replicas were used to read messages and recover keys. As the German rearmament programme gathered pace, so did the message volume and rhythm of rotor changes.

Machines were invented to provide additional capacity. The cyclometer, an electromechanical device linking Enigma rotors, was useful in recovering rotor orders and settings. An ice cream sundae called 'bomba' 'baptised' the 'bomby', a parallel processing machine inspired one day over dessert. Rejewski's process harnessed six Enigmas to try multiple rotor orders. A correct bomby 'stop' produced text.

Henryk Zygalski and Jerzy Royzcki were Rejewski's two closest collaborators. A notable innovation by Zygalski was a series of square, opaque punched sheets used to track changes introduced by the plugboard. More than 1000 precise holes were arranged in complex patterns on each sheet to mirror the 2601 possible locations. When a lamplight shone through overlaid sheets to illuminate a particular location, Zygalski had got a 'fix'. Rozycki, the third of the codebreaking triumvirate, catalogued wheel order permutations and devised a 'clock' to pinpoint which rotor occupied the right-hand position. All the while, Bertrand and Rex continued meeting Schmidt, supplying information to the allies. Yet the Poles had never reported any breakthroughs. Furthermore, the Polish cryptanalysts had not been given Bertrand's keys!

In December 1938, a new silence descended. Enigma messages became indecipherable because the Germans introduced a choice of five rotors, not the original three. Two of the rotors' wiring was unknown, but at this stage the Germans did not change their method of enciphering the message key and the ingenious Poles again reconstructed the rotor wiring using their tried and tested methods. Plugboard connections escalated to ten in January 1939. Schmidt's transfer to another office abruptly halted the access to Enigma keys. The Poles would have needed ten times their processing capacity to crunch the number of permutations. A gloomy Anglo-French meeting with the Polish cipher bureau in Paris, in January 1939, yielded no Enigma secrets as the Poles had been instructed to be less than forthcoming about their progress. Hitler occupied Czechoslovakia in March. At the month's end, British and French pledged to support Poland, followed by the Germans nullifying their treaty of non-aggression with Poland.

Tension between Poland and Germany stretched their relations to snapping point and once the French had agreed to attack Germany promptly should Poland be invaded, the Poles unilaterally resolved to share their Enigma revelations. The Pyry Forest (something of a misnomer as, while it has trees, it is heavily populated with buildings) was the venue for an historic meeting hosted by the Poles for the French and British in July 1939.

Britain's codes and ciphers organisation had made the transition from First World War and inter-war operations, to a country house in deepest Buckinghamshire. In the centre of a triangle between Oxford, Cambridge and London, lay what the locals called 'the hush-hush place'. The Government Code and Cypher School (GC&CS), had put down roots in Bletchley Park, the seeds of change having germinated some while before.

Early in 1919, realising its strategic importance and perhaps, because it controlled the radio intercept stations, the Admiralty laid claim to the British government's codebreaking agency. Hugh Sinclair, then director of naval intelligence, recruited experienced hands from Room 40 including Dillwyn Knox, Alastair Denniston and hand-picked First World War code-breaking veterans such as Oliver Strachey (brother of Lytton). On 1 November 1919, the Government Code and Cypher School was officially created.

However, by April 1921, the Foreign Office had gained control. Sinclair's successor at the Admiralty had proved weak and there had been an unfortunate political leak concerning Russian solutions. After Sinclair was appointed director of Special Intelligence Services in 1923, GC&CS sections were formed for the navy (1924), army (1930) and air force (1936). Dillywn (Dilly) Knox, one of the most impressive cryptanalysts, was impervious to Foreign Office routine. Like Champollion who deciphered the Rosetta Stone, Knox's training in classics and papyrology bestowed on him an unmatched ability to extract meaning and order from seemingly unrelated fragments of information.

Only Germany's codes and ciphers were problematic to GC&CS. The German Foreign Office used the 'one time pad' – the equivalent to a disposable camera with only one image on the film. It never knowingly repeated and was unbreakable except through espionage. Discouraged by a dearth of traffic in naval messages, GC&CS lost heart, lost touch and missed out on ten years of modifications. Nazi Germany and Fascist Italy assisted Franco's uprising in 1936. The growing aggression in the Mediterranean, fuelled by Mussolini, cranked up message production. By 1937, Knox had cracked into the Italian forces' traffic, which was using commercial Enigma machines supplied by the Germans.

GC&CS shared its premises with what Balliol recruit Charles Collins, who joined in 1938, called, 'another idiosyncratic agency, MI6 HQ'. Collins commented, 'I don't know that any of us had ever seen or signed any document related to the Official Secrets Act. Trust and discretion were taken for granted.' He describes the family-like atmosphere as cohesive and informal, though many of the staff worked independently of each other on a wide variety of tasks and targets.

We nearly all knew each other, at least within the walls. We were very private. Our house admitted no intruders. We were sheltered from public and Parliament. Our work being very secret, there was no ostensible overlap with our lives outside.

Oliver Strachey initiated Collins into the 'crafts of cryptanalysis,' and Collins said, 'I listened to Strachey and "Dilly" Knox discussing avenues into the Enigma problem.'

Recollecting the command chain, Collins said,

Alistair Denniston, himself a very able cryptanalyst, was the mildest of bosses. He had no need to be other. We were all responsible people doing jobs we enjoyed. The only element of authority was the shadow of Admiral Sinclair, the head of MI6, who would have had ferocious things to say if there had been the smallest lapse of security ...

Due to the general rise in international tension, the Admiralty initiated an operational intelligence centre, to which the original solutions of broken codes and ciphers were provided. Germany was about to start churning out a massive number of submarines towards the end of 1938 when, frustrated by red tape, Admiral Sinclair bought the Bletchley Park estate out of his own pocket. (There is no record of his ever being refunded.) Charles Collins was a founder member of Bletchley and attended 'Captain Ridley's shooting party', the rather tenuous cover-story for the group that reconnoitred Bletchley before Sinclair selected it as the new home for GC&CS and MI6 HQ. 'When we moved to Bletchley,' said Collins, 'it was just like the family moving house. Once there, we had an infusion from academic common rooms, people who readily fitted into our kind of society.' Temporary wooden huts were erected at Bletchley to deal with the influx of codebreakers and GC&CS moved there in July 1939. Dilly Knox initially operated within the newly created 'hut' system but by March 1940 he had installed himself and a research unit comprised of bright female staff in a cottage in the stable yard behind the distinctive Victorian house. Definitely a house rather than the 'mansion' it is often described as, Bletchley's ancestral home is a storey short of grandeur; an affectionate patchwork of disjointed architectural styles, each of which crowned a successful trade mission by Sir Herbert Leon, a previous owner. Around this Bletchley nucleus, a huge organisation was to accumulate in order to deal with the Second World War's secret challenges.

Bletchley Park director Commander Alastair Denniston, Dillwyn Knox and Commander Humphrey Sandwith set out to Poland in July 1939. They travelled the 10 kilometres from Warsaw to Pyry with the Polish cryptographers. Denniston's diary note is characteristically circumspect: 'Dinner, Warsaw', and the modest cost, even by today's standards. Dillwyn's youngest son Oliver, recalls as a child how,

still weak and ashen-faced from an operation for cancer, and also suffering from a bout of flu, he (Dillwyn) had silently and stubbornly insisted on making the journey. My mother (who had been his secretary in Room 40 in the First World War) had vainly pleaded with him to stay at home.

The astonishment was palpable when the Poles revealed their Enigma replicas and showed their allies the six bombys. It was like being given the key to a treasure chest. The Poles were unstinting with their knowledge and handed over, in the days after preliminary discussions, heaps of decrypts, Zygalski sheets, the principles of their bomby and, with great generosity, one Enigma replica each for the British and French.

Although, as Rejewski recognised, Dilly was close to breaking German Enigma when they first met, the order in which the typewriter keys and lamps were wired to the entry plate had proved intractable. The Germans were not using a QWERTZU diagonal and Dilly had assumed that the letter order would be random to compound the difficulty. He was wrong; it couldn't have been simpler and he was rendered speechless to discover that the running order was ABCDE. The Poles had made a model with an ABCDE keyboard for their own use. A letter of Dilly's unearthed by historian Dr Ralph Erskine confesses that a certain Mrs BB at GC&CS had been ignored when she made the very same suggestion.

Dilly Knox's record-keeping was even more minimalist than Denniston's, but Marian Rejewski spoke, in 1978, of the immediate rapport between the two: 'Knox grasped everything very quickly, almost as quick as lightning. It was evident that the British had been working on Enigma so they didn't require explanations.' Dilly had been similarly struck. A handwritten note on official stationery, congratulating the Polish cryptologists on beating Bletchley Park in solving key problems of early editions of Enigma was, to quote Oliver Knox, 'the sole code-related writing of my father ... I have ever seen, and that only lately (in 2000).' Dilly's note was accompanied by the present of a silk scarf with a picture of a horse winning the Derby race, a compliment to Marian Rejewski for reaching the winning post first. (The scarf is due to be recreated for exhibition at Bletchley Park.) Dilly also sent a souvenir set of rods, rodding being a technique in which cardboard strips with the cipher alphabet of each rotor were glued on to wooden rods to find message keys.

A few days after the Pyry encounter, Gustave Bertrand fêted Polish cipher bureau chief Bernhard Langer with a slap-up lunch at Drouant, a stylish Parisian brasserie. Commander Denniston twice crossed Nazi Germany in pursuit of Enigma. He arranged for a popular French thespian, Sacha Guitry, to bring back the Enigma machine destined for Bletchley. The box was consumed in Guitry's voluminous baggage and he was handsomely repaid by voyaging duty-free.

Denniston's goddaughter and niece Libby Buchanan recalls hearing her aunt say that, when Denniston returned from Poland, he settled straight back to routine domestic tasks. Customarily undemonstrative and British to the core, he was mowing the lawn – and whistling. 'Uncle Alastair *never* whistled,' said Libby. Denniston's wartime diaries scrupulously record his expenses and very little else. His report on the Polish meeting, released in April 2001, is more forthcoming.

> Bertrand was no cryptographer and never pretended that he was. Any technical staff under him must have been very second rate but he had a genius for making use of others ... Bertrand was, no doubt *inter alia*, a pedlar and purchaser of foreign government codes and I think that, as he never had an opportunity in his own organisation of obtaining results from crypt., he had decided to concentrate on careful purchase as his secret method. I would say he did not have access to very much cash and frequently asked us to go fifty-fifty in a possible deal.

Prior to the Pyry meeting ('I went over with (I think) Tiltman, Knox and Foss ...'), the account says,

> at last, we were intercepting a considerable volume of German naval material and a little military or air traffic. Knox was working on the naval material with intermittent assistance from Tiltman ... we had found that the Italian navy were using the commercial Enigma. This was cracked by Knox.

Knox had reacted badly at one stage in Warsaw and his explosive behaviour has been interpreted as sour grapes because the Poles had succeeded in breaking Enigma. It is true that Knox could be violently surprising. Bobby Osborn (now Lady Hooper) from Hut 8 came off a night shift at Bletchley into the breakfast room and describes an altercation in which Dilly and Angus Wilson suddenly seized a wooden chair each, raised them above their heads and engaged in 'a sort of stag fight with furniture. It was all rather too much after a night's work and we young girls were open-mouthed.' Angus Wilson, who went on to become a famous writer, was excused from Bletchley for a time and taken to some sort of 'lunatic asylum, completely overwrought', according to Bobby Osborn. When he returned, Wilson said words to the effect, 'Take me back there, I prefer it, it's less disturbing than Bletchley.'

'The Polish invitation specifically included Knox who was known both by the French and the Poles to be working on this subject,' wrote Denniston. On 26 July, the first day with the Poles, there was a 'prolonged full dress conference' during which an officer attempted to explain how the Poles had broken the *stekered* (plugboard) cipher, 'which took about three hours with a break for a cup of tea'. Knox 'reacted very badly to the explanation', and 'maintained a stony silence and was obviously extremely angry about something'. When the British got into a car to drive away, Knox, 'suddenly let himself go and assuming that no one understood any English raved and ranted that they were lying ...' The truth of the matter was, as reading Denniston's report reveals, having seen that the 'bigwigs' he so despised did not understand Enigma, Knox assumed they were lying and had 'pinched' the machine and the messages. Meeting Rejewski transformed Knox's opinion and he was full of admiration for what the Polish mathematician had achieved. 'On the second day Knox was really his own bright self and won the hearts and admiration of the young men with whom he was in touch.' If only the first day of formalities could have been avoided, 'and pompous declarations by senior officers had been omitted Knox's mind and personality in touch with men who really knew their job would have made that visit a very real success'. Had Dilly been at all furious, it would have been with himself for overlooking the simple discovery about the 'ABCDE' order, but his typically chivalrous behaviour in sending the scarf with the horse winning the Derby to the Poles better reveals Knox's nature.

Back in the cottage at Bletchley, Dilly applied himself to mass-producing Zygalski sheets, aided by 'his staff' in the Stakhanovite task of making the precise perforations – up to a thousand per sheet in sixty sets of twenty-six. The first set's completion was christened with a punch party. Mavis Lever later pointed out that, 'Knowing Dilly, he would have gone to a lot of trouble to acquire the right ingredients for the punch bowl.' Illness prevented Dilly from meeting Rejewski again and it was mathematician Alan Turing who took up the relay in due course.

The Poles then, through Rejewski, carried the honours for first reconstructing Enigma's wiring and working out a method for finding its message keys. The Polish contribution in making these inroads was not to be officially recognised until sixty years after the event, in an anniversary celebration at Bletchley Park on 25 July 1999.

CHAPTER SIX

Nonsense from letters

There was cause for celebration and concern at Bletchley Park. A letter had ruptured the long silence. On the morning of 5 September 2000, Merryl Jenkins opened an envelope addressed to me and I crossed the floor in the Trust's main office to read it. At the head of the letter was a copy of the identity plate for G312. Trying outwardly to show as much interest as had it been a piece of junk mail, I said to Merryl that we should get a second opinion on the correspondence. I measured the steps along the narrow corridor leading to my first-floor office, overlooking the park at the front of the mansion, and telephoned the police.

The letter looked as if it had been typed on a period typewriter. The characters were old-fashioned and the spacing between words was irregular. Several of the characters were damaged or worn, or the typewriter ribbon had faded in parts, as the text was intermittently indistinct. The author either needed English lessons, or was attempting to conceal his identity.

> I have been asked by the current owner the above Enigma machine, who purchased it in good faith … (in good faith being the operative words) to say and tell you now today, the unwitting person have no ultimate desire of depraving your august self or any one the pleasure to see it again.

The 'new owner' was not in a position, it seemed, 'to freely give the possession for nothing as the large sum is not to be lost (*sic*) that has been paid.' The next demand sent a shudder down my spine, for once the author had been notified that the terms were fully acceptable, there were to be 'no conditions of escape on your part or any other person or official body involved in this matter'.

The owner's representative demanded complete co-operation, money, privacy and immunity from prosecution. He insisted that a notice should be published 'by television and newspaper'. This condition was 'of utmost desire to him and must be done before any further word can be exchanged to you on this matter'. Furthermore, the media coverage was to be 'published nationally'. The self-styled new owner and his acolyte (assuming they were not one and the same person) had a burning thirst for media endorsement that was to be a turning point in the case.

Bizarre expressions peppered the vocabulary. The 'negotiating medium' expected the same 'freedom of entanglement' – in other words, not to be pursued in justice – as the person allegedly pulling the strings. The intermediary was 'not involved only on my insistence that they cotact (sic) you to make this offer and for no other reason which must be accepted by you'. A threat terminated the second and final paragraph. 'If no notice is to be seen by the day of Monday as the 18th day in September, then nothing else is to be said again.'

At the end of the letter was a codeword, 'Inshallah', which translates as 'If Allah wills'. This word and a few other key pieces of information were withheld as they could help determine whether the next contact, if it materialised, were genuine or a hoax. Fortuitously, Merryl had not read the letter thoroughly, though she had recognised it for what it was and had handed it to me.

Watching a party of schoolchildren spill from their coach, a number of thoughts were running through my mind. Hard to say exactly why, but I did not question whether the letter came from people who either had the Enigma machine in their possession, or knew where it was. The number plate could have been forged, but it was the right dimensions, with the appropriate type style and spacing; the two screws had been removed from the middle of the right and left sides, presumably to make the photocopy used as the letter heading, and the plate looked a little worn, as one would expect it to be. In tone, the letter veered from assertion to aggression and it alternated between sounding obsequious and bombastic. Precise in parts, it established principles that were to become recurring themes throughout the extraordinary saga, particularly the obsession to be recognised as acting 'in good faith'.

After making a statement to Detective Chief Inspector (DCI) Chesterman, who collected the letter, Merryl Jenkins and I were too preoccupied with the schedule of meetings, Board papers and visits, to pay much attention to the day's most unusual demands. English Heritage was making a series of tours in order to prepare an assessment of the Trust's new plans for the site; a planning application was mooted; the Bletchley regeneration partnership, which I chaired, had a meeting that week. Simon Chesterman telephoned me on my mobile phone that afternoon. A special summit with the police was proposed. It was to be kept secret from everyone else at the Bletchley Park Trust, or described as a routine meeting, if it became necessary.

Time was short and, mindful of the warning in the letter, the police and I agreed to discuss strategy for communicating with the media. Meanwhile, nothing was said, nothing at all. Modern-day Bletchley's ground fertilised the grapevine at an alarming rate and the swiftest way to start a story running was to ask someone to keep it quiet. Having learned from experience, the police decided to mention nothing of substance to anyone other than me. On the one hand, this meant that the vine withered overnight; on the other, it imposed an exacting burden that was, for the time being, impossible to rationalise or explain. My credibility with trustees depended on their belief in me. Whatever I felt in private, the proverbial British stiff upper lip had to be maintained in public; the trustees looked to me and I expected it of myself. However, the leaks did not entirely dry up. On a number of occasions, enterprising journalists tested out theories that had been launched by a police press officer trading snippets of information for personal prestige.

The person, who 'in good faith' had transmitted G312's new owner's instructions, had specified an 18 September deadline for national media coverage. On 11 September, Bletchley Park had decided to remind its supporters that the Trust's plans were making good progress. A news release of the day talked about an academic alliance with Royal Holloway's (part of London University) history department and a collaboration with the son of Alan Turing's mentor, Max Newman. Notably, a private collector of intelligence memorabilia had entrusted Bletchley to display an exceptionally fine original four-wheel Enigma from his collection. It could not replace the Abwehr machine, but it was a public vote of confidence.

Thames Valley Police issued two national news releases on 12 September. The first, entitled, 'Mysterious disappearance of wartime relic', referred confidently to three and four 'rota' (*sic*) machines and mentioned the ransom letter almost as an aside. Senior Thames Valley Police officers had commandeered a pile of books to study the Bletchley Park background but their knowledge of 'rotors' had not permeated the ranks. 'A "significant" development in Enigma investigation' publicised the press conference at Bletchley Park at 14.30 hours the same day. Despite the short notice and out-of-London (though just 50 miles north) venue, the library in the house at Bletchley Park could barely contain the rampant media interest.

'"Middleman" in ransom demand for Enigma.' 'Enigma thief's code baffles detectives.' 'I've got lost code machine.' According to the *Daily Telegraph*,

> Mrs Large said that the presence of the photocopy of the registration tag and 'something about the letter' persuaded her that it was genuine. It ended with a codeword which was 'not in the English dictionary' … it was being kept secret so that the trust could be certain of the author's identity in any further contact.

I had emphasised that the Trust's priority was to get the machine back and that the Trust was '… not in the business of getting the author of the letter prosecuted, particularly if he is trying to hand the machine back'. Police sources were also talking up the letter's importance, relayed in the press as 'significant'.

Anonymity and immunity from prosecution had been promised, according to the *Mirror*, 'if no crime has been committed'. The paper quoted 'director Christine Large',

> It seems to us that the author is stuck in the middle of a very difficult situation. The trust doesn't have that amount of money. But if we have to raise the money to get this very rare machine back, we will.

Detective Chief Inspector Simon Chesterman had the closing word, 'They signed the letter with an unusual word. We would encourage them to get back in touch using that word.'

The *Guardian* was one of the newspapers whose reporters had assiduously followed the investigation. In a report of 13 September, it poured cold water on the idea that the 'new owner' could be 'unwitting' and not know that the German Enigma machine was both valuable and stolen, because of 'the worldwide publicity that the theft in April provoked'. Neither the police nor the Trust had revealed the amount the author had demanded, but speculation was in the thousands of pounds. The fighting fund of pledges sent to me hovered just under £5000 and the letter writer's demand was, I had said, greatly in excess of the money available. Nevertheless, the *Guardian* reported, 'Mrs Large said she was prepared to do whatever was necessary to regain the machine for the public.' At the press conference on Tuesday 12 September, I had promised, said *Milton Keynes Citizen*, 'I will do anything safe and responsible to get the machine back,' though, the paper added, that could depend on police advice. Indeed it would. The *Citizen* also reported a 'Park insider' saying, without a hint of irony, 'It is almost as if this person is playing games with us.'

Before the media could give full rein to theories about foreign authors, innocent parties and financial negotiations, a second letter arrived. Posted from a Midlands address, as had been the first envelope, the letter was directed to Central Television News. Central sourced most of its information about Bletchley Park through Simon Garrett, a seasoned journalist with well-tuned news antennae. Garrett did not sacrifice his eventual scoops for short-term gain. Shrewdly, he took the police and me into his confidence before deciding how to respond to the letter's arrival. The media coverage on the day after the conference, 13 September, would have been hard to miss. The influential BBC Radio 4 *Today* programme's listeners took an intelligent and sympathetic interest in major developments at Bletchley Park. Comment in the national press was extensive and well informed. Just over a week since the first letter arrived and before the 18 September deadline was nigh, the author decided to flex his metaphorical muscles. He had been kept waiting. He was deeply 'offended'. 'The Master', his master, had spoken. The Master authorised another letter on 13 September.

> I am instructed by my estemed (*sic*), master to indicate this letter to your goodsel (*sic*) because of the arrogancy of the woman Christine Large, who despite a sincere offer of repatriation the Enigma machine ... has not deemed it fit to reply, a most grave insult to my master.

G312's apparently photocopied number plate again headed the letter. It continued by reiterating the terms set out to me in the original letter. The £25 000 it had demanded to 'repay' the 'new owner' was described as a good faith price, it being, 'not possible that this amount can be lost for an innocent act of the acquisition of this machine'. The closing line was chilling: '... not responding to this final offer will result in the machine to be destroyed as my master will not lose face by any means.'

Peter Spindler, a detective superintendent from the National Crime Squad (NCS), had been in touch with Simon Chesterman to enquire whether Chesterman might want to call on 'specialist resources'. Spindler was a bright-eyed, ambitious activist. His short, red-blond hair had receded to a half-pate whose shine reinforced the aura of a grown-up schoolboy, naturally a prefect and bursting with energy. He had had a hard job convincing his bosses to take on the brief. Usually, Spindler's cases were not the sort he could mention to friends and family, but this was different. 'It's a national treasure,' he had argued, 'and it's very high-profile.'

The summit was convened in Central Milton Keynes Police Station. Getting around the internally featureless building was like navigating the Minotaur's maze without Theseus's ball of string. The awaiting chocolate biscuit cornucopia and assembled acronyms signalled that the meeting was considered top priority. Flanking DCI Chesterman were Spindler of NCS; DI Gerry McGowan, also from NCS and a police hostage negotiator; DC David Jones, in charge of the kidnap and extortion desk at the National Criminal Intelligence Service (NCIS); David (Dave) Barker, the original case officer; and Kim Stowe from British Telecom Security, who had been responsible for guarding the gate at Bletchley Park on the day the Enigma 'took a walk'.

Chesterman explained to me that he and his team were about to take an unusual step. Chesterman was a thoughtful character; a man astute in assessing risk and understanding motivations. He was quite slim (but not as fit as he would have liked, due to the job pressures), and medium height; he had mousy hair whose short cut practically disguised its slight curl. He looked alert and studiously relaxed; not a man to jump to irrational conclusions and one likely to trawl endlessly over information to ascertain the truth. Nevertheless, he had raised my expectations that he was about to impart news of a breakthrough in the case. What came next was something of a surprise. The police had weighed up the options and decided that the most effective way to operate, not something they would generally do, was to take me into their confidence and include me on the investigation's inside track. After the present summit, the same group would be unlikely to meet again and everyone understood that the information divulged was not to be circulated outside the room. Some of the finer points are unlikely ever to be made public, as they were not recorded, except in police policy book decisions, personal action notes and in the file I decided to keep just in case it should be needed.

The National Crime Squad, the National Criminal Intelligence Service, Special Branch and ... Bletchley police? 'Who was in control of the investigation now?' I wondered. Were the specialist and security high-ups there by invitation? What were the underlying politics and financial constraints? Was BT Security red-faced? I concentrated on an impressive hand of business cards. One of them cautioned, 'This card is not proof of the bearer's identity.' The scene seemed straight out of a Hollywood B-movie screenplay. Departmental representatives were jockeying for position though they were there at the local force's invitation. I was reminded of wartime inter-service rivalries (worse in America than in Britain) and the wrangling for status and resources that had so damaged military intelligence prospects.

While the official turf was being marked out, I pieced together what I had researched about DCI Chesterman's background. Born in Cornwall, his youth was days on the beach and playing rugby. Chesterman's father, an Admiralty scientist, must have questioned his son's decision to join the army at eighteen, a misjudgement that made Simon homesick and unsettled. He returned to his Cornish roots, where an acceptable alternative to science was a career in antiques. His father restored them as a hobby and his mother used to work for a fine arts antiques house. Chesterman junior started to train as an auctioneer and valuer but the pendulum of practicality had swung too far. He found that world 'too airy-fairy.' He applied to join the Royal Marines, but torn knee ligaments from a rugby injury destroyed his chances. Loathe to take money for nothing, he decided to do voluntary work while recuperating and hobbled to the local Cheshire home. Public service had sidled up on Chesterman and the police became a logical choice. He tried local forces, but Thames Valley was first to offer the twenty-year-old an opening. Chesterman revelled in the life, at the expense of his personal relationships. His career took off after he came second nationally in the promotion examinations. Long hours on his chosen path into the CID and squad work, immersed in absorbing and covert operations, working hard and playing hard, cost him his first marriage; pain and disruption he had no desire to experience again. So Simon Chesterman was calm, humane, had excellent interpersonal skills; was, in a nutshell, on the ball and rather nicer than certain colleagues and superiors grappling with the greasy pole.

'... criminals' psychological profile ... press tactics ... someone involved has a grudge against you.' I was trying to 'play it cool' and stay objective and I did not know whether the summit was a kind of test to evaluate my reactions, see if I would 'crack'. One of the police business cards had warned me not to take the bearer at face value. Perhaps they were not who they said they were, could there be a couple of psychologists? My mind was whirling and I crumpled tiredly. The police were doing their job; what did they want of me? The meeting left as little as possible to chance and no available information unconsidered. Concern was expressed about the strain on me personally; the police knew I already had my job cut out to get off the ground the strategic plan agreed by Bletchley Park trustees, as things turned out, only a few weeks after the Enigma theft. The G312 incident had been a most unwelcome interruption to the work of a new Trust Board, appointed January 2000, after the previous board had very publicly imploded in the autumn of 1999.

'... the arrogancy of the woman Christine Large ... the machine to be destroyed ... my master will not lose face by any means.' In the forges of rancour, axes had been grinding.

CHAPTER SEVEN

Serpent!

'. . . The woman Christine Large' was appointed the first director of Bletchley Park since the end of the Second World War, in March 1998. It was a joyless appointment at the time, due to the infighting and petty politics that had preceded it. I had been a Bletchley Park volunteer for around eighteen months beforehand, seduced by the site's history and baffled by the inertia and gloom that encumbered its future. A failed Heritage Lottery Fund bid. Turned down by the Millennium Commission. I soon found myself in troubled waters with no propulsion for the foundering 'SS *Bletchley Park*'. The site's hopes rested on an underpowered craft that had been torpedoed by its own crew.

Towards the end of 1997, I had accepted an innocent 'invitation to take tea' with Sir Edward Tomkins, then a Bletchley Park trustee. A former ambassador to Paris, Sir Edward's diplomatic haute couture had dazzled the Establishment. I left his Buckinghamshire home, which had been crafted by St Paul's Cathedral maestro Sir Christopher Wren, under a cloud of moral obligation. Why 'a cloud'? Take the board meetings.

'I have in my hand a crucial communication,' said the trembling bearer. Although only middle-aged, he found it physically impossible to contain his emotion. 'I insist that the Board give it immediate attention.' In another environment, such an intervention could have caused consternation, but at the seventieth, eightieth or nth board meeting of the Bletchley Park Trust, all much of a muchness, the opportunity was either greeted as a welcome distraction from interminable reports about drains, or in the vain hope that something worth discussing might be on the horizon. Matters of importance were unlikely to appear on an agenda, having been overlooked, kept dark ('Don't worry, it'll be all right'; 'Trust me, I'll sort it out' were familiar credos) or buried in an off-piste 'deal'. In truth, there was no one agenda, there were multiple agendas – individual and shared. It had either always been, or had become, acceptable not to have common objectives, not to work as a team and for there to be no agreed plan mapping out the way ahead. I could see why supporters had got jaded, alienated or swept aside. As a volunteer, I could have walked away, but I didn't. Lots of other voluntary folk hated (and sometimes feared) the prevailing regime, the tantrums, the closed doors. They implored me to stay on and do what was necessary. I fretted that their enthusiasm would wane, because the financial minefield ahead would cause casualties.

The truth was that the Heritage Lottery Fund (HLF) had declined to back a plan invented by consultants and undeliverable by the self-appointed management. The Board's pièce de résistance had been to complain to the Parliamentary Ombudsman, whose technical assessment of the case exonerated HLF and clearly pinpointed where the deficiencies lay. British Telecom, a joint owner of the 58-acre site, had got extremely tired of gratuitous public insults from individuals at the trust and of being confronted with negotiators who, to BT and government landowner Property Advisers Civil Estate's mind, had a conflict of interest. As a matter of fact, drains did become rather important in the scheme of things, because the Trust had encouraged a form of 'heritage squatting' on the site, inviting bona fide hobby groups to occupy buildings without a by-your-leave from the landowners. Many of these stalwarts became volunteer exhibitors when the site opened to the public. Volunteers worked hard and loyally under the misapprehension that everything was under control, but neither they nor the old Trust ever paid a penny for utilities costs to their reluctant landlords and the current Trust brought together in 2000 was eventually saddled with the bill for arrears. Financial management in the early days of Bletchley Park Trust Boards consisted of checking the bank balance at the local cashpoint.

It would be unfair to say that there were no people of good quality on the Board or involved in Bletchley Park. Volunteers did and do play a valuable role and practically all the labour on the site was unpaid in the early years. The then chief executive, Councillor Roger Bristow, was well-meaning, an avid local historian and tireless ambassador, his office piled high with unanswered correspondence. He and Tony Sale, the 'museums director' of the exhibition that the Trust had opened up, were seen arguing over apparent trivia and countermanding one another's instructions while the impending financial and strategic crisis loomed. Sale had been released by the Science Museum, where he restored early electronic machines, to attend the codebreakers' reunion that launched the early campaign to save Bletchley Park. In 1991, the Park was deserted and only insiders or chroniclers of intelligence history knew about its wartime and technological significance. Peter Wescombe, who had worked overseas for the Foreign Office, was aware of the background and the imminent threat to demolish most of the unlovely Bletchley buildings and replace them with profitable housing. Peter and his wife Rowena mustered Dr Peter Jarvis and Sue Jarvis with Ena Halmos, good and trusted friends with a background in historical studies, around the kitchen table. The Wescombes' cosy house in Bletchley burgeons with archaeological finds poised to enthrall the curious visitor. Peter is challenging but kind and jovial. A high-and-low point in his career came in Iraq, where he incurred Saddam Hussein's displeasure and fled, once he had got his family clear. Rowena his wife is gracious, hospitable and wise. Their friends the Jarvises remind me of birds of paradise, resplendent with exotic knowledge. Sue is a linguist and authority on Japanese codes. Peter Jarvis's retirement passions are a redoubtable Welsh railway and Bletchley. They surely had an informed and heated discussion about Bletchley Park. Was it right that the place be saved or should the prime minister's post-war edict be allowed to come to fruition?

In 1991, the Bletchley Archaeological and Historical Society, led by the two Peters and Ena Halmos, brought together about 400 former codebreakers for a farewell party. Peter Wescombe used his Foreign Office and GCHQ contacts to start building a network of Bletchley Park alumni that might like to attend. An announcement in *The Times* advertised this original reunion of veterans. The Science Museum's director, Sir Neil Cossons, along with other organisations that might help, was invited to send an observer. Towards the end of the animated evening, Peter Wescombe posed the question, 'If we were to try to save Bletchley Park, would you give us your support?' There was stunned silence among the codebreakers. 'They thought,' Peter said, 'that we meant money.' Once that misunderstanding had been cleared up, most of the party offered their full moral support. The Bletchley Park Trust was formed in 1992 with the aim of preserving the site for posterity.

By the late 1990s, many distinguished and influential allies had drifted away from Bletchley Park because of the squabbling, arrogance, lack of open-mindedness and limited progress since the excitement of early campaigning. People had lost patience, got tired or had been excluded. I had been asked to attend a meeting convened by the Rt. Hon. Virginia Bottomley, Minister for Heritage in the Conservative Government at the time the Trust's Millennium Fund application was rejected. Apart from the Trust's representatives, Baroness Trumpington, a Bletchley veteran, was there and Robert Harris, author of the novel *Enigma*. Trumpington looked bored, Harris pleasantly baffled and the minister was helpful but firm. They had all heard the Bletchley Park apologia before. Bottomley chose to communicate through me after the meeting. 'You seem like a sensible person, with your feet on the ground,' said the minister.

This compliment contrasted with some insults slung around about me inside the Trust. The Board had changed chairman, Sir

Philip Duncombe took up arms and the Board decided to appoint a director. There were internal candidates; the post was known about in some heritage circles but regarded as a poisoned chalice because of the problematic background. I was asked to let my name go forward. For many reasons, I hesitated. To begin with, the Board was divided between mothballers and modernisers. There were those who wanted to keep the Park exactly as it was at the time, a ramshackle, quasi-military playground with disparate displays; and those who wanted the new director to preserve the most historically important features and give Bletchley Park a future purpose. Roger Bristow felt marginalised, though he and I spent hours in a teashop as I tried to persuade him that he could help mobilise community support and tourism. The Trust did not have funding either to pay a moderate salary or to advance its plans. It did not own the site and had never taken financial responsibility for its operation. Opposition to my appointment from within the Board would increase the difficulties. My husband Eric and I talked it over at length; it was a bigger risk than anything else I'd attempted. I was offered, but declined, a short-term contract because I thought it would take at least two years to begin the recovery. A foretaste of the vendetta to come is that (I was told), when eventually I was appointed, one trustee described me as a 'rattlesnake of a woman', burst into tears and stalked out of a board meeting, saying, 'That'll be the end of Bletchley Park.' It was a very unpleasant beginning.

Looking back, it is hard to say exactly why I persisted. My mother-in-law, who worked in wartime Bletchley's Hut 8, had been excited by my involvement in the Park. Volunteer friends urged me to 'go for it'. Sir Edward obviously thought that we could achieve a near miracle. The idea of Bletchley, what it had been and might yet become, thrilled me. I believed that to create 'places with cases', conventional museum exhibits, would not be an adequate tribute to the codebreakers (and the chances of that being financially viable would be slim). Bletchley Park's veterans warranted a tribute that would bring the moribund Park alive, make it intellectually vibrant, as it was in wartime, building on their work. The other major factor was that there did not seem to be anyone else around who could, or would, undertake the quest.

My instinct and friends went into overdrive, for little at Bletchley could be taken at face value. My mail was read on receipt, but not by me. Some of it went inexplicably missing, I deduced from telephoned reminders. I set to work with several willing volunteers and a drop of new blood on the Trust Board. Trustee Sir Philip Duncombe, propelled into the chair, insistently called in favours and recruited old friends who could bring skills and reality to bear.

Virtually as I came on board, British Telecom and government property agency PACE pulled out of negotiations, weary from seven unproductive years of botched attempts. Sir Edward Tomkins called on Sir Evelyn de Rothschild, whose deft inter-vention procured a stay of execution. 'They've got a new director, they're sorting themselves out, give them a few weeks,' Rothschild had said. As BT's banker, his influence counted. Within a few months, having had sight of an early strategic plan, the landowners relented and negotiations began in earnest. It was a rollercoaster ride, made more precarious by the baggage from its history. Dr Phyllis Starkey, Labour MP for Milton Keynes South-West, banged together heads in the government's property agency to good effect. In April 1999, Minister for the Cabinet Peter Kilfoyle MP, BT and the Trust signed an agreement for a 250-year lease (which would convert automatically to a freehold) on 28 acres of Bletchley Park land. It was a triumphant day and a great boost to the Park's long-suffering volunteers, but there was trouble afoot. As much was whispered at the press conference in D Block, and the target was me.

Reformers in the Trust wanted to set the past behind them, introduce an organisation more appropriate for the challenges ahead and particularly to focus trustees on making policy, not being hands-on. To this seemingly sensible notion, there was fierce resistance and talk of revolution. After a stormy meeting of the Trust's executive committee, I drove back to my family in London, hoping for a tranquil May bank holiday weekend. On the office answerphone I reserved for Bletchley Park, a message awaited. 'We'll kill you dead,' the caller threatened. I dismissed it, hoping that it was a tasteless joke, or even a wrong number. Over the weekend, the call came again. The voice sounded mechanical, disguised; it was male and the number could not be traced domestically. Apologetically, I phoned the police, filling them in on the general background. They were round within the hour and gave me some advice. I would park the car off site in future, just in case 'a nutter' tried to tamper with the brakes, and I would avoid being alone at Bletchley in the late evening shadows. Scotland Yard later checked out the caller's numbers to no avail. My husband Eric and I didn't say anything to our daughters Sofy (then thirteen) and Imogen (nine) at the time. With luck, the person concerned would have exorcised their bile. How wrong I was. This was a low, but the outlook darkened.

On 1 July 1999, there was a double-page spread in the London *Evening Standard*. Not especially flattering of Bletchley Park, it carried damaging allegations – Eric and I were out to profit personally from an unethical property deal involving Bletchley Park and BT. Or so the *Standard* said, for the BT executive implicated in the said deal, albeit not one of the alleged beneficiaries, was immediately authorised by his BT boss to refute the nonsense in the strongest possible terms. BT went further, stating that the allegations were part of a scurrilous campaign to undermine me. Max Hastings, the *Evening Standard's* editor, was permanently unavailable and no satisfactory response could be got from the newspaper's hierarchy. Perhaps people used to being in the public eye, politicians, can brush off this type of nastiness, I did my best impression while wondering who wanted me out of the way so much, how many were involved and why. It looked as if a campaign was underway. My arrival had been described in the *Milton Keynes Citizen* as 'the wind of change rustling anoraks in the corridors'. I could understand that change would be unwelcome in some quarters even though my motives were to glorify Bletchley Park. In my opinion, the place had been hijacked to satisfy personal interests, with insufficient regard for economic reality and Bletchley Park as a whole. 'Mud sticks' is a truism and the waters had been muddied by invisible hands. Eric and I had to take legal action against the *Standard* and the freelance journalist who had launched the article without ever contacting me. The full apology that finally appeared on 31 August was short, late and did not match up to the unprincipled rhetoric given headroom earlier.

Since the summer of 1999, I had been trying to assemble Bletchley Park's trustees to discuss a draft strategic plan on which I had consulted externally. There was never an opportune moment. In October, a group of trustees commandeered the board agenda and sent me and all but one of my colleagues out of the room. Sir Philip Duncombe emerged two hours later. He said he was crushed and deeply apologetic but the Board had sacked me on the spot. There was no reason given and I was asked to leave straightaway, which I did, taking only some family photographs. When I got back home I must have looked terrible. Imogen took my hand and stated, 'You've lost your job, haven't you?'

I couldn't reply and I couldn't stop the choking tears. Sofy and Imogen hugged me, upset but angry too.

The detail of what followed illustrates a seam of humanity that should, in my opinion, stay buried for a long time. Five trustees made it plain that they disassociated themselves from the Board's action and abhorred it: the chairman, Sir Philip Duncombe, vice-chairman Martin Findlay, Sir Edward Tomkins, Dr Peter Jarvis and Ken King. Their refutation and protest was published on the *Daily Telegraph*'s letters page. John Humphrys on the *Today* programme said rhetorically to Milton Keynes MP Dr Phyllis Starkey, 'A chief executive can't just be sacked like that?!' The Charity Commission was called in. The Trust commissioned an independent report into the functioning of the Trust from an eminent QC. By the board meeting of January 2000, seven trustees had departed and the Board had been reconstituted under the aegis of Sir Neil Cossons from London's Science Museum.

The new Board reinstated me. At their first meeting of the new millennium, I outlined the draft plan to get Bletchley's future back on track. Entitled, 'Last night I dissected a frog', my presentation confronted the major issues facing Bletchley Park: first and foremost, survival, in an environment where Bletchley's continuing relevance and role were questionable and scientific and historic experiences and information could be delivered remotely. My anatomically correct dissection of a frog had been painlessly carried out via the Internet site of a scientific institution thousands of miles away. How could Bletchley finance itself in a competitive marketplace and why would it matter to people who had no direct connection to the Second World War? The plan was unusual because it set out to celebrate the codebreakers' achievements while using them to inspire young scientists and stimulate technology development on the site. 'Large Back to Front' blared Milton Keynes' *Citizen* on Sunday. It was a favourite headline, from the paper that had described me as a 'housewife superstar' – the 'housewife' laughed out of court by my daughters. Nor was I a superstar or superwoman. I was doing my utmost, along with everyone else alongside the Trust, to reverse Bletchley's decline. Expectations ran high and, since my period of exile, personal anxieties had intensified.

Just before Christmas 1999, I had returned to meet colleagues at Bletchley to prepare for the new year and the forthcoming board meeting. We reviewed contingency planning and I speculated about activity that could be most damaging to Bletchley Park's mission. 'Someone,' I said, 'could steal an Enigma machine.'

CHAPTER EIGHT

The hunting

Stealing an Enigma machine might give the Allies a foothold on the ladder of comprehension, yet it was no guarantee of escalating to a full break. The machine itself posed problems whose difficulties became insurmountable when Enigma's separate defences were combined.

What made Enigma so difficult to break? The machines mustered a number of variable elements. In a typical, three-rotor Enigma, the plugboard was at a right angle to the user, visible at the front of the machine when the wooden flap covering it was pulled down. It had the appearance of a flat metal plate, into which rivets had been punched. There were three double-banked rows. By each plug hole was a letter, in the QWERTZU keyboard order, or a number. The twenty-six holes were designed to receive up to thirteen small, cylindrical metal plugs or 'jacks' sheathed in Bakelite-type material. From each plug protruded a short, double-wired cable. When a cable was inserted, it could make a connection between any pair of letters. Each cable therefore used two holes to make the connection between letters. To calculate the plugboard permutations depended on how many cables were used, which group of holes was selected and the interconnections between these sockets. The total of possible plugboard combinations was 532 985 208 2000 576 according to Dr A. Ray Miller of the National Security Agency's Center for Cryptologic History.

When the metal hood covering the workings of the Enigma machine was shut, only the very tops of the rotors' circumference were on show, smoothly serrated metal rings. Opening the hood and lifting out the rotors, which were ordered from left to right on the spindle, they could each be teased apart to reveal twenty-six input contact points on one face of the disc and twenty-six output contact points on its other side, connected in between by fixed wires that carried the electrical impulses. The variables were the choice and the order of the rotors.

The twenty-six serrations round the edge of the rotors were, of course, precision-engineered. They enabled the operator to set the rotors to an initial position by moving through a series of 'clicks'. The operator could set each rotor to any one of twenty-six positions, giving 17 576 possible combinations of rotor key settings.

On each of the rotors there was a movable ring inscribed with twenty-six sets of either double-digit numbers or letters. Where there were numbers, the first read 01 and the last was 26. With the Enigma hood down, three numbers were visible in three small windows to the left of each rotor. The function of each ring was to control its left-hand neighbour. The right-hand neighbour rotor on a three-rotor Enigma did this by means of one notch. To further complicate matters, the rings also displayed the alphabetic indicators, ordered A – Z, that were specified as part of the key-setting process. When a notched ring turned its left-hand neighbour, it also moved the alphabet indicators against the disc. The sequence of activity ran thus: a key on the keyboard was pressed; the right-hand rotor rotated. Every twenty-sixth time a key was pressed, the notch on the right-hand rotor would cause the rotor to its left (the middle one on a three-rotor machine) to rotate. For the rotor on the far left to rotate, the far right-hand rotor would have to move the middle rotor twenty-six times. Since it took the far right-hand rotor twenty-six rotations to move the middle rotor just once, it would need twenty-six times twenty-six rotations to force the far left-hand rotor to move. Mathematically, the far left-hand rotor was irrelevant in terms of causing rotor rotations or 'stepping' because when the rotors moved together it did not act on another rotor and the reflector ring was unaffected.

A three-rotor Enigma's reflector was not visible above its hood. Inside, it was a plain metal hollow cylinder around whose perimeter ran twenty-six metal contact points. A reflector was effectively a half-rotor because it had electrical contact points only on one face. The thirteen internal wires connected paired contact points. The effect was to send or 'reflect' an incoming electrical impulse back through the rotors but via a different route from the first time.

Dr A. Ray Miller has calculated the number of theoretically possible Enigma permutations by examining the maximum possible combinations for each component of a three-rotor Enigma and combining the values. He said, 'To see just how large that number is, consider that ... there are only about 10^{80} atoms in the entire observable universe.' The total of possible three-rotor Enigma combinations is approximately three times 10^{114}. That is:

3 283 883 513 796 974 198 700 882 069 882 752 878 379
955 261 095 623 685 444 055 315 226 006 433 615 627
409 666 933 182 371 174 802 769 920 000 000 000 000

It is a number that has no meaning in daily existence. Bletchley Park codebreaker and Dillwyn Knox protégé Mavis Lever (now Batey) modestly avowed, 'When we were breaking Enigma under Dilly's guidance, thank goodness no one explained exactly what we were doing. Had they done so, I don't know how we would have managed it.' Penelope Fitzgerald (*The Knox Brothers*) tells us that Dilly was a Lewis Carroll devotee. A short extract from Carroll's *Sylvie and Bruno* may give a clue to how Knox attacked problems,

> In Science – in fact, in most things – it is usually best *to begin at the beginning*. In *some* things, of course, it's better to begin at the *other* end. For instance, if you wanted to paint a dog green, it *might* be best to begin with the *tail*, as it doesn't bite at *that* end.

Fortunately, the Enigma machine's practical operation and development increased the chance of penetrating these astronomic potential configurations from the frankly impossible to the merely miraculous.

By the time that Scherbius's firm had delivered enough machines for the navy to put Enigma into service at the start of 1926, it was a much sleeker and more invulnerable proposition. The keyboard, rotor wiring, number of available rotors and number of electrical contacts had changed. Security had been beefed up and as the operating manual laid down, only officers could set rotor positions. There was always a possibility that the Germans' enemies might intercept a dangerous quantity of messages. If they did so and the messages were enciphered with the rotors in the same starting positions, the accumulated texts might overlap or superimpose and give away the information. To avoid this eventuality, the navy prescribed the rotors' starting positions that were far apart and distributed settings lists in booklets. The radioman who enciphered the message communicated these starting positions to the receiving radioman by transmitting enciphered groups of letters called 'indicators'. The more important and secret a message was, the fewer people were allowed access to its individual components and stages in the machine-setting, enciphering and deciphering routine.

Enigma was starting to repay the German navy's investment, and the chief of the army's cipher centre got wind of the incredible machine. The army's first three-rotor Enigmas went live in July 1928, adapted to suit army practice. The army's message key system did not use a booklet and the QWERTZU keyboard had twenty-six contacts. The former First World War signals officer who recommended introducing Enigma to the army was called Major Rudolf Schmidt, elder brother of spy Hans-Thilo.

Enigma failed to capture the imagination of the bankers or of the commercial market in general and Scherbius died in 1929 before seeing his invention's promise rewarded. His company and Enigma users continued to experiment with different versions, expanding the Enigma family. The army added plugboards in 1930, connecting six of the possible thirteen pairs and thus enciphering twelve letters through the board.

Enigma took off exponentially when Hitler denounced the Versailles treaty and began massively to expand Germany's armed forces. The railroad authorities, Abwehr (military intelligence) and Sicherdienst (party intelligence service) bought Enigma and instituted their own cryptographic systems. Some Abwehr traffic early in the Second World War still used manual ciphers and amateur cryptanalysts from the Radio Security Service (RSS) made some breaks into these messages. The Abwehr was not exclusively loyal to the Enigma cipher machine but the service developed one called a *Zählwerke* or 'counter' machine, which had a letter counter at the top right side.

Enigma variations were played in even before the Second World War. In 1934 the German navy adopted the army's plugboard model but used a set of seven rotors from which to choose the three. Second notches were added to two of the rotor rings, increasing the frequency of left-hand neighbours' ring 'steps'. Eventually, the navy was deploying machines with double-notched four rotors in the body, selected from a set of ten.

Machines used by some of the services occasionally had individual wiring. Reflectors were created for special-purpose Enigmas and some four-rotor Enigma machines had inter-changeable reflectors. Reflectors that were pluggable followed later and technicians in the field could rewire these. Had such refinements been implemented comprehensively and earlier, the machines and their traffic would have become an utter enigma.

As a general rule, cryptanalysts on the Allied side midway through the Second World War could expect to be contending with ten plugboard cables, a choice of five discs with known wiring, 17 576 possible rotational positions, single notched rings and a single reflector whose wiring was also known. Typically, computing these combinations yielded a still daunting 10^{23} possibilities.

The task the Allied cryptanalyst faced to break an Enigma cipher message was to work out from the available combinations which rotors were in use, their order in the machine, when the middle and left rotors would turn and how the plugboard had been set. From 1940 to 1945, these procedures, known as the 'key of the day', were determined monthly in advance by the Germans and changed every day. The radioman transmitting the message then chose the day's message setting, the position in which the rotors started, a further cryptographic bridge for the cryptanalyst to cross.

The cryptanalysts attacking Enigma would start by assuming what a ring setting, say XXX, might be and then test the assumption. The message setting would be found, relative to the assumed ring setting. As the ring setting determined how the left-hand rotors would turn over, the chances were that the actual turnover positions would differ from the ones designated by the assumed ring setting. The real turnover positions therefore had to be deduced through logic before completing this part of the break. Finding the rotor order was sometimes based on information from intelligence sources, but could be achieved through a systematic search. The most challenging part of the exercise was to whittle down the possibilities generated by the plugboard and the starting position of the rotors (the message setting). This monstrous number crunching was undertaken by the Bombe, an astounding machine inspired at Bletchley Park by Alan Turing and Gordon Welchman. This progeny of Rejewski's bomby had been radically re-engineered and had enjoyed unprecedented financial backing – £100 000 in all.

Hut 11 at Bletchley Park, the Enigma bombe room, was a codebreaking factory, pounding with Enigma simulators. Bold, clattering machines were choreographed in a powerful and remorseless hunt for rotor positions. Giant bronze frames encased thirty or more rotating drums, depending on how many Enigmas were being mimicked. More than 7 feet wide, 6 feet 6 inches high and two feet 6 inches deep, the lithe electrical giants performed like modern-day search engines. They blasted out ferocious heat that exhausted the Wrens (Women's Royal Naval Service) who operated them. Relays of young women 'plugged up' the bombes, taming the wire jungle that sprouted behind them. Their guide was a paper-and-pencil menu setting, concocted through guessing which enciphered letter might pair with a guessed German plaintext letter. Churning at high speed, the bombe was designed to track down rotor positions that satisfied the relationships supposed by the menus. Light as well as heat was generated, for when a menu relationship worked, the bombe stopped and the result was tested to see if it deciphered the entire message.

Gordon Welchman had the idea to incorporate a 'diagonal board' enabling many more letter loops to be tested. Running through all the potential rotor positions with up to sixty different combinations for rotor orders could take up to thirty hours. Welchman's diagonal board helped minimise the problem of false 'stops' that occurred when there were insufficient good guesses or 'cribs'. Turnovers caused by the rotor notches presented another problem that could be corrected through astute menu planning. However, it should be remembered that the bombe, brilliant as it was, could not have been used without the cribs (guesses) provided by early decodes in Bletchley Park's Hut 6 from May to September 1940. The honours for these decodes go to Welchman and John Herivel.

An outlandish number of possible combinations was not Enigma's only defence. Measures were taken to improve Enigma's physical security and to protect its true Achilles heel from the greatest risk – humans. During the mid-1930s, the lead metal seal on the machines was replaced with a lock. Hijacking the machine alone was not the main issue. The German navy began to print its cryptographic documents in red, water-soluble ink. Destruction by water would be swift and irreversible, so a precautionary backup copy was kept in case of spillage or condensation. Finally, there was an emergency procedure that changed the rotor order and the ring settings in the event that the enemy took possession of the current settings list, rotor settings and indicators booklet, indicator encipherment tables and the machine itself. The crisis action had either to be committed to memory or noted down in a way that would avoid enquiry or suspicion if it were discovered. The Germans had assiduously tried to remove or neutralise all the enemy's opportunities to break and enter Enigma.

Human error and Enigma radiomen's characteristics and quirks prompted some great codebreaking successes. David Kahn reported an instance in 1932 when an operator who was supposed to delete codewords that were unenciphered, crossed out the enciphered ones instead and transmitted the message in plaintext. Aghast, he reported his mistake, only to have it foolishly compounded by an order to retransmit the message with the correct, enciphered words. Anyone listening had the complete Enigma version, translated in 'clear'. Following this incident, the navy fortified and sharpened up its training, as well as changing keys.

Choosing keys that were easy to remember was a tendency first spotted by Rejewski. Girlfriends' names, personal initials and imprecations topped the user poll. Mavis Lever claims only half in jest to have been a world expert on wartime, dirty, four-letter German words! These foibles in Enigma message settings were named 'cillies'. Less frequently, the Germans 'blew' what were called 'kisses', by repeating parts of Enigma messages in a vulnerable cipher. Mavis Lever said,

> As soon as I picked up one long message I could see that it had no L in it; as traffic was so infrequent operators were told to send out the occasional dummy message and this one had just put his finger on the last key of the keyboard, probably relaxing with a fag in his mouth.

The sloppy operator had used L to encipher the whole message, giving the cryptanalyst the new wiring for the Enigma rotor.

Another great coup became known as the 'Herivel tip', although John Herivel refers to it as 'Herivelismus'. Gordon

Welchman had been Herivel's supervisor at Cambridge and it was his former supervisor who invited him to Bletchley in 1940, 'to do some very important work'. Herivel said,

> One thing I was very clear about in the beginning was, that it was much more likely to happen if the German operators were working under great stress. They were more likely to make mistakes if they were frightened, in a great hurry or very tired.

Herivelismus was inspired by an intuitive leap that put John Herivel in the shoes of the German operator. Herivel visualised the German sitting there, with the wheels and the book of keys. After he found the right wheels for the day, loaded them on the sprung spindle, fitted them into the machine and clicked the rotors round to the day's setting, his next task was to choose an indicator. What if the operator were afraid, in a hurry or distracted? Might he just bang down the hood, see the letters showing under the window in the top and use those? How did he actually deal with the ring settings? Rather than having set them, as he should have, at the outset, perhaps the anxious or lazy operator would set them after he placed the wheels in the machine. In that case, the indicator letters he chose as his message setting for the day would surely be close to the ring setting. It was an inspired guess whose net effect was to narrow down the 17 576 possible ring settings to maybe as few as twenty. Herivel remembers very clearly that his 'tip' worked properly for the first time on 1 May 1940. Welchman's thanks to Herivel was to ensure that Winston Churchill subsequently singled John out. In 2001, at Bletchley Park, Herivel reflected on his discovery:

> ... and when I thought about that more I realised the really vital move, was for me to want to find some new way of breaking Enigma. It was very strange as I'd only been there for three weeks and only just got to know under the instruction of Turing and Kendrick how the machine and the system worked.

Cryptanalysts' success with the messages depended heavily on other links in the Bletchley network. 'Y' stations – wireless intercept posts dotted around the country – listened in to Morse traffic and sent the fruits of their labour to Bletchley. The largely volunteer Radio Security Service had an outstanding record of culling Abwehr traffic. Radio interceptors recorded everything on two pads, one for messages and one for logs. Log readers had a 'control' function. Their logs showed the preambles to messages, which were vital to their interpretation and often, to decryption. 'Having found ways of breaking into the keys,' said Marie Le Blond (later, Bennett), 'it was often the log reader's interpretations of the traffic that enabled the cryptographers to continue to break them each day.' Le Blond worked on Luftwaffe Enigma traffic from the German airforce in the Middle East and later, the Balkans. 'We knew our groups by their frequencies, not by their German unit names,' she said. Units' positions could be plotted by taking bearings on incoming signals and where these crossed, 'On maps with coloured wool and pins we built up the patterns of the German airforce positions.' In addition to daytime and night-time frequencies and changed call signs every twenty-four hours, there was a periodic shake-up and all the frequencies changed. Breaking and sustaining intelligence from Enigma traffic was a massive logistical challenge.

Intercepting and analysing the traffic, the formidable permutations, the cryptographic security, the stringent procedures; for all these reasons, some variations of Enigma were strongly resistant to being broken. Yet while human resourcefulness could create awesome complexity and brilliant cryptanalytic inroads, it was the human factor that rendered Enigma most vulnerable.

CHAPTER NINE

A little bill

Vulnerability was not a trait evident in the negotiator's behaviour. At the strategy summit, the police disclosed their view of his psychological make-up. It was not rocket science. A profile had been drawn up by one of the force's experts. He believed the person, assumed to be male, had considerable knowledge of wartime cipher machines and a taste for gamesmanship. The letter's author showed obsessive personality traits and he had immersed himself in a world of secrets and intrigue. There were concerns about my personal safety, though my thoughts were about the impact that the theft and the media coverage were having on my family. Sofy's sunny demeanour had clouded over. 'I'm fed up with being asked at school whether you've got your machine back,' she had said, slamming the bedroom door behind her.

DCI Chesterman had researched the death threats of the previous year in meticulous detail and the meeting had picked over the familiar ground leading up to my appointment and tenure at Bletchley Park, paying special attention to the character traits of the key personalities involved. The letter writer or his 'master', unless they were one and the same, had a grudge against me and could not wait to make it public. The letters were fuelled by emotion and evinced a sense of self-righteousness. Emotion and reason are restless bedfellows. The transaction was not just about money, though that was certainly one of the objectives.

To my mind, the two letters' tone oscillated between Uriah Heap, the avaricious and grovelling character immortalised by Dickens, and the tantrums of a minor dictator. In my imagination and in my notes, the shadowy scribe had taken shape. He was in my perception a spiteful man with an obsessive personality who thought his value to society had been vastly underestimated. Perhaps, he thought he was at least brilliant, but could equally have been interpreted as unhinged. I imagined him to be self-important, unaccountable and image-conscious. Why else the convoluted and hectoring correspondence? Cloak-and-dagger activities obviously excited him and secrecy was power; a means of exercising control that could not be openly achieved. Was he paranoid?

It is hard to envisage exonerating circumstances for such demands for money. The act is calculated, it involves bullying and brave men do not indulge in it. The psychologist identified the obvious chinks in the letter writer's armour. Arrogant. Probably greedy. Resentment bubbled under the controlled surface. Was this a potentially combustible cocktail that could lead to an ill-judged step or a revealing mistake?

Tuesday 19 September 2000 happened to be the day of a quarterly Bletchley Park Board meeting. Merryl Jenkins had opened another special delivery for me. Merryl had followed the precautionary procedure that had become our standard practice. The letter was handled with thin plastic gloves on and the envelope was slit with a paperknife over a plastic folder that would preserve any forensic evidence. Police tests on the past correspondence had included ESDA, where the document is put on a magnetising machine, covered with plastic clingfilm and sprinkled with iron filings. Patterns in the metal show up indentations from other correspondence. Ninhydrin chemical fingerprint testing had been the last routine carried out because it makes the paper fragile and, over time, changes its colour to pink.

Merryl Jenkins shook the envelope in the folder and a letter dropped out. Over a clean desk (just in case) in a quiet room, I read a communication asking for £25 000 and stating how the cash was to be delivered. This time, a separate label with my name and the Bletchley Park address had been stuck with sticky tape on the envelope. It was an oddly professional-sounding letter. Matter-of-fact and businesslike, it stuck to the issue at hand. The vitriol of the second letter was missing from this cool and collected instruction list. The writer might well have been organising a routine collection. I was feeling under pressure.

According to the police psychologist, the same person had written all of the letters. Though I believed that another party had taken over, it was a matter of personal judgement and of little apparent significance. The police had the experience and I was very conscious that the police had to be seen to be taking the lead. Bletchley Park Trust, at a fragile stage in its recovery, could not afford to have its credibility damaged by making a false move in the operation to recover Enigma. The Trust had not got the funds to pay the sum demanded and, even if it had, could not have used money raised for charitable purposes to finance such a dubious activity. Visitors to Bletchley Park did not have such qualms. The overwhelming majority wanted the Trust to get the machine back, even if it meant raising the money to pay for it.

The police had intimated that the money could be made available but that the recipient would not be in a position to pocket it. The plan was to get the person into a position where negotiations could take place. Dealing by letters and through the media put the police at a great disadvantage, which the middleman surely realised. Clues from the correspondence were scarce and the blue fibre caught in Sellotape on a label was unrevealing.

Meanwhile, I had talked to a 'wise owl' at British Telecom. Alan White was then head of the division that ran BT's huge property portfolio. He had been personally involved in all the critical stages of negotiating the lease with Bletchley Park Trust and I rated him highly. He could be tough in business dealings but he was open-minded and fair, and empathised with the Trust's aspirations for Bletchley Park. Alan readily undertook to see whether his colleagues would agree to BT sponsoring a £5 000 pot of cash to be used in a way that would facilitate the machine's return. They put the money at Bletchley Park's disposal, but the negotiator wanted more.

I went in to the Trust's board meeting and said nothing about the letter or related developments. The Board was enthusiastically planning an awayday to thrash out its plan for the site's future. It was business as usual.

Simon Chesterman and I talked about strategy, tactics and the case's progress every day, often several times a day. Intriguing and important as the matter was, it had become a part-time job on top of my very full-time vocation. Chesterman and his team were also stretched. Criminals didn't suspend their activities just because a high-profile case had come along. They probably welcomed the distraction.

In the media, the police and Bletchley Park stuck to our carefully rehearsed mantra. The third party seemed to be a man in a difficult position and, assuming he was the honest broker he claimed to be, the police would have no reason to arrest him. Bletchley Park Trust couldn't pay the money from its own funds, but there was money available. The priority was to get the machine back and in good condition. Initially, I had feared that the machine had been outside overnight or, worse, heaved into the lake. The wiring inside the Abwehr Enigma was particularly fragile, a zinc-based alloy. Left prey to damp, the alloy would deteriorate. The machine's irreplaceable interior would become brittle and it would fracture when the lid was opened.

John Humphrys on the *Today* programme decided to turn up the burners. 'You're giving in to blackmail.' It was a statement. He was not unsympathetic but he had a job to do and it was a very fair question. Chesterman and I had to convince ourselves that the only way to stay in the game to recover the machine was to get ourselves almost believing that the 'honest broker' was what he claimed to be. The middleman's reactions were unpredictable and the temptation to gratify common sense was outweighed by a conviction that if the public line did not hold, the route to finding Enigma would be closed down.

CHAPTER TEN

Rules of battle

K eeping the wartime Enigma trail alive did not depend on one single factor but, naturally, there were dominant trends and themes. Empathising with the enemy, so that Bletchley Park could read the other side's mind, stimulated intuitive leaps that had a remarkable and sometimes lasting impact. Mechanising the elimination of inconsistencies with the Turing – Welchman bombe dramatically reduced the precious hours spent in testing rotor positions. In due course, a series of brave and selfless 'pinches' or hijacks of Enigma materials from U-boats stoked Bletchley's fires of invention and led codebreakers from a long cold period of information blackout. What sticks in the memory too is sheer intellectual brilliance.

They may not exactly have known it, but Bletchley's codebreakers were contending with a prolific and mutable Enigma family over the course of the Second World War. The German navy, army and airforce used different Enigma machine models. There were special adaptations for services such as the Abwehr, German military intelligence and utilities like the railways. Operating procedures and physical security measures varied within each service. There were individual communication 'nets' for services branches and units and the radio frequencies on which the encrypted messages were transmitted would change with the time of day. Overlaid on the basic communication structures were the preferences and quirks of the servicemen deputed to choose their own daily message settings. The first breaks into Enigma keys were called after colours. As the number of keys multiplied, new names proliferated. The Luftwaffe (German air force) key spawned flowers and insects. The army keys generated birds and naval keys were called after fish. Indeed, as the war advanced, German military command, notably Admiral Karl Dönitz, did everything conceivable to make the breaking of Enigma an even more remote possibility. Just in case ...

Just in case an unassuming young man or woman with an unarticulated ambition to break Enigma should happen to fix on one of its weaknesses. One such man was John Herivel, born in Belfast just after the end of the First World War. By his own account, Herivel was 'pretty average in school at most things, but gifted in maths'. Gordon Welchman had considered him an outstanding pupil at Cambridge. Charles Collins, a member of the group that had disguised itself as 'Captain Ridley's shooting party' in 1938 to reconnoitre Bletchley Park's suitability as a codebreaking centre said, self-effacingly in 2001, 'We were all at least decently intelligent and there were some high intelligences.' The young Herivel is easily recognisable in the Bletchley Park veteran, an intense, bright-blue-eyed man who uses language precisely and loves music. For almost three months after Herivel 'put himself in the other man's boots' to devise the Herivel tip, nothing happened. The unrelenting Blitzkrieg created the precondition for lax Enigma operating procedures and a powerful application of the principle, Herivelismus, was revealed, not by John Herivel but by a colleague, David Rees. The strength of the approach allowed the German airforce's Enigma codes to be broken for the rest of the war. Allies read the Luftwaffe's 'Red Enigma' (as they were called) throughout the rest of the war, including the Battle of Britain. It was from Red Enigma decrypts in Spring 1941 that the first clues came about the *Bismarck*'s real movements in the Baltic, leading a few weeks after to the mighty warship's sinking.

Dilly Knox was, said Charles Collins, 'the eccentric of eccentrics'. To stand out so in wartime Bletchley Park, Dilly must have been extreme. There is no doubt that the scope of his eccentricities was matched by his genius for codebreaking. Mavis Batey remembers vividly how Dilly introduced her to breaking Enigma. 'Hallo,' he said, 'we're breaking machines. Have you got a pencil? Here, have a go.'

Mavis was handed 'a pile of utter gibberish, made worse by Dilly's scrawls all over them'. She said, 'But I am afraid it's all Greek to me', at which Dilly 'burst into delighted laughter and replied, "I wish it were."' Mavis had been understandably puzzled by the hilarity at the time. The mystery was cleared up long after the war by Penelope Fitzgerald, Dilly's niece and the Knox family's biographer. 'It's all Greek to me' popped up in a skit, 'Alice in ID25', written by Bletchley contemporary Frank Birch. Dilly, who featured as the Dodo, contributed the verses and Mavis had unwittingly quoted what Alice had said when she met Dilly for the first time in Room 40 (the First World War precursor of GC&CS, which expanded into ID25 in 1917). 'Alice in ID25' had found herself among a series of 'odd creatures' who were researching by 'staring blankly at the tables in front of them and then scribbling away furiously on bits of paper'. The resemblance between 'Alice in ID25' and Dilly's Enigma codebreaking operation in the cottage at Bletchley Park was entirely intentional.

When Mavis Lever appeared on the scene in early May 1940 she was the fifth of 'Dilly's girls', whose number was soon to increase. Britain's fragile state was graphically brought home when, after Dunkirk, trains taking exhausted soldiers northwards all stopped at Bletchley on the way.

I was sitting next to a Frenchman when the fall of Paris came over on the radio. I wasn't sure what to do when he burst into tears so I went on eating my sausages; he must have thought me heartless, but with a long shift ahead and now the possibility of invasion, starving wouldn't help.

New Enigma systems were brought in for specific purposes. They included a communications link between a German research establishment and a German airforce base in France. When 'Brown Enigma' had been broken, the British professor, R. V.

Jones, was able to devise countermeasures that deflected the navigational beams guiding German aircraft.

German railways used an Enigma cipher called 'Rocket'. Its value to the Allies lay in the long-distance troops and weapons movements revealed by railway schedules.

The Enigma machine used by Mussolini's naval forces when he entered the war in June 1940 turned out to be one without a plugboard and to which Knox had already found his theoretical rodding solution. However, the volume of daily traffic was extremely thin and there was a dearth of 'cribs' to facilitate a break. Months of frustration culminated one evening in Mavis Lever trying inspired guesswork in rodding procedures. By the morning shift she had not only identified the right-hand rotor position. She had 'exceeded instructions' and broken the entire message. 'Being trained on Dilly's *Alice in Wonderland* thought processes was,' she said, 'it seems better than wrestling with a Turing treatise.'

Dilly's cottage team also triumphed in March 1941 with Enigma breaks that revealed the battle plan for Matapan, to the far south of Greece. Breaking this Italian naval Enigma traffic made possible an early British success in the Balkans campaign. Admiral Cunningham used the Royal Navy's Mediterranean fleet to sink three heavy cruisers and two destroyers. Cunningham came down to 'meet Dilly's girls' at Bletchley. The deciphered message had allowed Cunningham to scupper the Trieste division that had planned to attack a British convoy en route to Crete. Famously, the admiral had gone ashore the night before the battle and, by ostentatiously carrying a suitcase and dallying on Alexandria's golf course, had gulled the Japanese consul (who was guaranteed to send word – interceptable word – to the enemy) into thinking that nothing was suspected. Dilly penned an epitaph on Matapan to Mussolini,

These have knelled your fall and ruin, but your ears were
    far away
English lassies rustling papers through the sodden
    Bletchley day.

Abwehr Enigma traffic was available to Bletchley Park in an intermittent dribble from late 1939 and Dilly was asked to look at the Abwehr messages in early 1941.

The purpose of maintaining the large Abwehr establishment was to supply Germany with intelligence. First in 1940, spies like 'Tate' had to report on the state of Britain after Dunkirk and the Battle of Britain, in order for Germany to form a view on the likelihood of it mounting a successful invasion. The Abwehr also had to take a view on the timing, nature and strength of the Allies' prospective invasion of Europe. The tactics employed by the Allies were equally accessible to the enemy: secret agents, double agents and informants, prisoners, reconnaissance, intercepted and deciphered messages; the Germans used every instrument at their disposal and deployed their own 'black propaganda' or disinformation.

Forging ahead on scant information, Dilly discovered a novel feature of this four-rotor Enigma – its reflector moved during enciphering. Unusually, the rotors had frequent turnovers so that all four rotors might turn over together. Dilly set his girls, including Miss Lever, to what he dubbed a lobster hunt.

In his 'Report on the "Lobster Enigma"', Dilly's bravura intellect, Carrollian thinking and endearing qualities shine through. He begins by setting out his methodology, comprising 'a theory, and observation devised by the head of the section' (himself). 'The keyblocks were too scanty to be evaluated', despite 'a sufficient hunt ...' so he devised a way of comparing all available keyblocks to find two that were essentially the same. The search failed, but he found one keyblock in which the indicator letters in columns 1, 2, 5 and 6 had a special relationship. To Dilly it was no great surprise that 'he found what was wanted standing, like the abomination of desolation, precisely where it should not – on a single setting ...' From this he deduced that the diagonal was 'QWERTZU,' all rotors turned over together at places four machine positions apart (a 'crab') and hence that the machine had frequent turnovers (otherwise crabs would occur very rarely). Dilly then decided that '... as

everything that has a middle has also a beginning and an end ...'
there would be places where all rotors turned together without
turning together four positions later; these he called 'lobsters'.
Dismissing the 'useless' crab, he had ordered the lobster hunt.

> The hunt was up and scent was good. One very fine 'lobster'
> (among others) was caught, and after two days Miss Lever,
> by very good and careful work, succeeded in an evaluation
> which contained sufficient non-carry units to ascertain
> the green wheel. (Dilly describing how Mavis Lever
> recovered the wiring for the first wheel).

The relationship between the cipher and plaintext alphabets
when a lobster position occurred would help with deductions
about letter pairs. Mavis Lever's 'good and careful work'
had resulted in a breakthrough; others followed. Dilly's report
to Bletchley's inured commander, Denniston, contained firm
requests on staffing:

> ... at least two more linguists must be chosen and have time
> to learn (a) what we know we want, (b) what might be
> useful. All hunters must know the tricks of the machine.

There were other recommendations, justified by an explanation
rewarding its study:

> The existing system of crib-hunting by proxy has yielded
> the Italian enigma in two years the total of 0 (nought)
> cribs. I should add that I am using 'cribs' in the widest
> sense of the term. A long 'crib' in the ordinary sense is no
> longer necessary. We must proceed as with the Italian
> enigma with the careful study and correction of messages
> before they leave us. Any other system of arbitrary
> correction by those who do not understand machine plans
> and cannot avail themselves of Morse corrections is
> repugnant and unthinkable.

With difficulty, Dilly did the complete sequence of turnovers and
tackled the question of how the letters on the alphabet rings

related to the turnovers. Incredibly, helped by a mathematician called Margaret Rock, he deciphered a message, never having had sight of the machine. Exactly how he did it is not known and Dilly was generous in his success. 'Give me a Lever and a Rock and I will move the universe,' he said. Sadly, the codebreaking universe slid away from Dilly, who was dying of cancer, though he worked from his home to the last.

Dilly's friend since Room 40 days in the First World War, Nobby Clark, head of BP naval section, wrote a postscript to Dilly's Matapan poem,

> When Cunningham won at Matapan by the grace of God
>   and Dilly,
> He was the brains behind them all
> And should ne'er be forgotten. Will he?

Dilly had been a leading light in Enigma breaks up to the end of December 1941 when the Abwehr cipher was first laid bare. He did not live to see the *coup de grâce* in the 1944 theatre of war. It was to be a product of his achievement with Abwehr Enigma.

Italian naval Enigma had been broken in 1941, but since the beginning of the war, German naval Enigma had proved a very tough nut. Alan Turing and Peter Twinn set up a small group to explore naval Enigma solutions around the start of 1940, when a bombe by the name of 'Victory' came on stream. Installed in March, Victory was engaged for five months trying to break naval Enigma. Agnus Dei, or Agnes for short, was the second bombe to be drafted in. A crib recovered from a German patrol boat in 1940 provided an opening and Turing, undoubtedly a genius if marginally less eccentric than Knox, made several minor inroads in April. There was worryingly little sign of a substantive break in the German naval code.

CHAPTER ELEVEN

Dream of money-bags

The coded signature was absent from the third letter, which arrived on 28 September and concluded with eight exclamation marks: '!!!!!!!!' There no sign of a break in his defences. Negotiations for the return of the Enigma had been terminated. Disobedience would not be tolerated by the Master. The Enigma machine would be destroyed.

News reached me in London, where I had to make hurried alternative arrangements for our younger daughter's visit to a prospective new school in Streatham. '!!!!!!!!' Communications had been guillotined. Was it to be a brutal ending? Could the situation be reprieved? It was difficult to make sense of the middleman's erratic behaviour and the pressure on me was beginning to tell. I felt nauseous, a combination of chronic weariness and worry. Fear that malice or mental instability would propel him to hurl away the machine in a rage. Splintered wood and mangled keys flashed into my mind; visions of a remote quarry or stagnant pool where Enigma would be left to rot for eternity. Media attention flickered on and off like thrumming stroboscope blades. In the dark intervals, anxiety gnawed at my confidence. Usually a positive character, I was burdened with doubts, none of which I was in a position to influence. Simon Chesterman was committed; he was focused. I could not envisage him being diverted from his search for the truth but I was becoming aware that the investigation's success depended on multiple uncertainties including police politics. Did the police have the resources and staying power to get a result? My reports to the Bletchley Park Trust consisted only of information that could have been found in the newspapers. Trustees were sympathetic and interested, but unaware to a man of the time being consumed in servicing the investigation and supplying information to the media.

The Trust had begun looking for another new chairman at the beginning of 2000. Sir Philip had agreed to continue as a trustee but he had wanted a respite after the trauma and turbulence that his effective leadership had helped resolve. The vice-chairman Martin Findlay had two main worries about the Enigma demands. Because Bletchley Park Trust is a charity, the use of its scarce funds was governed by its constitution. As I knew, trustees could not in any way endorse giving money under such unusual circumstances, even though the Park's visitors would probably have supported such a move. From a policy point of view, it would have been a deeply dangerous precedent; open day for assaults on the Park's historic collections. For the Trust even to be seen contemplating a donation through such unconventional methods was unacceptable.

Second, the vice-chairman was insistent that the Enigma theft should not distract me and my overstretched small team from turning around the existing operation and from delivering the ambitious plan behind which the trustees had united. It was a tough proposition for I was bound to keep silent and I wondered how the Second World War codebreakers would have contended with the media's attentions.

Earlier in the week, DCI Chesterman had appealed for the mystery man to contact him direct so talks could progress. Privately, I wondered what was the probability that this was a game – warped, to be sure – and that our Enigma would disappear along with the Master.

Like the first two letters, which had been sent from the Midlands, the third letter had been postmarked Birmingham. After the *Daily Mail*'s article on 27 September which clearly said something that pricked the middleman, I received a sharp response via a West London post office. 'I have been instructed to inform you that negotiations for the return of G312 are hereby terminated and further, that the machine will now be destroyed.' Horribly unambiguous.

I did not doubt that 'the Master's' intermediary was a vital link in the chain leading to Enigma's recovery. As the press reported on Sunday 1 October, I found it hard to accept that someone who had paid a substantial amount for the Enigma machine would destroy it. My deep concern centred on the psyche behind the author of the letters. 'Implacable' and 'psychopathic' were the adjectives that came to mind when I revisited the first two letters. Their author was obsessed with control and power. He (almost certainly) relished having the whip hand and directing the circus that comprised police, media and me. Giving him top billing as ringmaster was essential to the police's and Bletchley Park's strategy and we had no alternative at that time. In a dialogue of the dumb, one party only could give voice.

To solve the Enigma mystery, the negotiator had to be persuaded into breaking cover, at least enough to start a conversation. Chesterman and I sang from the same hymn sheet, Chesterman taking up the refrain in another report of Sunday 1 October,

I don't believe it's been destroyed. I don't think it would be by someone who pays a five-figure sum for it. I can see no threats in this and if the author is prepared to contact me direct, I believe I can provide the reassurances he requires.

The writer of the letter was urged to contact the control room at Milton Keynes Police Station using a telephone number widely reproduced in news reports. 'Would I do that in his shoes?' I mused. 'I think not.'

Keen to get the middleman to comply with one of their standard procedures, the police had fixed on a hotline to the Thames Valley Police main switchboard. Chesterman came across very plausibly in press and radio interviews. He was having to tread an indistinct line that separated investigative success from illegality and lies. Immunity from prosecution is the prerogative of innocent parties. Therefore, Chesterman could guarantee that the self-acclaimed 'innocent' intermediary who was 'acting in good faith', would not be pursued in justice. Chesterman could 'provide the reassurances he (the "third party") requires.' Would the other party be sufficiently convinced to make direct contact, especially through the mechanism of a police station?

Regularly during the investigation, Chesterman took care to inscribe his thought processes and the consultation he had undertaken before agreeing the measures he put into practice in a policy book. The Crown Prosecution Service had been asked about the potential pitfalls of a 'no prosecution' offer. Colleagues based at Bletchley and in the main police offices right in the centre of Milton Keynes had their views taken into account, as did the psychologists, representatives from specialist national agencies and I. Procedures and debates devoured time. To the other side consumed by impatience and suspicion, the delay was troublesome and infuriating.

Less than five days after the fourth letter came the next, its envelope postmarked Milton Keynes. 'As a result of news reports asking the owner of G312 to reconsider his decision to destroy the machine ... he has reluctantly agreed to me contacting you further', wrote the 'owner's' representative to me, the director. The decision to destroy the machine had been made, 'because no agreement either by you, or the officer in charge of the investigation has been published in the press accepting the terms sent to you in a previous letter'.

On Wednesday 27 September, 'page 11', specified the author, the *Mail*'s article had produced an unintended affect, for in the minds of the 'client and the broker', it was obvious that the new 'owner' would have to prove his innocence. Feigning – or feeling – outrage at the aspersion that the machine might not have been bought in good faith, the letter sought to justify the violent response to the piece in the *Mail*. The transaction had never 'been about the money, but about not losing face'. The writer's client had 'unwittingly been drawn into this sordid affair', and if destroying the object of the client's 'anguish' was the only remedy, '... then so be it'. Bletchley Park received the letter just over twenty-four hours before a final deadline, Friday 6 October. By that time, the writer demanded media coverage proving that I and the police had fully acceded to his previously notified terms. Failure to perform would result in G312's destruction.

Undoubtedly the announcement made a good story, but the media responded instantly to the letter's ultimatum of Thursday 5 October: a notice was to be published and they obliged with blanket coverage. 'Thief gives museum 24 hours to find £25 000 and save Enigma machine,' ran the *Mail*. The paper elaborated, 'The museum has now decided to agree to the ransom demand because they are convinced that the author is genuine.' Tellingly, the Mail did not specify in what respect the author was believed to be 'genuine', whether in his claim to be representing the machine's 'new owner' or of acting in good faith. The explanation offered in the letters remained consistent. The fifth letter said that an intermediary was acting on behalf of 'the present owner (who is) of high office and is not prepared to become involved with the police who are clearly attempting to prove his complicity in an offence committed by others'. As usual, the author recycled his refrain about the client having unwittingly bought the machine in good faith only to discover that it had been stolen. The 'man of high office' was a new feature. A hectoring tone had returned and, this time, the author was not prepared to tolerate the niceties of extended consultation. Bletchley Park had been given twenty-four hours to publish guarantees and the deadline would expire at midnight on Friday 6 October. Sealed with the codeword, the timebomb's countdown ticked away.

'Enigma ransom shocker.' 'Enigma owners to pay ransom.' 'CID agree to Enigma cash.' 'New hope on Enigma.' Simon Chesterman and I had taken the deadline seriously and the bulk of Friday's coverage concentrated on the revelation that Bletchley Park had found enough money to pay the ransom. Off the record, I revealed to certain contacts that funds had been pledged by a single donor, who insisted on remaining anonymous.

In a couple of instances, I intimated that the donor was a company, not a person. Indeed, that was the case. 'We did not have the money,' I said, 'but we have been given funds by a private donor', which was reported by Sam Lister in *The Times*. Anyone who followed the coverage attentively might have deduced that all was not quite as it seemed. Chesterman and I had lost little time prevaricating. A friend and informed onlooker in a British multinational had offered to put up the funds on the basis that they would not be called for. In private, the police operations team and I were under no illusions about the author's credentials. 'Honest' and 'broker' in the current circumstances were opposing concepts.

Having the funds available enabled me and Chesterman to say so publicly with a clear conscience. 'My overriding priority has always been the safe return of the Enigma, a machine which has great historical importance,' said Chesterman in the *Mail*. A rapport had developed between the police spokesman and the newspaper, which had been given an early interview. The news was displayed with relish. 'To this end,' Chesterman went on, 'I am prepared to agree to the author's terms, and I hope now that the author will feel sufficiently reassured to telephone me to talk about how we can progress to the next stage.' According to the *Mail*, detectives and Bletchley Park had agreed the night before to meet the ransom in order to save the machine. In the *Mail*'s opinion, the author was a 'thief'. That was incorrect and did not go unnoticed.

Other newspapers focused on the latest letter sent to me, the ransom demand and the fact that Bletchley Park Trust was playing ball with an individual perceived by some to be a blackmailer. The *Mirror* described the police's decision to endorse the ransom as 'unprecedented', nevertheless acknowledging that 'A mystery man threatened to smash up the device if he did not get the cash by midnight tonight'. Yet the reports were balanced and accurate, as if understanding that a delicate game were underway, with one side's team blindfolded.

Details of how the £25 000 would be exchanged for the Abwehr Enigma had not been disclosed, and with good reason.

Neither the police nor Bletchley Park intended there to be a handover until they could engage in negotiations with the intermediary. It was a gamble, but we had resolved to let the midnight deadline expire if need be, while making it clear that we had the cash to hand. So far, the letters' author had declined either to meet or speak to me, his 'penpal', or my advisers. *The Times* recorded my hope, 'the museum had found enough money to pay the ransom but had no way of contacting the person making the demands ... We have to make contact before the deadline.' Chesterman offered himself as a conduit, 'I hope now that the author will feel sufficiently reassured to telephone me to talk about how we progress to the next stage.'

Live radio interviews that morning had been a little taxing. From the *Today* programme's swanky new glass apartment in the BBC's West London studios, I had been wheeled around other studios where live broadcasts had been stacked up. Guests for *Today* wait in a small, adjacent, transparent room, from which the famous journalists are visible. The mounting tension is more palpable than in a dentist's waiting room. A trolley in the anteroom is gradually relieved of toast, cereals and orange juice throughout the morning. Interviewees have either to be very hungry or very confident to plunder the trolley before they have been grilled. For some reason, the coffee machine was playing up, which was perhaps as well, given the adrenalin surfeit already in my system. I mused about when is blackmail not blackmail. 'When an honest broker is playing white knight?' Later, I learned that *Today* had done its best to roast Simon Chesterman with a tough line of questioning. Afterwards, I was glad that the programme had been only insistent, but not unreasonable. BBC Three Counties Radio was a different proposition. 'Running the gauntlet' sums up the tone of a regional radio news show hosted by John Gaunt. 'Gaunty' was swinging his axe that day, in a bid to chop away the ambiguity surrounding the case and reveal a clearing of common sense. It was a struggle to hold the party line without sounding either foolish or inept. 'Come on, Christine,' he said, 'it stands out a mile that this bloke is holding you to ransom and you're giving in.' He had a point, which I was powerless to acknowledge.

I headed off for some television interviews in studios at Millbank. Afterwards, I caught a train to Herne Hill and walked back to the office at the top of our family home. There was a development budget to be put to bed that day for the Trust, several fundraising letters had to be prepared and I needed to speak with Paul Davis, global marketing chief at Intermedia, the company organising finance and distribution for the forthcoming film of Robert Harris's novel, *Enigma*. My real state of mind was starting to be reflected in my health. The day before, I had visited an osteopath, Jonathan Le Bon, who had treated me while I was expecting our second daughter Imogen and to whom I had gone to be 'tuned up' from time to time. A perceptive practitioner, Jonathan did not need to read newspaper reports to understand what was going on in the Bletchley Park workplace. I had attributed the severe back pains I had been suffering to bad posture at computers. Le Bon disagreed and was forthright. 'You've got an acute kidney problem brought on by stress. I'll treat you now and give you some advice. If it doesn't improve dramatically in the next twenty-four hours, you'll need to be hospitalised.'

Back in the office at home in London on Friday, the answerphone was engorged with awaiting messages, which were mainly press enquiries. My mobile had a backlog of calls. The budget might have to wait till Sunday. Tomorrow would be important for Bletchley Park's historical development. I expected to be away for the day, meeting William Newman, son of the great Max Newman, Alan Turing's tutor at Cambridge. I would have to make up to Imogen, later, for missing two open days for prospective schools, on Saturday. With any luck, once the late afternoon press deadlines had passed, Eric and I could slip out for supper at a local restaurant.

Late afternoon sunlight caught the yellow blind's edge and the absent-minded cord furled round the roller, in a jig with the breeze. A clear, plate-glass desk top reposed in its rectangular cradle, two flat black metal legs straddling the white wooden floorboards at either end. The idle computer screen reflected the busy room, magnifying the view across the desk, its back to the sash window framing Victorian rooftops. At the computer's left stood a regiment of discs. A dark-wood Scandinavian stool was positioned in front of the desk, its sienna hessian kneepads and cushion poised to receive my grateful back. Face cupped in hand, elbow on desk, I gazed across white eaves to the two cages sitting on a varnished wood trunk at the right-hand end. There cavorted 'Someone' (a male rat) and the hyperactive female, 'No one', produced when Sofy's veterinary breeding programme had got out of hand. Rats are intelligent creatures, sociable and responsive to mood and voice. Generally, they sleep during the day but now they were rustling through straw, alert and inquisitive. My pulse rate slowed, they had a calming effect. Home.

Against the wall opposite to the desk rested a sofa clad in autumn's colours. Above it was a vast map of the world. The irregular alcoves were crammed with books, papers and project archives. A large, dark wardrobe divided two thirds of the room, the work area, from an enclave dubbed 'Aladdin's cave' by Imogen because a clothes rail and shelves against the room's far wall were hunting ground for art and craft materials and fancy dress clothes. Aladdin's cave had produced costumes ranging from a peacock to a pizza, at very short notice.

A matt mahogany-varnished door, two tall panels inset at the top, two smaller ones below, isolated the room from the house. Down two old-fashioned thinly carpeted staircases lay the emptiness of children at school. Shifting to the round black table in between desk and sofa, I swivelled in the orange office chair to process the latest batch of enquiries. 'You must be so tired of answering the same questions. Thanks for getting back to me,' said one of the considerate callers. The chair enveloped me; I am diminutive despite the surname.

Sofy disrupted the temporary peace, bursting in to regale me with the latest from school. The headmaster had enlivened a talk about pastoral care by describing how a pupil (it was Sofy) had arrived one day with bright turquoise hair. About to be reprimanded and sent home, she had interjected with, 'Do you think I should sue the manufacturers, sir? It should have come out in twenty washes.' In fact, the dye was permanent and had to be disguised, but Sofy's quick wit got her off the hook. 'Lighten up, bag lady,' she proclaimed, bouncing out of the room. Eric, Sofy and Imogen forced me to keep a sense of proportion, not least by teasing me about Bletchley. I cared about it intensely and felt personally responsible for imperfections. By now, taxi drivers had cross-questioned me about the Abwehr machine and more than once I had been yelled at across the street, 'You got that Enigma machine back yet?' The dusk smoothed out a furrow across my brow that had deepened with the years and with responsibility, in contrast to the fine laughter lines at the corners of eyes and mouth. I narrowed my eyes, deep blue, almond-shaped, set against quite prominent cheekbones and a pointed chin (especially when I am in a determined mood) but softened by a dimple. A button nose, just turned up, often failed fully to retain my bronze-rimmed spectacles. I had stretched the telephone wires to the table, where it was easier to focus exclusively on Enigma and, notes at the ready, I sat up straight to respond to the next incoming call.

'Christine *Large*.' A strange voice sliced through the routine. Metallic, low, male.

'Yes,' she said, 'I heard you!'

'Christine *Large*. Inshallah,' he rasped. The secret code word. 'You will be contacted further.'

The line went dead.

CHAPTER TWELVE

Cold, cold sea

Dead; stone cold; in 1940 there was little prospect of bringing alive the German Enigma trail. Chess champion Hugh Alexander had become Alan Turing's assistant in 1941 in Bletchley Park's Hut 8, where the naval cryptanalysts worked. Hut 4 was dealing with naval intelligence, Hut 6 tackled army and air force intercepts and Hut 3 occupants were the analysts for Hut 6.

Breaking German naval Enigma was to depend on a series of daring hijacks from enemy ships. In February 1940, submarine *U-33* yielded its most important secret. About to be captured by the British, the rotors from the U-boat's Enigma machine were parcelled out among officers, with orders to jettison them. By early morning, she had been sunk and the German survivors in the know believed that the rotors had been dropped into the sea. In the rush to deal with the crisis, two rotors were forgotten and subsequently discovered in a pair of leather trousers. Bletchley Park rejoiced in the knowledge released to Hut 8 by the hitherto unknown rotors.

However, the German navy's version of Enigma expunged the machine and procedural weaknesses that had delighted the British codebreakers. There were no crabs, lobsters, or crashes – when the same letter worked in a crib (clue) and in a cryptogram (coded message). These supposed Enigma complications some-times had the directly opposite effect from that intended. Naval Enigma operators were not foolishly prone to cillies such as lifting a message key sequence from a keyboard or using a pet name. During the 'Phoney War' of December 1939 to June 1940, the British produced 83 per cent of Enigma solutions without assistance from allies, amounting to several thousand messages. From May 1940, the Red Enigma Luftwaffe key, the airforce cipher system, was read regularly by the Allies. Breaks into Red and other messages could not in themselves guarantee military success and in June 1940, Paris fell to the Nazi régime.

A trawler flying the Dutch flag provided the first break into naval Enigma. On closer investigation, it turned out to be German and from one of the canvas bags flung overboard, notes for four days' worth of Enigma keys were retrieved. Bletchley Park quickly latched onto the precious material. In June, *U-13* ceded regulations for the use of naval Enigma.

Ian Fleming, the novelist later famed for 'James Bond', devised an imaginative if somewhat reckless plan to capture Enigma keys, but Operation Ruthless, planned for the autumn, perhaps fortunately never materialised. The spectre of losing the war against the U-boats was more serious than the Blitz, a truth that Churchill shared with the House of Commons towards the end of 1940.

One of a new class of destroyer, the *Somalia*, had engaged in a raid in Norwegian waters early in the next year, 1941. Without realising the significance of her find, she captured a wooden box containing some rotors and documents from the *Krebs*, a whaling trawler converted to a patrol vessel and disabled in action by *Somalia*. Bletchley's Hut 8 already had that particular version of rotors, but the paperwork included the Enigma tables for February and the number of solutions tripled to over thirty. Earlier messages could also be read because of the information seized. Eighteenth-century mathematicians inspired one form of detective tool devised by Hut 8 scions. Banburismus – sheets so called because they were prepared in Banbury, near Oxford – were a substitute for cribs and they relied on a form of statistical analysis used to track rotor movements. 'Romsing' was the tongue-in-cheek name for another technique that drew on the 'resources of modern science'.

Between January and April 1941, the number of German U-boats in the Atlantic escalated by one third and the crib-supplying kisses (identical messages, one of which was in a breakable cipher system) provided too little comfort, often too late. The British never had fewer than 2000 ships afloat and up to 15 per cent would be in the danger zone at any one time. German attacks on British convoys of food-importing ships precipitated rationing, first of petrol (September 1939) and then of food. From January 1940, all basic foods were rationed and nutrients less in demand were governed by a points system. The Allies would have to win the Battle of the Atlantic if they were to procure victory. If German U-boats established and maintained a stranglehold on essential supplies, the length of the war and even its outcome would be extremely uncertain.

Harry Hinsley, who had come to Bletchley from Cambridge and who had been working to improve GC&CS's communications with the Admiralty in London, hit upon a novel idea. Weather is an important factor in planning battles, Hinsley reasoned. Although U-boat command disapproved, the submarine fleet had been ordered to transmit weather reports, naturally enciphered in Enigma. The receiving weather ships would, logically, have to carry Enigma. Unlike the U-boats, the weather ships might have to be at sea for long periods of time. They would not be able to pick up new sets of Enigma keys. Hinsley realised that weather ships would be carrying several months' worth of Enigma keys. He hatched a plot with the Admiralty.

Weather ship *Munchen*, sailing along in April 1941, spotted hostile masts on the horizon and made an unsuccessful bid to flee. As she strove to escape, emergency drill kicked in and the boat's Enigma machine was bundled overboard in a lead-bottomed bag. Under fire, *Munchen* was abandoned but not sunk. Also abandoned were the short weather cipher and the inner and outer Enigma settings for home waters June keys. Strangely, the German navy deemed *Munchen's* loss insignificant. It had been a very fortunate British coup.

Within two days, there was a major step forward in the hunt for Enigma clues. It happened off the Icelandic coast in the North Atlantic in May 1941. S. W. Roskill, a British sea captain, chronicled the official history in his volumes, *The War at Sea*. The first edition merely states that '*U-110* was sunk by British surface warships on 9 May, 1941'. *The Secret Capture*, Roskill's book published in 1959, is the first mention of a spectacular hijack that Roskill regarded as immensely more important than subsequent U-boat captures. His daughter, Claire Dean, recalled Roskill's quest for the full story underlying the 'one small file which, doubtless for reasons of security, was kept apart from the main mass of the wartime archives'. Until 1959, the Royal Navy had never been given any credit for its role in the crucial retrieval and Roskill commented, 'We British are notoriously slow and diffident about publicising our successes, and by thus hiding our light under a bushel we not uncommonly allow others to claim a disproportionate share of the credit.' Bletchley Park in current times was almost lost because of reticence but it is an endearing and admirable trait of the great Bletchley Park codebreakers – those who were actually there rather than think they should have or would have been – that they emphasise teamwork and luck, rather than grabbing for glory.

Prominent figures in the *U-110* episode are Captain Baker-Cresswell and then Sub-Lieutenant David Balme. It was Balme who, in November 2001, represented all those engaged in breaking Enigma, at a Royal British Legion Festival of Remembrance in the Albert Hall, London.

'Hearty congratulations, the petals of your flower are of rare beauty', is not perhaps the language one would expect from a First Sea Lord, but that was the message sent to Baker-Cresswell late on 13 May 1941.

A maritime safari to track down submarine *U-110* had been launched on 9 May, just after noon. The quarry was a magnificent specimen, sleek of build and powerfully equipped. A notorious captain commanded her. Fritz-Julius Lemp had begun his war by sinking the *Athenia* on the day after war was declared. After the war, the Germans ranked Lemp in the top twenty most successful of the country's U-boat commanders.

Baker-Cresswell's convoy escort group attacked and forced *U-110* to the surface. Fearing that the submarine was about to be rammed by a destroyer heading straight at it, Lemp ordered his crew to abandon ship. Baker-Cresswell remembered the *Magdeburg*'s intelligence value in the First World War and, at the last moment, the British ship veered away. Only light damage, or so it appeared, was sustained by *U-110*.

Riding the huge swell in an otherwise calm sea, Sub-Lieutenant David Balme's whaler rolled up to the submarine. Floundering Germans bobbed in the glacial sea, but Balme wondered whether the U-boat contained a trap. It was reluctantly that he stowed his revolver in its holster and, conscious that he made a perfect target, he cautiously grappled his way down inside the conning tower, which was heaving with the waves. Baker-Cresswell strained to monitor their progress from his ship, *Bulldog*, while *Broadway* and *Aubretia* looked on.

U-110 was set like a stage, with no actors and no sign of an audience. Lights blazed. Depth charges thudded distantly. Antisubmarine signals anxiously pinged from time to time. Dönitz's German naval command in Lorient on the French north-west shore might, if alerted, call up nearby reinforcements that could speed to the kill in under an hour. As the boarding party indiscriminately gathered working documents and technical equipment, *U-110*'s injured plates creaked and quiet water bubbled slowly.

In the radio room, there was a typewriter-like device, bolted to the table. Its normal keys produced peculiar results and the machine was recognised as cipher equipment. Many hours passed on the ship and, in the late afternoon, officers debated how to take her in tow. Her sharp bow could knife through the destroyer's thin armour if the submarine were wrongly aligned. Three-and-a-half-inch wire through *U-110*'s towing eye tied her to the *Bulldog* as they progressed towards the misty horizon. A stray periscope set off an Asdic scare but the underwater messenger signals returned no threatening news and the convoy proceeded. There were two days' travelling – over 400 miles – to go and the sea and the wind began rising with the dawn. On 10 May, German command concluded that *U-110* had been lost, just as the outgoing crew had assumed.

During the morning *U-110* listed towards the far-off destination. Suddenly, she reared like a frightened animal, froze vertically and pierced downwards into the ocean. Rapidly, the tow was slipped. *Bulldog* did not plunge with *U-110*, but Baker-Cresswell thought that his precious cargo had been lost. On the contrary, the quality of the material that had been recovered was exceptional. Cryptographers in Bletchley's Hut 8 received key tables for general- and officer-grade Enigma messages, books of indicators, details of how the cue word emergency system worked to replace compromised keys and a U-boat short signal book. Of course, there was also a prized naval Enigma machine.

With the benefit of *U-110*'s hoard, Bletchley Park at the end of May was translating and teleprinting messages to the Admiralty on average thirty-four hours after they had been intercepted. They were hot on German heels.

CHAPTER THIRTEEN

Cat and mouse

At last, the middleman had appeared on the sonar. Before I could reach my mobile phone to call the police, the land line rang again. I held my breath and snatched the receiver before the answerphone interrupted. 'Christine Large.' Did I sound out what I was thinking? Pause. 'It's Sam, Sam Lister. *The Times*.' He was finishing off his report and wanted to find out if there had been any developments.

'Developments? Right.' I released my breath gently, heart thumping. Sorry! I explained that I'd just run upstairs. No, there was no change in the situation since this morning. The midnight deadline stood and we were appealing to the middleman to get in touch direct. 'Thanks for calling.'

The next journalist left a message for the electronic android. I was talking to Chesterman. 'Are you all right?' he asked.

'I think so. Wasn't expecting it.' The impact had been like the shock of discovering plaintext in the middle of a cipher.

'... and we'll send you some support, just in case he calls again,' Chesterman was saying. 'Just sit tight and a colleague will be in touch.' Ever the professional, he wanted to agree a password and restrict it on a tight need-to-know basis. What would be easy to remember? 'OK, "bravo" it is.' Chesterman advised me to bear in mind that the other side could check us out by pretending to be a police officer. He said he would talk to me later.

On a piece of paper swept aside in the flurry, I wrote down the call's time and meagre content. 'Withheld number' flashed on the mobile. 'Bravo. This is Gerry speaking. Is there a back door into your house?'

'I ... pardon?' I stuttered.

'A back door?' Gerry repeated. 'The place may be being watched and we want to come in undetected.'

'We, *we?*' I puzzled. Yes ... there is a back door but no, 'they' couldn't access it from the street.

Gerry asked how well I knew our neighbours. 'Can we enter through their back garden?'

I replied that the neighbours had just moved out. We hadn't met the new ones, they were too busy fortifying their house with window bars and security devices. They came and went, and Gerry and cohort would anyway have to climb over their fence. In all probability the police would set off a pack of alarms and have the local squad piling in. This struck me as adding unnecessary drama to an already tense situation. Had Gerry's team had an imagination-bypass? They could pretend to be council maintenance workers, window cleaners, gardeners or one of the scams regularly flagged up in police 'Neighbourhood Watch' bulletins.

Conscious I might be treading on their toes, I suggested that there might be an easier way. Eric, my husband and I, were supposed to be going out but we could be having friends in, to dinner. Why didn't they – how many people? – pretend they were coming for supper? They could walk up to the front door then, I said. 'And,' I added, spicing up the menu, 'why don't you bring a bottle of wine from the local off-licence at the top of the road in Herne Hill?' The shop was on the way from the station (would they be travelling by car?) and they'd seem like guests.

'Cheers, Christine,' grinned Gerry's voice. They would get there as soon as they could. Meanwhile, Gerry asked me to sit tight, write down all the details if he called again and play for time. 'Keep him on the line.'

Press calls were petering out and I went downstairs to explain the news to my husband. I was really sorry; it looked like we would be late going out. I was not sure how long the imminent visitors would expect to stay. 'Let's play it by ear,' said Eric. We would have to tell the girls something, though we did not want to complicate things. The mood in our back lounge was disgruntled. From the room, through dark-stained wooden French windows set with small-leaded, clear diamond glass, we would have had a splendid view of the police performance, had they chosen to crash over the neighbouring fences into our back garden. I dare say that Eric would not have relished a brace of regulation boots chomping through his carefully tended shrubs. Still, they were only doing their job, how could they have known?

I broached the tidings to Sofy and Imogen. They were not impressed by the idea of my having another meeting, in their home and on a Friday evening. 'Here Bletchley Park goes again, poor you,' said Sofy, ever the elder statesman. She had installed herself in a favourite cocoa-coloured two-seater sofa at the back of the room. Eric had repaired its sagging frame and no one but Sofy could bear to inhabit it, having moulded it to her shape. Light from a bronze-capped floor lamp emphasised the bright blonde streaks in her auburn bob and she gave me a glance, saw my expression and let the challenge drop. Sofy, Imogen, Eric – their humour and loyalty kept me going. They could be critical too, it was that sort of family environment; we are all independent, have different interests (some overlapping, some antagonistic) and an innocuous meal can quickly turn to heated debate. Imogen's naturally blonde head raised itself from her reading on the safari sofa by the doors. She pursed her full lips, an irritated flush set on fair cheeks. Our second daughter peered imperiously over her spectacles, a storm in her blue-green-hazel eyes. 'I don't suppose there's any chance of our supper?' came the voice from the depths of Imogen's book.

It was gone seven when the doorbell rang. Three deliberately cheerful guests ostentatiously proffered a bag from the off-licence. They 'hoped they were not too early'. (What polite 'guests' indeed.) Inside, Gerry introduced himself as being from NCIS, the criminal investigation squad, with Jo and Mick. Their technical guy Paul Ballard was just getting some 'stuff' out of the car. 'Sorry about the wine, it's the cheapest plonk we could find,' grimaced Jo. A glass of wine was beginning to sound like a remarkably good idea, though police budgets being what they are, I reckoned that their 'plonk' wasn't fit for cooking.

Upstairs in the office, Gerry sat amiably on the sofa, the technician examined the telephone and computer sockets and Jo busied herself with papers. I wondered how to entertain my unexpected guests. 'Tea? Coffee, how do you take it?'

They had distinct preferences. I sensed that Gerry was studying my reactions. He had an open, inquisitive face and confident body language. In the corner, the rats had been animated by the new arrivals. 'An animal lover, are you?' he enquired.

I replied that rats were a bit of a new thing, but that I did chair a national charity that investigated human – animal interactions, *just like he's doing*, I thought. The middleman's call had come like a guillotine cutting through the easy conversations with journalists. 'You will be contacted further.' Covert operations, back door tactics, might be being watched; I felt under surveillance, by which side I was not sure. Worried for my family – it was nothing to do with them – I related the sequence to Gerry and the equally intent Jo.

In the background, the technician was clicking his tongue. 'Dear oh me, can't do what I need here, haven't got the parts. It'll have to be a bodge job for the moment. I'm off now,' he said. He was sorry to spoil the party, but he would be back later with the proper kit. Probably tomorrow, the depot would be closed now. It could have been a routine maintenance job although to my ears, it began to have the ring of brain surgery without the patient's consent. 'Bye, mate,' chorused Gerry and Jo.

The phone had stopped ringing and a comparative calm was established. 'Just go on as normal,' said Gerry, 'don't mind us.' (Don't mind them. He couldn't be serious). 'If we could just brief you about the next stage, then we'll all be ready.' Gerry was medium height, of athletic build, a swimmer rather than a runner, perhaps, and had the demeanour of a muscular cat poised to spring. The 'dress-down-Friday' mode could easily be his natural habitat. He had clean-cut jaw, crew-cut light hair and his direct gaze held my attention. 'This is like a hostage situation. The Enigma has been kidnapped. It's cat and mouse. We need to trace his call; so the longer he's on the phone, the better chance we'll have. He probably knows that too. When he comes through, we'll prompt you by holding up notices. Take it easy, take your time. Let's have a rehearsal.'

It was after 21.00 and I offered to make the team a bite of supper, or order in a takeaway. 'I had something earlier, thanks,' said Jo. 'We're used to eating on the move.' My sister, Caroline, who was staying with us, put her blonde head gingerly round the office door. 'Eric and I are going for fish and chips. Fancy some?' I certainly did. How about Gerry and Jo? Gerry didn't see any harm in it; no one seemed to be monitoring the house.

Shortly afterwards, Caroline hovered at the office door, wondering whether to provide room service. I thanked her, but I didn't want to eat with the rats. 'Oh, Gerry's not as bad as all that,' responded Caroline, retreating from the slightly pungent rodent odour and clattering downstairs with the tray. I found this hysterically funny, it relieved the tension.

Squeezed together, four on a three-seater sofa in the family lounge downstairs, Gerry, Eric, Caroline, daughters Sofy and Imogen and I pretended to be distracted by the television and the takeaway, but not for long. Back up in the office, Gerry proposed a run-through. 'We're hooked up now to the outside unit, so we will be able to trace a call if contact can be maintained for long enough. What we'd like you to do is keep him talking. The whole purpose of the exercise is to get into a negotiating position. It would have been easier if he'd gone direct to Simon, but I'm very confident that you can handle whatever is thrown at you.' I let the vote of confidence ride. 'There's a private dick who's been phoning in to give us advice,' said Gerry, 'bit of a smart Alec. We'd like you to check him out. Jo here will be listening in and we'll use this pad to scribble down instructions if we need you to steer the conversation in a particular direction. Wave your hand when you think you're getting into trouble. Just relax, you'll be fine.' The three huddled by the circular stage. Jo was cross-legged on the floor, pressing earphones to one side of her finely boned, tilted face, folk singer's hair screening her expression. Gerry sat opposite on the sofa left of me. He concentrated, leaning forward. In the orange chair I sat, left arm protectively around abandoned correspondence and right hand resting on the hotline handle. Within sight was an unlined paper sheet on which I had scribbled the key instructions in case of a repeat call. 'Can I just say that I can't get the money?' In a rectangular block were capitalised words, piled one underneath the other: 'Write. Extend. Be Even. Commit.' They were instructions in conducting the next conversation with the middleman. In an uneven lozenge in the page centre was a telephone number, the one I had been told that would connect to a BT security negotiator.

Prodding in the number as Gerry read it out, I blanked out the studio set-up, focusing on the handset. 'Evening, apologies for calling this late, it's Christine Large, Bletchley Park Trust. I understand that you might be willing to give me some advice and I'm phoning first and foremost to say "thanks".' I paused. Did it sound as script-like to him as it did to me? Every profession has its protective shorthand; this was, well, 'plod-speak'.

The private detective paused to suck in breath and told me that, well, love, he appreciated my call. It was just that he had had quite a lot of experience with this sort of thing and that I might not be getting the best advice from the police. Gerry made a picturesque face and motioned to continue. I confessed that this was all completely new to me, I was a total novice and if he could spare the time now, I'd be grateful for some guidance. He cleared his throat and I almost heard the private investigator tilt back in his seat, expand his chest and take a lungful of breath. Now there, he had every sympathy. He had assisted his clients with similar situations and they could, he underlined, be very nasty indeed. No person in this position was going to want to talk to the police; they couldn't be trusted, so he'd homed in on me. What I needed to do first is to establish a codeword that I could use between trusted people, as proof of identity, he advised.

('Hadn't he read the papers? I wondered. Gerry was quietly exploding beside me.) That was an interesting idea; I asked, how did it work?

The ace sleuth continued to hold forth, '... and I wouldn't advise you to deliver the money alone ...'

I gradually became conscious of a piece of paper being waved to my right. It said, 'Stop!' I cut into the guru's pronouncements and thanked him ever so much for really putting me wise to the options. 'Look, may I call you again if need be?' Click. The call concluded.

'Unbelievable,' said Gerry. 'I thought you were going to go on all night.'

'The boys have got the source,' confirmed Jo.

'Think we'll pay our friend a visit,' said Gerry, 'He could be a former policemen, quite a few of them go into that line. We'll check him out.' I did not think that the previously anonymous adviser would enjoy their appraisal.

At 23.30, the phone rang. 'Follow the drill, don't overreact,' went the chant in my mind as I picked it up. My, a journalist was working late. No, we hadn't heard, the deadline was close but we were still hoping I replied to the enquiry. The Press Association had been following up.

As the hour advanced, the prospect of a contact declined. Gerry was the last 'dinner guest' to leave and he had stayed to witness the embers of the day. In his absence, wire basketry nested on the central table and the expanse of glass. The technology trail ran from the desks, across the office, down the Edwardian wood balustrades and connected to a suitable socket in the first-floor bedroom overlooking the street. It looked as if a plate of spaghetti had been tipped over the banisters. ('How am I going to explain that to Sofy and Imogen?' I wondered. 'BP' [short for Bletchley Park] trialling some new technology?) A rather basic answerphone had supplanted the original, which had been removed for evidence, swept like redundant body parts into a plastic bag. Too late in the day to buy spare answerphone tapes, and the visitors had suggested that a supply might be useful.

Theoretical discussions about phone calls could be light-heartedly dismissed, but when the moment had come, it made a sick knot in my stomach. I felt I was being stalked and I was worried for the family's security and, to a degree, my own safety. Sleep was out of the question and work not in short supply. At 04.00, I turned in. William Newman was making a special visit to Bletchley later that morning and it was essential to maintain a semblance of normality.

CHAPTER FOURTEEN

Misunderstanding

Later that morning, but still early, the *Today* programme bent its rules and allowed me to appear two days running to appeal to the incommunicative middleman. Midnight had passed without a call and no repetition of the threat to destroy the machine. Would the story end there, suspended on a cruel joke? I travelled on to Bletchley.

Codebreakers' progeny can be unpredictable. The fear that the great Max Newman's son might be unimpressed by Bletchley Park's efforts to commemorate his father's work was unfounded and William Newman was a courteous and attentive guest. He was notably sympathetic to the additional pressures imposed by the Enigma theft, as journalists turned up for interviews or speculatively. After lunch, there was a call from my husband. 'There's a message, I think you ought to listen to it,' he said. I excused myself from the middle of an interview with Anglia Television's Penny Wright. I listened from Bletchley, on my mobile, as Eric held the telephone handpiece to the answerphone in my office. On Saturday 7 October, the muffled instructions came,

> Christine Large — Inshallah. Notify BBC Television that the Enigma will be returned to them minus coding wheels. You will be contacted further. Goodbye.

I had been 'contacted further' and the caller had presaged future communication.

Bletchley Park and the police decided to take the BBC into our confidence, in a manner of speaking. With Penny Wright's help, directors and security chiefs were prised from their weekend comforts to confront the peculiar news. The BBC's chief crime correspondent, Stephen Cape, assured DCI Chesterman and me that the whole of BBC security was on red alert. Over the telephone, the message had been indistinct, so the question was, where in the BBC? Local to Bletchley Park? From one of the demand letter's mailing points? The BBC would 'take no chances'. Having heard that BBC security had a propensity to explode suspicious packages, I had visions of the rescued, priceless Enigma machine being destroyed in an ignorant accident.

Stephen Cape had insisted on a news blackout at the BBC. There were whispers circulating round the BBC's regional offices and Three Counties Radio's Paul Meurice was fast to check them out. He had an uncanny knack of being able to find me almost anywhere; even, I ruefully reflected, on a wedding anniversary by the Patriarch's Ponds in Moscow. Without repudiating his information, I metaphorically shrugged and suggested that whoever had transcribed the idea on the BBC's internal news-gathering system might have got confused with the message of the previous day. The rumours faded out.

Three theories were still doing the rounds. *Milton Keynes on Sunday* reported my reactions to them. First, the theft was a sophisticated hoax. 'I don't buy this theory,' I said. 'Everything we've seen in the letter and evidence suggest that this person(s) has got the machine in their possession or knows the person who has.'

Second, it was a complicated game. I was less dismissive of this notion, saying, 'It could be that whoever it is, is playing some sort of game we don't understand, in which case there's not a lot we can do except follow up the clues we already have.' Third, the idea that the machine had been destroyed, I found 'hard to believe. Anyone who has gone to these lengths to get it is hardly likely to destroy it.'

'Short, specific and businesslike,' was how I had described the telephone call. My public stance was that when the call had come in, I had not been in a position to deal with the whereabouts of the funds at the time. Now, I was ready for discussions and awaiting developments. The money had been donated by 'an anonymous, kind benefactor'. The media quoted me, 'We are not viewing this as blackmail. We are viewing it as buying something from someone who acquired it in good faith.' At least, until the evidence might prove otherwise.

Cheerful chaos swirled around Simon Chesterman as he weathered Sunday evening in with four children and in-laws. Mrs Chesterman tried to subdue the rioting youngsters as she answered the phone. 'Simon, it's for you. Can you get a move on, the kids' bath will overflow.'

'Who is it, then?' asked Chesterman.

'Pollard, I think he said, a Charles Pollard.' The only Pollard that came to mind was the head of the force, Sir Charles Pollard. It was unprecedented for even a senior officer to be called direct without cascading through the hierarchy, let alone be called on leave and at home.

'I thought one of my mates was taking the piss,' said Chesterman. He went to the kitchen to take the call.

'It's Charles Pollard here. I'm phoning about the Enigma case.'

Chesterman tried to compute the voice but didn't recognise it. 'How can I help ... Sir?' he hesitantly asked. There was to be a meeting the next day with the chairman of the Police Authority. The chairman, who also chaired the local magistrates' bench, was very interested in the case. This was hardly surprising. Having returned from a rudely interrupted beach respite, Police Authority chief Mac Hobley, a longstanding Bletchley Park guide, had discovered that the Enigma theft was no mirage.

'Have major crime got involved?' enquired Sir Charles. Chesterman had in fact already scheduled a meeting, but it was brought forward, a sure sign of top-level support. Sir Charles had visited Bletchley Park with his wife and this experience had sparked off a genuine interest that was maintained from that point on.

Sir Charles's enthusiasm for Bletchley was far from unique in the force. Chief Superintendent Mick Page, area commander of the Milton Keynes police area, had studied Enigma as part of his degree in Second World War history and had since continued to read avidly about battles and battlefields. Sir Philip Duncombe had 'picked up the blower to Commander Page' shortly after news broke of the theft, inviting him to witness the lie of the land at first hand. Page had had no hesitation in accepting and he had exhorted his colleagues to get under the investigation's skin by delving into Bletchley's library.

Meanwhile, Gerry and I spent another cosy evening in the London office, nursing an unresponsive phone.

Press reports heralding the week ahead mentioned that I was, 'sure that the machine will be back at Bletchley Park soon for all to enjoy'. The *International HeraldTribune* ran a feature. In it, 'Ms. Large' said, 'Clearly, the machine was stolen, but we don't believe it was stolen by the people who are in possession of it now.' I confirmed that the police had given certain assurances (about immunity from prosecution) and that, 'they have gone some way to being accepted'.

It was Monday 9 October. Arranging the terms of transfer for a full-size replica submarine section from the *Enigma* film provided me with light relief amidst budgets and contracts. That afternoon, Carol Moon, a loyal lieutenant in charge of the Bletchley Park shop, picked up a call intended for me. Something about its brevity, anonymity and tone prompted her to keep it quiet and to notify me and the police. It was a moment that tipped the investigation into overdrive.

Simon Chesterman was enjoying the responsibility of the job, but he needed support and additional resources. Dave Buckenham, a detective superintendent with whom Chesterman had worked, was appointed senior investigating officer (SIO) on the Monday. Buckenham viewed himself in the mould of a television detective, something of an 'Inspector Morse'. He had a carefully cultivated casual air, designed to put the suspect at ease while Buckenham conducted a character appraisal. Sandy-haired and slightly balding, his ruddy cheeks balanced a smiling mouth and still eyes. Respectable chain-store suits polished his already shiny shoes and he ran an unaware finger between his crisp, blue shirt collar and prolific hairline. The SIO kept himself in the background. He was a mite political; a bit of a string-puller; nearly very senior but not quite.

It was weeks since the meeting with the national crime, high-tech and criminal investigation teams. David Jones from the blackmail unit had monitored a couple of the letters that were trying to use the media as brokers. Peter Spindler had already contacted Chesterman, offering NCS services, only available by invitation. 'They came to me before I went to them,' said Chesterman. The nationals were coming in to support the home force. Careers could be riding on it.

DS Buckenham appointed a team to man the incident room he had set up. There had been three phone calls and suspects were slowly coalescing in the investigative frame. Detective Constable Fulton and his moderator Tim Dickinson did not deal with just one job; they had a number of assignments on the go at any one time and they were responsible for managing the intelligence. 'Everyone is a potential target,' said Fulton, 'until we've written them in or out, proven them guilty or innocent. Christine Large is first on my list.'

Fulton set about profiling me. I had a motive – publicity for Bletchley Park. The theft could be a stunt to bring attention to Bletchley's plight and raise funds. The intelligence officer compiled my background. What had I done before and why? Good academically, law degree, part-time lecturing, business, voluntary work. Smart enough to head up the suspects list. Had I or my husband had compromising business connections? Did I carry out every instruction from the police? Was I fully co-operative or just playing along? Where was I when the machine had been stolen? Could I be under financial pressure? Fulton couldn't see any major problem in the bank and credit statements …

I had a newsless, birthday night in. There was no further information for the trust board on Wednesday 11 October. My vigil towards the weekend was lonely. The police reckoned I could deal with a call and they expressed a mobile telephone to me from Oxford to London by Detective Sergeant Gary Grewal, late one evening. It was to be used exclusively for priority operational calls. Police economics baffled me. Not only had the phone been rushed from Oxford to London by car; it also lacked a spare battery or power source. The chunky traditional model would have exhausted its energies without the vintage charger cannibalised from a cupboard at home. However, radio silence reigned. The BBC relaxed its guard. The middleman had gone to ground with his unreadable code.

CHAPTER FIFTEEN

Knots

The U-boat code was the most difficult of all to crack. It was used extensively by the German navy and the Allies had struggled to find a way in, for failure to penetrate the U-boats' defences could lose the war. Even when, thanks to *Bulldog* and others rounding up *U-110*, intercepted messages could be read, a fresh supply of keys was needed to rejuvenate the codebreaking effort. Captured keys had a sell-by date and once expired, another supplier was required.

Late in May 1941, a converted motorised fishing vessel, *Lauenberg*, was selected as the Allies' next prey. Her captain was a former fisherman skilled in evading the treacherous icebergs that crystallised the northern waters' depths. On *Lauenberg's* trail was an eccentric hunter called Lionel P. Skipwith and known as 'Kim'. To relax, he embroidered and distinguished his craft with unconventional design schemes, rendering his cabin and the deck tropical yellow and lime green. His equally disconcerting tactics might have impressed the young Ludovic Kennedy, a sub-lieutenant aboard Kim's HMS *Tartar*. Firing high-explosive practice shells above *Lauenberg*, Skipwith persuaded its crew to abandon ship. As was the norm, their Enigma machine was relinquished to the deep. Some documents had been burned but the surviving sacks held the July home waters key and internal Enigma settings sheets. Intelligence penetration time crashed from two days to less than two hundred minutes.

At the end of August 1941, the Allies gained an unexpectedly useful casualty, a submarine that had surfaced south of Iceland as a spotter plane was flying overhead. *U-570* yielded a curious find. The Enigma machine hood had four windows for key letters, not the usual three. Messages recovered with the Enigma had been enciphered in three- and four-rotor mode, which allowed Hut 8 to deduce the wiring of the fourth rotor. It was an omen.

When Churchill visited Bletchley Park in September 1941, he had reason to be glad that the efforts to break Enigma were gradually paying off. The prime minister had been enamoured of secret intelligence since the power of *Magdeburg's* codebook had been placed in his hands in 1914. He attached more importance to intercepts as a means of gauging public policy's direction than to any other source of knowledge at the government's disposal. A daily selection of several dozen Enigma messages was supplied to Churchill in a buff-coloured dispatch box disguised as 'Boniface' but converted in due course to 'Ultra'. Ultra was the name for the secret intelligence produced at Bletchley Park from the breaking of high-grade enemy ciphers (such as Enigma) and the analysis of intercepted signals. Churchill (for example in communications with Roosevelt) referred to information from signals intelligence (Sigint) as 'Boniface', the mythical secret agent from whom, to camouflage the source, it was supposedly obtained.

Papers from 1940 show that on 8 November that year, thirty-one people received Ultra, supplemented in December by a judge. Almost all the names are familiar. Apart from Churchill, there was General Ismay, Lord Halifax, 'C' (Colonel Menzies), Anthony Eden, Clement Attlee, Lord Beaverbrook, Ernest Bevin, the king's ADC, Air Chief Marshal Sir Hugh Dowding and others. Churchill set great store by his intelligence goldmine and visited it quite often, though it was rare for him to do so officially.

Standing astride the trunk of a tree felled outside Hut 6, Churchill beamed at the startled Bletchley mob. 'You all look very innocent,' he addressed them in stentorian tones, praising his 'geese that laid the golden eggs and never cackled'. In an aside later, he revealed that, while he had told the recruiters to take anyone able they could lay hands on, he had not expected to plumb the barrel to *that* extent. 'You don't have to be mad to work here, but it helps,' summed up Malcolm Muggeridge, a Bletchley alumnus.

The codebreaking game went backwards and forwards like the balls over the tennis court available to distract the Bletchley folk in their precious leisure time. One day a new U-boat net, one day not enough bombe operators to decipher the normal Luftwaffe code. The codebreakers at the heart of Bletchley's operation were themselves close to breaking. 'Dear Prime Minister,' wrote Turing, Welchman, Alexander and Milner-Barry on 21 October 1941. Nelson had saved England from Napoleon's invasion on that very date in 1805, commemorated as Trafalgar day.

> Our reason for writing to you direct is that for months we have done everything that we possibly can through the normal channels, and that we despair of any early improvement without your intervention.

The letter was headed, 'Secret and Confidential. Prime Minister only'. Flouting convention by going straight to the top, the four 'wicked uncles', as they were known, set out the case for more people and equipment to discharge their pressing tasks. They talked of bottlenecks in breaking naval Enigma. Overnight shifts in Hut 8 had been stopped due to a severe shortage of clerks. The skilled male staff, which had been working on bombe production and at Bletchley, was liable to be called up at any moment. There was a log jam in military and air force Enigma; the decoding personnel were exhausted and there were insufficient typists to deal with the rich crop of wireless traffic being intercepted in the Middle East. There was no sign of the Wrens who had been promised to take over testing results from the bombes, causing valuable people from Huts 6 and 8 to be diverted from urgent jobs. 'We have written this letter entirely on our own initiative. We do not know who or what is responsible for our difficulties,' though the four were at pains to stress that the fault did not lie with the Park's deputy boss, the forceful and effective 'Jumbo' Travis. 'But if we are to do our job as well as it could and should be done it is absolutely vital that our wants, small as they are, should be promptly attended to.' The tactic worked. Churchill wrote to his chief of staff, the secretary of the Committee of Imperial Defence, General Ismay, 'Secret. In a locked box. Make sure that they have all that they need in extreme priority and report to me that this has been done.' 'ACTION THIS DAY' the note was stamped. By 19 November, Ismay was able to report that his instructions to the Ministry of Labour and the department of the Admiralty, which dealt with WRNS, had unblocked the supply of labour for Bletchley.

Four not-so-wicked uncles' action had set Bletchley on the path of mass-production. From the unlikely shooting party in autumn 1938, the operation had expanded to 1500 people. The demands of breaking Enigma were straining scarce housing, food and transport. There were political battles to fight if Hut 8 was to stay focused on protecting the grain, sugar, fuel oil and essential metals destined for Britain. Commander Travis was appointed to create the environment in which the modern world could develop, at Bletchley. A massive and sustained attack would be needed to destroy the Germans' central nervous system, the Enigma.

Enigma guarded the heart of the enemy's war at sea, the U-boats. As the navy's main cipher method, it was the brain controlling the fleet's movements and the Germans constantly strove to protect its security. There had been two major investigations in 1941, prompted by fears that the Allies had hijacked naval Enigma. U-boat and destroyer losses that were geographically far apart but close in time had fuelled suspicions. *Bismarck* was a case in point. The British had learned the position of German support ships in May and tried to cover their codebreaking tracks by deliberately choosing not to sink two ships. Unfortunately, Royal Navy warships came across them unexpectedly and boosted the haul. *U-570*'s capture, prompted by a lucky spotter plane, triggered another German investigation. The conclusions reassured German high command. Indeed, the

Germans were breaking codes too and had found the Royal Navy's ubiquitous five-digit code easy meat, breaking it in 1935. Wilhelm Tranow led the team of 900 Germans and his seafaring knowledge proved invaluable in breaking more complex codes. Mid-1940, the Germans were already reading up to 50 per cent of the British Navy's intercepted messages. The extreme security surrounding Ultra and its use was its salvation, for British messages never gave away the fact that Enigma had been infiltrated.

Yet the watchful Dönitz did not rest on his laurels. Germany might think that its Enigma system was, as one report asserted, sixty times better than their enemy's. It was strange, he thought, that U-boat wolf packs were less successful than individual submarines in hunting down convoys. Were German procedures getting sloppy? Could a spy be passing out details on planned attacks and routes? Or had the British developed some new radar or reconnaissance technique? Whatever the reason, Dönitz was conscious of the risks inherent in the growing traffic volume, which was on course for a ten-fold increase over 1939. The admiral played a master card. On 1 February 1942, the whole German naval Enigma traffic blacked out. There would be no light at Bletchley until the Allies were to spring an Enigma trap.

CHAPTER SIXTEEN

Man at the helm

Wartime Bletchley had managed to conceal the secret sources of its intelligence amidst seemingly innocent British naval message traffic, which the Germans intercepted. The modern-day Master and his accomplice in signals were not so clever. Their telephone communications started to reveal an interesting pattern. Enquiries revolved around two telephone kiosks in quite close proximity and from which calls to me had been made on two separate dates. Police data at the time indicated that immediately after each demand, a certain mobile phone had been called. The logical conclusion was that the person making the demand calls also telephoned the mobile number. It would be too much of a coincidence otherwise. Enquiries were made into the mobile phone and its itemised billing. Having identified the mobile's user, the police had no option but to believe that the person must in some way be involved in the crime. Investigators discovered that the mobile phone had been in contact with a person in close proximity to the telephone kiosk. At face value, it looked as if the person identified had been making demand calls and reporting back afterwards, presumably to the Master.

Tuesday 17 October was a grey and grainy London affair. Late on, never far from at least two telephones, I sat at my desk, preparing material for a lunchtime speech with trustee Peter Wescombe the next day, at a conference organised by City bankers Kleinwort Benson. Enigma was not top of mind. Oddly, it was something of a relief that the middleman had not delivered.

In addition to a monthly Trust Executive meeting, top-level discussions were underway with the regional development agency about establishing a technology incubator in the Park. It was a facet of the Trust's strategic plan, important for the future, and I could not afford to be distracted. Fortunately, the pressure of news gathering had abated. The telephone rang, but I let the answerphone kick in.

A public school male voice announced itself, 'This is Jeremy Paxman.' Pause. Thinking that 'enough is enough', words formed in my throat. 'And this is the Archbishop of Canterbury,' I was about to say but I didn't, because the confident tone continued, 'I believe we have something that belongs to you.'

'I hear that Christmas has come early for Bletchley Park,' I said as I picked up Paxman's call.

It had been 'a hell of a day' for Dave Barker. To cap it all, he was told that *Newsnight* was going to, ' "do" the Enigma' on that night's show. Barker drove from Milton Keynes to London in a carefully selected and specially cleaned, four-door Corsa, a serviceable but unostentatious small car. 'They could at least have managed a Ford Sierra,' he grumbled under his breath as he set off to recover the Enigma machine's shell in the bright blue vehicle. His mates had, he muttered 'enjoyed taking the urine'. Outside the BBC Television Centre in Wood Lane there was a camera reception committee fit for a royal wedding. Barker pulled up and parked right outside the door, relieved of the usual unwelcoming.

While he was away on holiday, Paxman's post had gathered dust in some unobserved BBC corridor. It hadn't struck anyone as strange (although the illustrious television presenter, feared for training his microscope on political specimens, never received anything larger than review books) that a large typewriter-sized box, posted in Derbyshire, had been languishing for his attention. For six days, I and the police had waited, expecting a low-key call from BBC security. The *Newsnight* unit manager had not been unduly bothered by the parcel. Having seen it in her office, she thought, 'Books. Usually parcels have been scanned before anything gets to the studio, so that's what made me think it was books. Jeremy gets hundreds of them.'

Paxman had dropped in for a chat after he got back from holiday. He looked at the parcel and gave the manager a hand to unpack it, 'It was so well wrapped,' she said, 'that it took us half an hour to get the outside off, what with the plastic parcel tape it was bound up in – lots of bubble wrap after that when we got down to the wooden bit.'

'What's this?' Paxman had said as they released the Abwehr Enigma hull from its bubble and tape wrappings.

'We both had our hands on it, me cutting back the layers and Jeremy peeling it back.'

'Someone has sent you something for fishing,' said the manager ('Jeremy's a great fisherman'). She squeaked as they realised what it was, 'what with G312 on the front'.

Prior to that, a week or ten days before, the unit had actually had a phone call to say 'they' were going to deliver the machine, it was not expected to come through the post.

We do get a lot of these sorts of calls, so we don't take a great deal of notice of them – mostly hoaxes. Anyway, as I had expected it to be delivered I had alerted all the security people to be on the lookout and give me a call the minute it came in. So the last thing I thought of was it coming through the post – I was really embarrassed about this. It was after that I thought if it was scanned, why didn't it show up? It showed that the security people were not doing their jobs – we weren't at all happy about that.

Paxman had been unaware of his awaiting post. It was understandable that his famously forensic mind adhered to its priority: the story. 'The moment we realised what it was we alerted everybody and got the photographer in, as the shots would be quite good publicity and stuff like that,' said the manager.

Paxman handled G312 approvingly, offering it round the office. 'I wonder why it was sent to me?' he mused.

'Then of course,' said the manager, 'they rung the lady who runs Bletchley Park. She was going to come on the programme that night ...' My telephone conversation with Jeremy Paxman had been diverting. He was bright and charming. After I had agreed to go to the studio, identify the machine and be interviewed, he asked where I lived; they would organise a car to collect me.

'Herne Hill if you're buying, Dulwich if you're selling.'

'Then I'll send two cars,' he had replied.

The police were less impressed with *Newsnight* and with good reason. Preserving the evidence potentially embalmed with the machine was not a consideration for the production team, which vastly complicated the investigation's job. The police's hopes of finding incriminating evidence on the Enigma body had been dashed. According to the unit manager, 'The police said, "Please don't touch the thing", by which time we had our fingerprints all over it.'

Thrust into a room full of reporters, Barker radiated under lights and the camera glare. Beads of sweat punctuated his forehead as journalists gestured towards the Enigma. He got through to me on the landline.

'Prove who you are,' I challenged, unaware of his exact predicament. 'What is the codeword?' I asked, following instructions to the letter.

'I'm in the television studios, surrounded by media,' Barker protested softly. 'I can't say the codeword,' he underlined. 'Christine, just take it on trust?' Light blanched Barker's face, rubbing out the features like a permanent flashbulb. The room fell totally silent.

I thought it was Dave Barker, but I had wanted to be sure. Was he OK? Was the machine all right?

Jeremy Paxman popped his head around the corner, addressing his audience at an angle to DC Barker. 'You look after my Enigma,' he admonished the policeman. Fingerprints were taken – in the time-honoured fashion – from Paxman and colleagues. Paxman thought he had seen the machine before, and first of all, they were unsure whether it was genuine or not.

In order to establish that it was the genuine article, they had telephoned me and I had said I thought it was the one, 'but for some reason she didn't come on the programme,' remembers a BBC executive. 'We heard, even before it was delivered, who it was had stolen it. The word was about that it was someone slightly disaffected,' she said.

The Enigma was repossessed and put in the back of the Corsa 1.1. On the way back to Milton Keynes Central Police Station, Barker collected a speeding ticket.

Paxman had asked me to be interviewed on his programme. Conscious that the *Newsnight* slant might not be entirely complimentary, I nevertheless judged that it would be an opportunity to impress Bletchley Park's importance in the minds of influential viewers and I accepted. Simon Chesterman was on the phone again, urging me to withdraw. 'We're concerned about your security,' he said.

I recollected a conversation with Chesterman shortly after the summit at his police HQ. 'We've been thinking about sending you away,' he had said. 'Sending me away? I like your sense of humour, I haven't exactly got time for a holiday!' I'd retorted, half-joking. 'Quite seriously,' had said Chesterman. 'What with the death threats and the personal nature of the letters, we were wondering whether it might be a good idea to remove you from the scene for a while. We've done it in other cases.' Eyebrow raised, I had asked him what he had in mind, perhaps the Seychelles? I hadn't been there, it sounded lovely. Unfortunately, Chesterman had said, their budget ran to something more like Butlins, the holiday camp. I had told him wryly I would take my chances closer to home, all the same.

Within minutes, Gerry McGowan was on the other line. 'I think you made the right decision,' he said. 'The negotiator is more likely to trust you and it's a chance to make a direct appeal. It will reinforce his sense of control and flatter him.' The directly contradictory opinions from two valued advisers were more than I could bear and I rushed downstairs into the back garden to get some air. Keeping the secret was getting to me.

At a recent meeting, Bletchley Park trustee Dr Peter Jarvis, a medical doctor, had ignored the other attendees, leaned across the table and pulled down the bottom rim of my eye to inspect its colour. He had been so swift that I hadn't had time to avoid it. 'You're looking pasty,' he announced, to the other attendees' astonishment. 'Anaemic. I prescribe sleep, proper food and fresh air. She's like a daughter, you know,' he added to nods of approval. The Enigma case was taking its toll. There was unremitting psychological pressure; servicing the media demand, as much as circumstances allowed, and being at the centre of the investigation was time-consuming. The extra hours that I usually devoted to Bletchley Park were no longer available. I was a prisoner to the telephone and without divulging details that the police wanted to stay private, it was hard to justify the course of events to colleagues. Well-intentioned deadlines from one of the trustees were building up a head of steam. That evening, I reached a point when I thought I couldn't go on pretending that I would be all right. I asked Chesterman to telephone the trustee and to explain why the police considered it was necessary to rely on me and the extent to which I was part of their plans. The call was made and after that, the strain eased off.

Jeremy Paxman's producer followed up the invitation and pressed me to go to the studios and identify the machine on camera. From the USA, David Hamer had briefed me and the police on how to be absolutely sure that the Enigma was the genuine article. In the time that had elapsed since the theft, it would have been possible to make a deceptively accurate replica. 'The machine has been dismembered,' I said, hearing that the rotors were missing.

The *Newsnight* driver was waiting for me to join him. I was dealing with telephone calls and weighing up the merits of a television appearance. From the Trust's point of view, the police had to remain in the driving seat. In practice, the relationship between Chesterman and me was collaborative; he was advising me, not giving instructions, and he would accept a reasoned argument, especially if it were backed up by another experienced specialist's opinion. Maybe the crucial factor was not personal security or communications with the Master's intermediary; it was police motivation that could be the key. In order to continue to keep police resources behind the investigation, the top brass needed to be seen to take charge and collect the credit. So was it a public relations fit-up for the police? Paxman's producer was not a happy man when I told him that I felt obliged to withdraw from the programme because the police had advised me to do so for security reasons. He telephoned a further two times, attempting to persuade me to change my mind. The star's extreme irritation was impressed upon the police. *Newsnight's* Enigma hot seat stayed vacant. The next day, I telephoned Peter Wescombe to apologise for bowing out of the Kleinwort Benson seminar. I had developed a pile of 'urgent paperwork'. Wescombe, a career diplomatic traffic expert, had an unspoken question in his voice. He understood the code. 'Saw you on *Newsnight* last night,' he said. 'Or rather, heard.' Paxman had recorded his telephone conversation with me and had played back the disembodied tape on the air.

'Jeremy Paxman has never been known for sitting on the fence,' wrote Brian Viner in the *Independent*, the morning after Paxman's Oscar-style performance, 'which makes it all the more marvellous that he has, however innocently, become one.' Viner's witty column went on to propose an hierarchy of television journalists to whom items too hot to handle might be 'fenced off'. 'There are so many juicy dimensions to this story,' he observed, going on to ask all the obvious and pertinent questions. 'Who on earth nicked it? Why send it to Paxman? Is the date of the theft – 1 April – in any way relevant?' Viner also enquired whether the stolen machine might itself be used to solve the theft – a rather remote possibility. The cartoonist Nick Newman later suggested an altogether more plausible use of Enigma's properties – working out the result of the US election in the year that George W. Bush and Al Gore were tussling over dimpled chads.

The *Financial Times* depicted Paxman in a sketch with the Enigma machine, saying that, at last, the BBC had given him a laptop computer. BBC security was put under the spotlight and journalists freely asked the questions that I had refrained from asking. 'How come Paxman opens his own post, especially mysterious large packages? With all the people he's roughed up on *Newsnight*, that's just asking for trouble.'

Wednesday 18 October was a media field day. Paxman put on a bravura performance that delighted me and countless others. 'I haven't a clue why they sent it to me,' he told *Telegraph* defence correspondent Michael Smith. 'As far as I know, I haven't got a reputation as a receiver of stolen goods,' quipped Paxman. He switched to a serious note. 'They are very poignant machines. I think what they did at Bletchley Park during the war was quite outstanding.'

Paxman's post had 'solved' the Enigma mystery, according to the *Daily Express* and *The Times*. He was described by *The Times* as delighted and astonished that he had been chosen to receive the machine. 'As soon as I opened it, I realised what it was,' he said. 'It smelt and felt like the real thing.' He added that he could smell oil and that he had spotted the G312 serial mark. The *Express* quoted him as saying, 'The moment I opened it about an inch I thought, "God, it's the missing Enigma machine!" ... If it's a replica it's not a very modern replica.' Admitting that there were 'lots of people they could have sent it to' such as, Robert Harris (the author of a novel on Enigma and a close friend of Paxman's), Paxman had been inextricably wrapped in the Enigma mystery.

The story bubbled away through heavy-duty news programmes to diary columns. A producer on *Today* was disappointed that I would not come on air to denounce Paxman's supposedly intemperate treatment of the evidence, but would anyone but a crime correspondent or detective have acted otherwise? It was true that *Newsnight*'s team had flourished their scoop early. The morning papers referred to Paxman's conversation with me.

> I called the director of Bletchley Park and she was hopeful. She's on her way here now to try to identify it.

> Christine Large, director of Bletchley Park Trust at the wartime decoding centre in Buckinghamshire ... was last night on her way to the *Newsnight* studio in London's White City where she was expected to verify the machine's authenticity.

No seasoned journalist would have missed the chance to file the story before the newspapers' early evening deadlines. My appearance was a reasonable bet. On the other hand, it is never wise to take the advance text of a speech and run it as delivered until it actually has been.

The London *Evening Standard* claimed to have unearthed a revolutionary plot. The package had been labelled with a fictitious address in Edgbaston, Birmingham, with the sender identified as 'P. Smith'. In a bizarre plot twist, P. Smith turned out to be an Old Etonian socialist in P. G. Wodehouse's novels. P. Smith was trying to overthrow society and the character believed that property was theft. The *Observer*'s literary editor, Robert McCrum, advised Thames Valley Police to 'read all of Wodehouse's ninety-nine works before they take further action. P. Smith could be a vital clue and a major breakthrough. They should concentrate their inquiries on the region of Blandings Castle.'

After the drama and tension of the theft and the letters, it was party time in the media. John Humphrys was not the only eminent public figure to be disappointed at not being the anointed one. Robert Harris professed his chagrin. 'I wish they had sent it to me,' he said. 'I'd have opened it quicker and kept it for longer. The fact they sent it to Paxman makes it look like a practical joke or a publicity stunt ... I wish,' he added wistfully, 'they had thought of it when the movie (of his novel *Enigma*) came out.'

There was the whiff of scores being settled and points being made, albeit obliquely, lest the object of their unwilling admiration might turn the tables. 'The strange case of the Enigmatic Mr Paxman' was a diary piece masquerading as conspiracy theory. The London *Evening Standard* suggested:

> At first sight, nothing could be less suspicious than Jeremy looking studiedly uncomfortable as the *Newsnight* cameras follow him round the office, and then mumbling a confession that the package was left lying around for days.

'Paxo', they noted, said he hadn't got a reputation for receiving stolen goods. 'Well, no you haven't, Paxo. Not yet. But it's very early days.' Irreverently, the article explored the possible connection between Robert Harris, Paxman and their joint friend Peter Mandelson, who 'would want to encrypt every political memoir of the next forty years'.

The *Standard* dismissed the notion of Germans having been sent to rescue an important piece of Nazi memorabilia. Their theorising was not to be taken seriously, but they did almost hit the spot with one observation, 'No one knows who has kept the three rotors, or why.'

'Following this act of faith by the new owner of G312, we are now attempting to put him in touch with representatives of the benefactor who has come forward with the £25 000 ransom,' I repeated as often as I could. Three of the four rotors were missing, as were all but one of the lamps that lit the circular encrypted letters on the flat panel behind the Enigma's keyboard. 'Without the rotors,' I said, 'the Enigma machine is like a car without its engine.' I let it be understood that a British company had come forward with the cash. 'Whatever happens,' wrote Steve Larner in the Milton Keynes *Sunday Citizen*, 'there can be few crimes where the name of the stolen item has so effectively described its impact.'

But the middleman and his master had overplayed their hand. Their desire to boast and to 'call the shots' showed a fatal character weakness. Either an innocent party or a professional intermediary would not have given up such an important bargaining chip as the machine hull and would certainly not have fawned on the media attention. Getting the rotors back was the next objective. The police and Bletchley Park were planning to spring a trap. With any luck, the possessor and his shadowy retinue would be crucified on the altar of their own egos.

'Mince pies out at ex-Min spies base' tortuously proclaimed *Milton Keynes on Sunday* (the *Citizen*'s streetwise rival). 'Bletchley Park is to enrol its own army of spies in a bid to ensure its Enigma machine isn't stolen again,' they explained. Twenty-four hour Internet surveillance was the park's proposed way of maintaining security. Allegedly, I said, 'Before too long, webcams will be installed to look at various points of the park. People accessing our website will be able to keep an eye on the Enigma.' The often outrageous newspaper was prescient. The trap in the making had both a real and a virtual dimension.

CHAPTER SEVENTEEN

The landing

The ship that was to trap and hijack the Second World War's mightiest Enigma secrets was an unlovely creature whose name, *Petard*, conjured up unreliable explosives and was even more ignominious in French. *Petard* was a fleet destroyer. Fast and fully armed, she had been crafted by Geordies, as Newcastle-upon-Tyne natives are known, in Walker's Shipyard on the river. From the first rivet in 1939, it had taken almost two and a half years till *Petard* rolled into action, mid-1942.

While *Petard* was churning through her first duty tour round the Cape of Good Hope's rough waters to the Middle East, Bletchley Park's naval Enigma squad was mired in its darkest hour. The difficulty of breaking four-rotor Enigma had multiplied sixteen-fold and the intelligence blackout was absolute. Devoid of Ultra, the Allies' ability to avoid predatory U-boats had atrophied and sightings by the enemy had increased threefold in spring 1942. Bletchley's three-wheel bombes had crumpled under the weight of four-rotor Enigma's combinations. The three solutions produced in early 1942 had relied on guesswork and over fifty days' processing time on the three wheel bombes. German aggressors were pulverising four times the 1941 level of Allied craft by the middle of the following year. Ultra might not, alone, be the decisive factor in winning the war but lack of it would lose the Battle of the Atlantic, the campaign in which the war would be lost. All the Admiralty's exhortations to the Enigma codebreakers were in vain. Given infinite time, they could solve the machine. In the short time available, they lacked the processing capacity and the materials.

Fortunately, fate was working with the Allies to some extent. Other forms of intelligence compensated for Ultra's loss, though inadequately. Dönitz's wolf packs had started to be called off to the Mediterranean due to a direct order from Hitler. In January 1942, *U-559* set off to join them.

Petard's captain was tough, focused and living close to the edge after two years' stressful duties on Atlantic convoys. Mark Thornton was hungry for the hunt and he wanted U-boats. His largely inexperienced and awestruck crew hesitated to describe the inadequacies of submarine detection techniques to their overpowering leader. Radio detection finding (RDF) was hit-and-miss, made more unreliable by adverse weather conditions. Asdic, named after the First World War Allied Submarine Detection and Investigation Committee when it was invented, was an echo-sounding device whose signal bounced off submerged submarines and registered on a screen at the transmission source. In stormy weather, Asdic could be inaccurate and deceptive.

The fleet that *Petard* eventually joined in August 1942 off Alexandria was a shadow of its former self, wasted by Hitler's resurgence into Crete. Over the next weeks, Thornton moulded his team as they participated in manoeuvres and fleet action off the North African shore. El Alamein's birth illuminated the late October skies. Just before the month end, a radar contact in the Eastern Mediterranean between Port Said and Tel Aviv marked the beginning of *Petard*'s greatest adventure.

Five destroyers and an RAF aircraft converged on the search area. The plane had spotted a periscope and telltale hull but the depth charges it dropped had warned the submarine to take avoiding action and it dived for cover. The ships formed an attentive ring around the search area, straining to catch an Asdic 'ping' in the restless waters. Fair weather was a bonus but beneath the surface, the Mediterranean swirled with fluctuating temperature bands and pockets of Nile discharge. An hour later, there was contact. *Petard* catapulted depth charges into the air and, as they plunged into the sea, columns of water rose in opposition. Another destroyer unleashed a flurry of depth charges and *Petard* quickly followed with a salvo. For several hours they pursued the camouflaged prey, with only intermittent sightings.

An equally brilliant enemy captain, Heidtmann, had a grip on *U-559*'s situation and its crew's morale. He had managed to maintain a commendably calm atmosphere in the throes of a punishing assault. *U-559* had plunged deeply and lain low. Depth charges shuddered through the German adversary but Heidtmann had positioned his submarine sufficiently far below to resist the siren call to the surface.

Depth charge attacks tunnelled into the deep, wave after wave distorting the glassy black depths like a melting mirror. Each tubular metal can bore downwards, hitting its limit with a punch and releasing a fearsome, growling 'boom'. Light was growing thin and absent echoes suggested that the wily *U-559* might have made its escape. Five hundred feet was the maximum depth charge drop and it was possible that the submarine skulked just below their reach. An ingenious crew member stuffed soap into the holes in the depth charge primers, knowing that water pressure would build more slowly inside the explosive, which would sink deeper, emitting its impact further below. *Petard* unleashed ten soaped depth charges. There was a long, attentive pause and the explosions bit. *U-559* was rocked violently in her cradle and she moved, awakening the Asdic.

Celebratory fountains played atop the sea, marking repeated attacks by the surrounding destroyers. *Petard*'s weary crew had been at their posts for almost ten hours, but they exulted to see the seawater eruptions that signalled an enemy at bay. *U-559* was trapped between the depth-charged deep and an umbrella of shallow explosions overhead. The submarine was in trouble. Diesel fuel odours permeated the salt air above. Below, the rank air had become intolerable. Holed in the bow and with her starboard plates caved in, *U-559* had endured almost 300 depth bomb attacks. A jet of white water tore upwards through the waves. *U-559* was blowing her tanks and coming up.

Seconds later, the submarine was frozen in the glare of a searchlight. A white symbol on the conning tower reflected a port beam lamp. Flickering white mariners dashed for the U-boat's armaments, or flung themselves into the water's chill embrace. Destroyer gunfire chewed into the conning tower until First Lieutenant Antony Fasson, aboard *Petard*, realised that the submarine had stopped moving and saw her crew abandoning ship. If the damaged U-boat sank, Commander Thornton would be denied his codebreaking spoils. *Petard* cleaved alongside *U-559* and prepared to board.

The absolute darkness was pierced by one beam of light from *Petard*. A fellow destroyer circled protectively around as Thornton's men enacted the drill they had rehearsed. First Lieutenant Fasson flung off his cap, pushed his feet from his Wellington boots and scrambled out of his uniform as he hurried to swim to the U-boat. Among his party were Colin Grazier and Tommy Brown, a fifteen-year-old canteen assistant. The roughening sea snapped three or four ropes as the men struggled to secure the submarine alongside their ship. A chain was thrown across the conning tower to prevent it being closed. Inside the U-boat, the pitch black was sliced by the first lieutenant's torch beam. Water lapped around their ankles, gradually rising as sea poured through a hole just forward of the conning tower and the damaged plates that flanked it. The men smashed open glass cabinets and unlocked drawers to retrieve the confidential books within, pulling them up on a line and passing them across to a whaling boat tight by.

On the third visit, Grazier and First Lieutenant Fasson were absorbed in liberating a box containing some instrument. The water was flowing in fast. 'Box coming up. Be careful, it looks important,' yelled Fasson. 'Go carefully with this instrument,' he ordered. 'It is very delicate.'

Brown and a fellow crewman fixed a line to the box and began hauling it up the tower with some urgency.

'Slow down!' said Fasson. 'You're hauling it up too fast, it's very delicate.'

Brown shouted down to his seniors, 'You'd better come up. You'd better come up!' and jumped away from the submarine. Suction from the rising water tugged the swimmers back.

'Abandon ship!' came the cry and suddenly U-559 was gone, burying Fasson and Grazier with her. The hapless German survivors were too exhausted to climb up the scrambling nets thrown over Petard's side and they were hauled up like a shoal of fish.

Petard was originally to have been called 'Persistent' and it was persistence that had won the ten-hour battle across 30 miles of Mediterranean. Commander Heidtmann was among the fourteen survivors and could confirm that by the time his ship had reached the surface, there had been no choice but to abandon ship as the breathable air had been exhausted. One of Petard's crew, Reg Crang, kept an illicit diary. He recorded, in tribute to the dead Fasson,

> Jimmy, as we all knew him, was a real man's man. Handsome and arrogant, but deadly efficient, he was admired by everyone. He was ready with a smile and a joke for the humblest. We cannot imagine there's a finer first lieutenant in the Navy.

Even in the tragedy, there was humour. U-559's lighted conning tower was distinguished by a motif, which at first sight passed for a horse. In reality, it was a donkey, chosen because the crew believed they had eaten the poor creature as salami while they were stationed in Greece.

Petard headed for the nearest port, Haifa, where awaiting naval officers set the hijacked secret information on course for Bletchley Park's Enigma team. Sadly, the Enigma machine for which Fasson and Grazier had sacrificed their lives was less important than the documents previously secured aboard the whaler. HMS Petard's trophies included a current short signal book, which reached Bletchley within four days, and one of the current edition short weather ciphers. Mysteriously, the short weather cipher's arrival was delayed by three weeks.

U-559's documents did not list the rotor settings for the machine the Germans named M4 Enigma Triton. In Greek mythology, Triton was the son of sea god Poseidon, who could raise mighty storms by blowing through his conch shell. At Bletchley, it was codenamed 'Shark'. Bombe machines modified by Harold 'Doc' Keen at the British Tabulating Company in Letchworth were used to test the short weather cipher process. Doc Keen's modifications enabled the bombes to do twenty-six times as many tests as the three-rotor bombes but in only double the time. The codebreakers were apprehensive that four rotors were being used to encipher weather messages. As it turned out, there was one letter's variation between the four-letter indicators for U-boats and the three-letter weather messages, so once Bletchley had the daily weather key, only a twenty-six position bombe test was needed to find the full key for four rotors.

Hut 8 was cock-a-hoop on 13 December 1942, when one of the weather cribs yielded a key. Bletchley Park had forty-nine bombes at its disposal then, but Hut 8 codebreaker Shaun Wylie wanted to commandeer six and they were in short supply. Later that day, just six weeks after the *U-559* coup, Shark solutions of the four-rotor Enigma key began to emerge. Within an hour of decrypting U-boat signals, fifteen U-boat positions were revealed. From December to January 1943, Ultra is estimated to have halved the Allied convoy sinkings, saving up to 750 000 tons of vital supply ships, including US supplies for forces in North Africa.

Bletchley netted and read Shark traffic almost without interruption. Short of fuel, a convoy captain unaware of Ultra's credentials chose to ignore the intelligence source and the revised course that would confront rough weather to the south. Nine full tankers of men and commodities were scuppered. A forty-eight-hour break in U-boat traffic due to a Triton setting change blanked out messages that might have saved seven tankers. These were exceptions.

U-559's documents had facilitated Bletchley's break into the four-rotor Triton code and within six weeks, the Enigma sleuths were fluently reading much U-boat traffic. Thanks to *Petard*'s hijack strategy and its leaders' bravery, new knowledge from U-559 had illuminated the ten-month blackout, reducing the menace in the Battle of the Atlantic and strongly influencing the eventual outcome of the Second World War. Salvation had come in the shape of keys to the missing rotor.

CHAPTER EIGHTEEN

A cunning conspiracy

News of the missing rotors awaited me on Wednesday 18 October. Late back after chairing a community forum at Bletchley Park, I dropped my papers on the London office sofa and noticed the answerphone light blinking from the desk corner. I was to await instructions about the rotor handover. The call sounded as if it came from one remove away, distant, perhaps itself a tape recording. Hoping that there might be further contact, I took my time about unpacking and arranging documents for the next day, more operating on autopilot than actually waiting.

No message came and over the next couple of days, I endeavoured to lower the media's expectations of imminent delivery. News that the rotors had not been returned with the Enigma's body had filtered out and prompted offers that might provide solutions if contact with the intermediary and his 'client' were terminated. Zyg Nilski, who edited *Morsum Magnificat*, the Morse aficionado's magazine, had been told by an ex-user of Enigma machines that the Swiss Air Force Museum in Dubendorf had 'about a dozen' four-rotor-wheel machines in stock. In 1939, the Swiss government had bought eighty Enigma machines that did not have the *steker* or plugboard in front like the German forces' machines. The rotors would not fit the Abwehr, but could be displayed alongside to demonstrate the principles.

Even better, James Taylor, a one-time branch chairman of IEE north-west (IEE being the Institute of Electrical and Electronics

Engineers) offered his company's services – at their own expense – to manufacture the missing rotors. 'We would make them as authentic as possible but would need the loan of a sample rotor, naturally with whatever security arrangements you feel you would need to impose,' said James's email. His unsolicited and altruistic gesture concluded in a way that I rejoiced to see, 'I ask nothing in return but the honour of assisting your cause and perhaps one day the chance of looking at an authentic machine.' It was in charming contrast to my erstwhile 'honest broker' correspondent.

Joe and Barbara Eachus were in town at the weekend. They had met at Bletchley during the war, when Barbara had her maiden name, Abernethy. Joe, an American and Barbara, a member of the shooting party that had first surveyed Bletchley, had both been prominent in its activities. They were celebrating Joe's ninetieth and Barbara's eightieth birthdays with a party in stylish Kensington. Their hospitality is legendary and close friends, many from intelligence and diplomatic circles, ventured far to share the colourful occasion. Shaun Wylie, a codebreaker's codebreaker, was there and Reg Parker, who had been in Hut 6. Reg told a story about Enigma at Christmas, swearing without a hint of a twinkle that Enigma lamps were removed from the machines to make Yuletide decorations. It sounded in character. Barbara checked outside the room, closed the doors, stationed a safe pair of hands at each and asked me, 'You wouldn't mind putting us in the picture about the Enigma machine, would you, Christine? We're all dying to know.' It was not an everyday assembly. Constrained in the outside world, I felt relatively free to brief friendly insiders who, better than anyone, understood and respected the need for secrecy.

Bletchley's post arrived unusually early on Monday 23 October and I fished a home-made-looking effort from the pile. There was a moment to telephone the police before the trust's Executive Board went into session. A sixth letter had started the week. My name and address had been typed on a separate piece of paper and stuck to the envelope with adhesive tape.

'My client has given the following instructions for depositing the £25 000 which is required for the repatriation of the three coding wheels belonging to Enigma G312', opened the correspondent. The list of instructions was a page long and specific. The Master (though that term had ceased to appear in the text) made it quite clear that 'no useful purpose will be served by surveillance, tracking, arrest or other form of interference against the persons retrieving the money', who, the writer claimed, had no knowledge of the rotors' whereabouts. The courier who would collect the money was 'as distant in these final negotiations as is every other person involved in their return'. If the intermediary were to be apprehended, 'the coding wheels (would) be destroyed immediately'.

£25 000 ransom money, in ten bank-sealed packets of £50 notes, was to be bound with waterproof tape, placed in a plastic bag and again sealed with waterproof tape. Either the author had read thrillers avidly, or he was on familiar ground. A businesslike, detached tone, displaying only an occasional quirk of language, distinguished the later letters from the first and second. Linguistics professors, cryptanalysts and inventive amateurs had searched, but failed to find, hidden depths in the first two scripts. There had been suggestions that 'deprave and deprive' had been mislooked up by an inept translator. 'Your august self' was judged to be a German term of respect and the use of the subjunctive was intriguing (but possibly inadvertent). 'Freely' could translate as *freilich*, in which case it meant 'of course' and the German *grossum* equated to 'the large sum'. 'Conditions of escape' apparently referred to a term used in television contracting. It had been a fascinating but fruitless debate. The current author was specific, authoritarian and in a hurry. He had no intention of being misunderstood.

'Behind the headstone, bury the £25 000.00 by digging a hole ...' The repository behind Alice Fletcher's grave was to be deep enough to ensure that rodents would not uncover the package and the ground was to be reinstated so as not to arouse suspicion. The middleman made his second mistake. 'On completion the following message is to be placed on the Bletchley Park website: "Would the new owner of Enigma G312 please contact Alice Fletcher."' The Master's envoy asserted that, as soon as he had recovered the funds, the news would be relayed to G312's new owner and the rotors would be returned to the director at Bletchley Park. 'Under no circumstances are you to question the integrity of either my client or any other person concerned in restoring the wheels to their rightful owner.' The identity of the 'rightful owner' was a moot point. 'They are all,' said the middleman, 'men whose word is their honour. INSHALLAH!!!'

Unwittingly, the Master and his minion had introduced an element into the equation that would help break their code: technology.

CHAPTER NINETEEN

The professor's song

Japanese airborne technology assembled in force on 7 December 1941 and at 07.55 launched the first wave of an assault that pulverised the United States Pacific Fleet as it lay in anchor at Pearl Harbour. America entered the Second World War at around the moment when HMS *Petard* was in her final stage of manufacture and *U-559* had been ordered to the Mediterranean to support General Rommel.

Already, the world's first electric codebreaking had taken place at Bletchley Park, with a bevy of bombes pressed into service by WRNS at Bletchley and further afield. By August 1942, GC&CS had thirty bombes in operation and its chiefs established a bombe station on the London Road at Stanmore, to the west of London. Some of the bombes at country stations such as Wavendon and Gayhurst manors and Crawley Grange were relocated to a similar facility built about five miles from Stanmore.

During the Second World War, the need for women to serve was as acute, if not more so, than in the First World War. President Franklin D. Roosevelt signed a law in July 1942 creating a women's reserve component in the US navy. Initially, 10 000 women were requested to serve in the branch named 'Women Accepted for Voluntary Emergency Service' or 'Waves' and they became a vital part of the naval force. Like many of their counterparts in the British WRNS, the Waves joined for love of their country and because, as single, adventurous girls, they rather liked the uniform (designed for the Waves by a

The Abwehr G312 Enigma machine in its box (with thanks to Thames Valley Police)

The Enigma machine from the front, showing plugboard sockets with cables removed (with thanks to Dr David Hamer)

The Enigma machine with and without the rotors (with thanks to Thames Valley Police)

Close-up of a rotor (with thanks to Dr David Hamer)

Bletchley Park mansion, 'the house' (copyright 1995 Bletchley Park Trust)

Simon Chesterman and Dave Buckenham with me at the entrance to Bletchley Park mansion (with thanks to Thames Valley Police)

Alice Fletcher's tombstone (with thanks to Thames Valley Police)

The telecoms and recording kit packed away after the alleged blackmailer was charged

My answerphone and associated evidence

Dave Barker taking my fingerprints

The post office from which the Enigma machine was posted to the BBC (with thanks to Thames Valley Police)

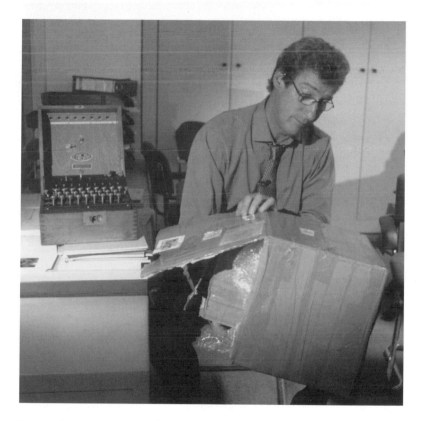

Jeremy Paxman receiving the Enigma machine at his office (with thanks to the BBC and Jeremy Paxman, October 2000)

The telephone box in which the suspect was apprehended (with thanks to
Thames Valley Police)

Dougray Scott and myself at Bletchley Park for a screening of *Enigma* (with
thanks to Dougray Scott and Victoria Pearman)

Parisian couturier) and thought it would be an exciting life. After a spell at boot camp in either Iowa or New York, the new Waves were sent for aptitude testing in Washington DC. A carefully selected group was told that it had been chosen to work on a special project, details of which could not be divulged. British Wrens who had been similarly addressed at the beginning of their war speculated about the thrilling exploits they might share on the high seas. Bletchley Park, therefore, had been a rude shock, but they adapted cheerfully enough. The Waves were surprised to a woman when, after a discreet journey on secondary rail lines, they pulled up at a station in Ohio. 'When we arrived in Dayton I thought,' said Betty Bernis Robarts, 'Dayton, well, it isn't even on the ocean.' The entire contingent must have wondered, as did the Bletchley Wrens, what was so special, in the heat of the Second World War, that they would be stationed in such an isolated and unexpected location?

'Confidential contact with the USA,' said Charles Collins,

> ... to call it 'covert liaison' would be misleading – had been established almost from the first. Alistair Denniston, the head of GC & CS, made, in a bomb rack (literally), his first transatlantic crossing, for talks with the pioneers of what was eventually to be the vast National Security Agency, NSA. Never Say Anything!

At the end of 1942, a contingent of US army officers, including some former IBM (the computer company International Business Machines) staffers, was sent to help Bletchley Park. The seeds of the intimate intelligence relationship that developed had been sowed in 1940 when a reconstruction of 'Purple', the main Japanese diplomatic cipher machine, was swapped by the Americans for British cryptanalytic information on Enigma.

Intelligence from Purple decrypts was called 'Magic', the US equivalent to British Ultra. Americans posted to Bletchley Park were first acclimatised by a period in Berkeley or Grosvenor Square premises in the centre of London. Robert (Bob) Button, one of the advance party, confirmed a courteous albeit cautious welcome to the effective but idiosyncratic British codebreaking centre in Grosvenor Square. The US team began a five-week stint at Bletchley in January 1941. The British did not disclose their Enigma machine, but they provided a paper version. After twelve months, the Americans left, having exchanged further direction-finding information.

Between 1942 and 1943, in the crucible of the Second World War, Britain and America forged a set of policies governing co-operation on intelligence. A US report for the National Security Agency's Center for Cryptologic History observes,

> The emphasis on British Intelligence is an absolute must for a policy and administrative history, because there is no understanding of US COMINT (communications intelligence policy) without continually reporting and examining the role of the British.

A declassified but then secret document dated 1 October 1942 set out the nature of the collaboration between British and US radio intelligence organisations on Japanese and German projects. Commander Travis negotiated for the British and, having thoroughly discussed the radio and intelligence problems in the Pacific and the Atlantic, he had made a number of Admiralty-approved proposals, incorporated into the agreement known as 'BRUSA'. The key points covered personnel deployed in Australia and how best to use the scarce and specialist cryptanalysts at the nations' joint disposal. America agreed to pass radio intelligence from Japanese communications to the British and all the recovered Japanese codes and ciphers, as well as raw traffic where practical. The British were to provide technical assistance to develop cryptanalytic machinery and agreed in principle fully to collaborate by exchanging all pertinent details of German submarine and naval cryptanalysis problems. 'The British treat German material on a far higher plane than any other which they handle,' stated the paper. 'It must be realised that since the outbreak of war the British success has literally been their life blood,' BRUSA continued and it emphasised that before America engaged in the work, 'the US must be prepared to accept their (the British) standards of security.' At risk would be not only Britain's empire but, as America threw its might behind its European allies, 'the future of the US may also be at stake.'

The 1942 BRUSA agreement had strengthened the case for collaboration and in autumn that year, Lieutenant Joe Eachus found himself bound for Bletchley. For months he was the only American there, forging ever closer links between the transatlantic codebreakers as secure transmissions by radio and cable sped between Britain and America, passing through New York's Rockefeller Center. Relations between the British and the Americans were competitive but cordial. In Robert (Bob) Baker's section of Hut 6, the atmosphere could be positively convivial.

> I had the top six US sergeants in my section. They were extremely useful in bringing in unsmokable awful American cigarettes. They paid about one shilling and sixpence. When they invited us to the US canteen we always got steak, followed by the same, favourite plate of peaches and creamed milk. What a treat. They enjoyed our British hospitality but, oh, they did complain about the British beer.

In a letter to Professor Sir Harry Hinsley, Bob Button, a member of Bletchley's US contingent and General Omar Bradley's liaison officer, wrote,

> we always accorded BP and its people the status of Senior Service, having in mind that HMG had been at this sort of thing ever since Walsingham and Queen Elizabeth I. It took us a long time to learn how to use the product properly.

Bletchley's *Petard*-inspired break into Shark at the 1942 year end was a triumph that highlighted a galloping trend in Enigma solutions: the power of technology.

Dayton, Ohio, was not quite as ordinary as it first appeared. It was endowed with a company that inspired the love of electronics and research: the National Cash Register Company. Within NCR was an electrical engineer called Joseph Desch, who was hired in 1938 to found the company's electrical research laboratory. Desch was experimenting with ways to build an electrical counter and he briefed MIT (Massachusetts Institute of Technology) to develop a 'rapid arithmetical selector'. Commissioned to produce defence electronic equipment by the National Defense Research Committee in 1940, the NCR laboratory was pinpointed by the US navy in 1941. The resulting Naval Computing Machine Laboratory opened for business in March 1942, with Desch as its director. The Americans wanted codebreaking technology.

Hut 8 was jubilant in December 1942. Shark solutions, the Atlantic U-boat key, often took less than twenty-four hours early in 1943 and when the Germans brought an alternative fourth rotor into service during July, Bletchley's Enigma experts gave it short shrift. Within a few days, Hut 8 had cryptanalytically reconstructed its wiring, though this 'alpha' wheel type was never recovered in any operation. Kisses were in season at this time and Hut 8 exploited the three-rotor messages transmitted to land forces and shore stations, then sent again to the U-boats in the four-rotor mode. British technology was not, however, keeping pace with the codebreakers. Demand for bombes far outstripped supply, and solutions for the four-rotor Enigma key consumed processing power.

Waves had begun to be beached in Dayton, Ohio, from April 1943. Their new home was called Sugar Camp and it had first been opened by NCR's founder, John Patterson, in 1894 to train his company's salesmen. 'It felt,' said Sue Eskey, 'like a little country club. We were more or less a bunch of overgrown Girl Scouts. We loved it.' Sugar Camp was as striking to the Waves as Bletchley's rural idyll to the Wrens. 'Living in a cabin surrounded by those huge trees was quite a change from the boot school in the Bronx,' remembered Jimmie Lee Long.

Building 26 at NCR was where the Waves began assembling parts for the bombes. They were taught how to solder, lace harnesses and terminal boards and generally schooled in electronics skills. The rotor wheels were known as commentators, each of which had two sets of twenty-six wires. Plastic did not exist, so the wheels were Bakelite; with each wire a different length and colour. The rotors' function was never officially discussed and it was forbidden to talk about the work. Nevertheless, 'If you had any intuition or deep thoughts you could sort of figure it out,' said Sue Eskey. 'There's twenty-six wires and twenty-six digits on the wheels and, oh yeah, the alphabet has twenty-six digits too.'

The Waves were building bombes designed to deal with four-rotor Enigma. The US testing machines were bigger than their British cousins, weighing about two-and-a-half tons and they ran much faster. Large air conditioners were installed every 10 feet and the US bombes ran twenty-four hours, seven days a week.

By mid-1943, the American and British cryptanalysts had become so proficient at finding cribs, due to their familiarity with German naval signals, that naval Enigma was almost an open book. The availability of bombes at last matched the abundant cribs.

Waves returning to Washington in the autumn of 1943 might be invited to a little chapel and addressed by a navy officer. They probably thought that they were going to have a thanksgiving service. Instead, they were ominously told never to divulge the work in which they had been engaged. 'And don't think because you're women you'll get special privileges. If you talk about what goes on here, you'll be shot,' was the message imprinted on them. Then Waves were warned about the possibility that they might be kidnapped, before being indoctrinated in the ultra-security-conscious Washington drill. Running the entry gauntlet involved two security passes, checks by two towering marines and a navy man and then admittance to a room that held several bombes. 'Grey elephants', as the Waves called them, lined the rooms, lumbering 6 feet high, 3 feet deep and 10 feet wide. The operators were given charts that explained how to set the rotors and switches on the machines, thirty-six of each. The bombes' accuracy relied on the efficient women hand-picked to run them. 'We worked in ungodly hot buildings with those machines,' said Beatrice Dunphy. 'Salt dispensers were near the water fountains. And the noise was terrific.'

Then they waited for a so-called strike, when the machine would print out a piece of paper, used by cryptanalysts to decipher intercepted messages. The equivalent English call was, 'The job's up.'

Cipher machines and the technology required to break them were at the heart of a communications revolution engendered by the Second World War. Warring countries competed for technological supremacy, pitting their finest scientific and engineering resources against each other. The results were to have an impact far beyond the immediate arena and nowhere more so than in the field of secret communications, where the latest information on advanced planes, submarines, weaponry and defences was for the taking.

By mid-1943, the American and British cryptanalysts had become very conversant with German naval signals and they were generally able to locate a crib. A sufficient quantity of high-speed bombes enabled the Allies to test these cribs comprehensively and the bombe operators' success was manifest in multiple calls of, 'strike', or 'the job's up'.

CHAPTER TWENTY

White knight

The 'job' was far from 'up' for Milton Keynes police. Darren Wray, then Bletchley Park Trust's webmaster, was asked to publish a message on the Bletchley Park website home page, www.bletchleypark.org.uk. It read,

> Message to new owner of Abwehr Enigma G312.
>
> The Bletchley Park Trust thanks you for your letter. We understand that you have bought the machine in good faith. The police have publicly stated that having acquired the machine in good faith, there is no reason to prosecute you. The Trust's priority is to get the missing Enigma machine back in good condition. We accept that you will need to be reimbursed for the purchase price. Please let me know how you would like to take matters forward.
>
> Christine Large

During the Enigma investigation, Jack Straw, then Home Secretary, was considering the case for a national high tech crime unit (NHTCU) to combat wrongdoers (with an emphasis on pornographers, paedophiles and blackmailers) who used the Internet for criminal purposes. A multimillion-pound investment was shortly to be made in the team, which was presently operating as an experimental project group. NHCTU's skills and methods were progressive and the government saw the importance of the 'virtual' dimension in tracing and tackling organised crime. Wray liaised with these police technologists about where to position the message so that it would not attract a horde of media enquiries. They opted for discretion, overly so, because the hidden message stayed secret. I had been away at Bletchley Park and had returned late to my London office. I caught up with the answerphone the next morning. A curt message from a caller informed me that I had not put a proper message on the website and the caller required this to be done. Even colleagues in Special Branch had been unable to find the covert response to the 'honest broker's' latest instruction. Wray and the police technicians went back to the drawing board. In theory, the webmaster and I were not supposed to be in touch with each other once I had approved the police's use of the Trust's website. In practice, I kept a detailed record, for I was concerned that the police might overstep the mark in a way that was detrimental to the Trust's reputation. For example, in reacting to the 'invisible' message, the police were advocating a website posting so blatant that most virtual visitors could not fail to notice it.

Around the same time as website communications were attempted, the media-savvy middleman added another string to his bow. Two journalists on the *Sunday Times*, Jack Grimston and Nick Fielding, had earned his approbation for their insightful coverage of the missing Enigma saga. On 20 October, the two reporters received a letter at their office.

> I wish to make it crystal clear that I act purely as an honest broker and that at all material times neither I, nor anyone else involved in the return of the machine have taken part in its theft, disposal, or been in possession of any material facts which could have assisted in identifying the thieves.

The writer specified that before any negotiations could take place, the journalists must

> make it clear to the police ... they have to give a categoric assurance that they accept this statement as a matter of fact and give me, as writer of this letter, their unequivocal

assurance that I will not be arrested or prosecuted for my involvement in brokering the safe return of first the machine and now the rotors.

The legalistic tone contrasted with the querulous early letters sent to me. No further correspondence or discussion would take place, the writer averred, until 'the vague promises to this effect which have so far been given' were replaced by cast-iron guarantees. 'How do you prove a negative?' queried the lawyerly scribe, when the police had said only that 'if "they" (presumably myself and others involved in the return) can prove they had no hand in the theft, then no action will be taken'.

Negotiations, according to the writer, were in the final stages for the £25 000 to be paid to G312's innocent buyer. Instructions had been relayed to me at Bletchley Park, saying precisely where the money was to be deposited and giving the strongest possible threat – the rotors' destruction – were there to be any attempt to watch or apprehend the transaction. 'Only after safe recovery of the money,' he wrote, would 'a message be relayed to the keeper who will give instructions for their (the rotors) return'. He again warned that if the police made any attempt to interfere, 'the rotors would be lost for all time, something,' he went on, 'I am sure none of us would wish to see happen.'

According to the letter writer, he had been given permission by the person at the head of the chain of command to approach the press. He offered the *Sunday Times* the opportunity to get involved in the final retrieval of the money and subsequent handover of the rotors. The honest broker was going for a dénouement in the media spotlight, in return for a flash of chequebook journalism.

Fielding and Grimston were also asked to contact me and ask me to confirm that

the code word used in all communications contains eight capital letters beginning with I, ends with a number of exclamation marks, and that a burial place is involved in the repatriation of the money.

Finally, should the reporters wish to learn what the letter writer called 'the true story', they were told to make their interest known via the personal column of *The Times*, on three consecutive days, starting Monday 30 October.

Fielding telephoned me. The investigative journalist and I had a long conversation about how the case was being handled and the psychology of the opposition. We arranged to meet and spoke face to face over tea in the Howard Hotel, overlooking London's Embankment and, thereafter, the reporter and I stayed closely in touch, discussing tactics and piecing together as full a picture of the investigation as our pooled knowledge and contacts would permit.

I was seriously concerned about the length of time it was taking the police to make and implement decisions. In the enquiry's early days, with fewer people and a closer-knit team, the operation had steamed ahead and communications had been good. As more agencies became involved and more senior personnel were exposed to decisions that might affect their careers – financial resources, cross-border policing and, most of all, public relations – the pace was committee-like. Dave Buckenham had kept himself in the background, plugged into the investigations room and mentoring Simon Chesterman. He was a name on a piece of paper until I obtained his mobile phone number and called him direct. I wanted a meeting.

Buckenham was courteous but guarded when he and Chesterman met me in Bletchley Police Station on the evening of 2 November. He apologised for having put me in a difficult position with the media, the police having twice failed to pass on 'need-to-know' information. In my own mind I queried whether the police were still vainly trying to persuade the Master's man to communicate with them purely in the interests of the investigation. The high-profile publicity that would emanate from a positive result in the case had to be a driving factor in their approach. Delays in responding to letters and phone calls had caused a breakdown of trust and communications, as was shortly to become apparent.

Announcements had duly appeared in *The Times's* personal column on 30 October and the next two days. The wording would not have been amiss in a St Valentine's Day greeting. 'I.......!!! Delighted with your message please contact Nick,' it ran on each occasion. Buckenham and Chesterman had arranged the details with Fielding, who had thought it prudent to involve Richard Caseby, the *Sunday Times* managing editor. The newspaper's management had been extraordinarily co-operative: editor-in-chief John Witherow had sanctioned the exercise. In return for negligible advertising space and the temporary loan of a journalist, they would earn the rights to a sensational true story. Fielding and the policemen had crafted the advertisement with care and their efforts gained swift appreciation.

'Thankyou for your response', wrote the 'broker'. He had again lost patience with me, and Fielding had opened up an alternative route to accomplishing his master's objectives. 'My client is not prepared to engage in further correspondence with Christine Large ...' Despite the act of faith in returning what he oddly called G312's 'carcase' to Jeremy Paxman, the intermediary believed that his client's suspicions about the existence of an anonymous benefactor had been borne out. 'Unfortunately, no message has been received from Christine Large concerning payment ...' Master and author believed that 'this was a cynical attempt by the police in a desperate attempt to flush someone out into the open so that they could be arrested and charged with theft ...' The police would then, he argued, 'be seen not to have given in to what he (the Master) feels they always considered to have been a straightforward case of blackmail ...' For this reason, stated the letter, the terms, location and method for the funds to be deposited and subsequently recovered, were chosen. Pouring scorn on what they considered as clumsy police efforts, it went on,

We are certain that their sympathies do not lie with either G312 or the pages of history. They have been outwitted at every turn from day one by both the persons responsible for the theft, and now those attempting to return it, and are obviously incandescent with rage because they have been ignored in all negotiations so far.

The letter bristled with hostility and naked condescension. It contradicted itself too, as the conclusion was to ask Fielding to relay a message to me,

> unless the police give the required assertions and Christine Large complies with the terms of the letter setting out the conditions that must be adhered to for the rotors to be returned, before midnight on Sunday 12 November 2000, then the situation of stalemate which now exists will result in their destruction.

A satisfactory response from either me or the police would open the door to a handover which, for a price, the *Sunday Times* would have the opportunity to witness and 'control'.

'I.......!!!!!' concluded the text, having asked Fielding to confirm this letter's receipt in the announcements section of *The Times* personal column on Friday 3 November.

'I.......!!!!! Message received, thanks. Nick,' replied the newspaper.

The police went over some of the same ground that they had covered with me after the first phone call. Transcam, a security company whose negotiators were skilled in dealing with blackmail demands, had been brought into the loop. Once again, the police strategy was to get the rotor keeper or his associates in touch with a negotiator, Gary Brent. Brent would pose as the representative of the benefactor company. Fielding, like me before him, was allocated a mobile phone, which was to be used to talk to the letter writer, if indeed the number could be communicated. Yet before the third advertisement had run in *The Times* on 1 November, Fielding had received another letter in which the keeper cast doubt on the existence of a benefactor. The Master had set a deadline of Sunday 12 November for compliance with his orders. He pressed home the point in a third letter to Fielding. The full story surrounding G312's theft had been told to his client 'by the person responsible', and the letter writer was massaging his information as a prelude to going public.

Five elements of a plan were in play: Fielding and the *Sunday Times*, Transcam, *The Times* personal column, the proposed cash delivery and the Trust's website. In the background were the awaiting police and me. As the first letter to the *Sunday Times* had referred to 'a burial', the police told Fielding that they did not plan to bury the money. A video would be substituted with details of how to get in touch with the benefactor. Expecting the letter writer to ask the journalist to be involved in the pick-up, the police asked the *Sunday Times* to clarify where on the Trust's website the special instructions could be found. Fielding was thanked for acknowledging the scribe's correspondence that had registered doubts about the existence of a benefactor. This letter went on,

> It is now quite patently clear that the police and Christine Large have acted foolishly with their false claim that an offer to refund my client had been made by an 'anonymous benefactor.' It must therefore be accepted that by their actions, they, and they alone are responsible for the loss of the rotors to both scholars and the nation.

The writer claimed now,

> to know the full facts and circumstances surrounding the theft of G312, as told to my client by the person responsible ... However, they cannot now be told by me even though I have the consent of my client to capitalise on it as I would wish, presumably because my involvement would be seen as criminal.

In the author's mind, the text stated, was the idea that the police might arrest him out of malice and he would thereby forfeit any payment. 'Do the *Sunday Times* lawyers take a different view?

Please advise me of their opinion,' he enquired. On Friday 10 November, *The Times* advertisement stated, 'I.......!!!!! From Nick. Let's keep talking. Alice F. needs to make urgent contact. Please check "How to help, Meeting Point" for a message.'

What the middleman had not realised was that there was a double agent in the equation: Fielding. While the Master and his associates had bargained for a double-cross by police, they had not anticipated that their media contacts would prove immune to blandishments and capable of the necessary patient discretion. A classic double-cross was in the making and the bait was set on the Bletchley Park website. The electronic circle was closing in.

CHAPTER TWENTY-ONE

Lobster quadrille

Agents were an integral part of the vast intelligence agency maintained by the Germans to find out when, where and how the counteroffensive against them would occur. 'Abwehr' was the organisation's name, which the British gave to the Enigma variant used to communicate its high-level, top-secret messages. The Abwehr had at its disposal the same sources available to Germany's enemies: spies and informants, of course, photo reconnaissance, cryptographers, information seized from the opposition, news from the media and details extracted from prisoners of war captured in occupied territory.

Britain's 'black propagandists' sowed misleading information and tried to deceive the Germans by broadcasting fake radio bulletins, setting up bogus military establishments, leaking inaccurate or untrue information and planting false stories through double agents. The surest way to ascertain whether the deception had been effective was through intelligence garnered in various ways. Here, in Ultra, the British had a trump card that, due to Dilly Knox and his team, they had been able to exploit since the end of 1941. Reading Abwehr Enigma traffic enabled the Allies to look over the Abwehr's shoulder and learn how German military intelligence was responding to the deception and misinformation and whether the Germans were aware of or worried by developments on the Allied front.

The Americans made an extremely useful contribution by having broken the Japanese diplomatic cipher Purple, for the Allies were able to monitor the Japanese ambassador to Berlin,

Baron Oshima. Oshima was both garrulous and indiscreet. He retransmitted summaries of enciphered messages in breakable form, offering the Allies such gems as an overview of Germany's defences on the French coast.

MI5 is the British agency responsible for security within British shores. Abwehr messages obliged MI5 with details that equipped them to anticipate the time and place at which German spies would arrive in Britain, usually by parachute or in a submarine. Oliver Strachey's section (known as 'ISOS' – Intelligence, or 'Illicit' Services Oliver Strachey) dealt with Abwehr hand cipher (that is, where machines were not used to encrypt) and reported on the spies being sent. ISOS broke the hand cipher early in 1940 and thereafter, in an operation unparalleled in its comprehensiveness, MI5 located each and every agent that the Germans tried to insert into Britain. MI5 agents were on the spot to apprehend the incoming spies, all in all about 120. These active German agents were either 'turned' – meaning converted into double agents – or, if necessary, executed.

The double agents were run under a system known as 'Double Cross'. Ironically, Double Cross originated when the Germans had tried to convert a Welsh electrical engineer who was approached by the Abwehr while travelling in their country. Arthur Owens, a civilian employed by the navy, contacted MI5 on his return to England, only to have confiscated the radio that he had accepted from the Abwehr. Owens was added to a list of detainees when war broke out but he agreed to use the radio as a channel for MI5 to access Abwehr plans. Owens's prison warden was an amateur radio buff and he ran the Welshman as an agent, making contact with the delighted Abwehr in Hamburg. After Owens, codenamed 'Snow', there followed a downpour of other, colourfully described agents such as Bronx, Lipstick, Teapot and the most successful of all, Garbo.

The strategy for establishing double agents' credentials was devised by the Oxford don who chaired the Twenty Committee (XX), which controlled the double agents from within MI5. A polymath who was a novelist, mystery-story writer and famed amateur athlete, John Masterman was ideally equipped to manoeuvre through the complex plots, weaving together plausible lies and dispensable truths in a manner that would build the false agents' credibility and feed the Germans' appetite for information. Each week, the Twenty Committee conferred on the information to be dispensed to the enemy, by personal contact, intermediaries, couriers or wireless communications.

Revelations from ISOS and ISK (Intelligence or 'Illicit' Services Knox, Dilly Knox's operation in Bletchley Park) work comforted the British in their ability to run the Germans' spy network. The communications, when seamless, worked as follows: the double agent's case officer directed him to send out false information using a hand cipher (not machine) given to him by the Germans. The hand-enciphered message was sent by wireless transmitter in Morse to Abwehr controllers in neutral capital cities, usually Madrid or Lisbon. The controllers received and analysed the message intelligence, which was crucial for Double Cross. At this point, Bletchley's Enigma capability came into play, for the controller used the Enigma machine to encipher the analysed intelligence and then transmitted it by wireless either to the Abwehr headquarters in Hamburg or, if very urgent, direct to German High Command in Berlin. En route between the Abwehr controller and either headquarters, it was intercepted and sent to ISK. A land line was the communication link between Berlin and Hamburg, so the message traffic could not be intercepted. A wireless transmitter was, however, used when Berlin or Hamburg wanted to raise questions with Madrid or Lisbon. This traffic was intercepted, and the enquiries sent back to double agents enabled the British to see whether the Germans had swallowed the double-cross and how best to proceed. It might be supposed that, because the British knew what was being sent in their agents' messages, the Enigma-enciphered material would be easily read, but far from it. Having cribs did not necessarily help break the machine, because the rotor turnovers particular to the Abwehr model could occur after a key of three had been inputted, too 'early' to get the benefit.

Intercepting the radio messages was an integral part of the strategy. Radio amateurs were recruited to listen for the enemy agents' Morse transmissions and for German radio beacons within the United Kingdom. They were volunteers in an MI5 department set up in spring 1939 and initially known as the Illicit Wireless Intercept Organisation, later as the Radio Security Service (RSS). They were mostly volunteers, radio 'hams' who had picked up weak signals from occupied Europe and the South Americas. The discovery that these communications were from the Abwehr was of paramount importance and when war broke out, RSS established temporary headquarters in Wormwood Scrubs prison and in 1941, a twenty-four-hour intercept station in the luxuriant north-Buckinghamshire grounds of Hanslope Park. It was to Hanslope Park that the radio transmitter formerly located in a castellated room at the top of Bletchley's mansion was relocated. Known as 'Station X,' the 'X' being the Roman numeral for the tenth outlet, it was an unacceptable risk for Bletchley to carry on this function. Brigadier Sir Richard Gambier-Parry was the genial and far-seeing boss who developed RSS and its Special Liaison Units (SLUs) to operate in the field. By 1945, RSS employed some 1700 volunteers and 300 full-time interceptors. Hanslope Park monitored the more promising enemy stations on a twenty-four-hour basis and, together with Bletchley Park, they had remarkable success. One estimate suggests that the Abwehr traffic intercepted and analysed comprised around 10 per cent of Bletchley's total decrypt volume during the war – an astonishing 268 000 broken messages.

Ingenuity and quirkiness were not unusual characteristics among the British double agents. One of them, Garbo, was noted for his acting ability and prolific, imaginative correspondence. He arrived in England in spring 1942 and in his first year wrote over 63 000 words to his German contacts in Lisbon. By the end of the war, Garbo, or Juan Pujol, his true Spanish identity, filled over fifty volumes with his inventions. For inventions they were. Garbo fabricated a completely fictitious network of agents, and when he invented messages before he left Lisbon, he padded out his letters and transmissions with travel and geographic information collated from often outdated timetables and holiday guides. This breathtaking audacity completely fooled his German masters who, as Abwehr Ultra revealed, said in autumn 1943,

> Your activity and that of your informants gives us a perfect idea of what is taking place over there; these reports, as you can imagine, have an incalculable value and for this reason I beg of you to proceed with the greatest care so as not to endanger in these momentous times either yourself or your organisation.

Of the 'organisation', only Garbo was real. Instructed by his masters to uncover the full military picture, Garbo played a significant role in deceiving Germany about the Allies' coming invasion. The aim of the deception operation was to persuade the Germans that the Allies had built up enough land, sea and air forces to mount attacks in the north, against Scandinavia and in the south, against France. The two-pronged bogus operation was dubbed 'Fortitude', north and south. Garbo and another outstanding double agent, Brutus, cultivated the enemy's belief in fictitious Allied military units stationed around Britain. Imaginary agents were engaged to monitor the invented garrisons. Down in Dover, the First US Army Group (FUSAG) was positioned ready to create a diversion from the real landings in Normandy, persisting with the Pas de Calais deception even after D-day. Fortitude's success depended on a deliberate misconception that the Allied troops were over 50 per cent more numerous than the reality. Four hundred men sending one another radio messages were deployed to establish the falsehood. Nonexistent divisions carried out exercises and trained together, and double-agent radio operators reported their endeavours.

Pretending to be gainfully employed in London's Ministry of Information, Garbo kept the Madrid-based Abwehr fully briefed on the fantasy armies and their activities. While men in jeeps drove around the countryside feigning military units on the move, double agents relayed reports from military inspections that built up an image of the mighty phantom forces awaiting the day of engagement. Top commanders including the US General Patton and Britain's Montgomery made high-profile visits to their shadow soldiers. These illustrious names and their presence in the field contributed to the completely false image that was insinuated into German thinking. Abwehr decrypts show how readily the bait was digested.

Fearing that the Germans might cover the options and despatch reinforcements to secure Normandy before they concentrated on the Allies' fictitious diversion in the Pas de Calais, the deceptionists went into overdrive. The airwaves were bombarded with intense military preparations for an assault on Belgium and the Pas de Calais. It was the Double Cross system's sternest test and it passed with fictitiously flying colours. Garbo's pièce de résistance was an imaginary meeting with three of his hand-picked agents. They 'concluded' that soldiers reinforced by nearby British air bases were a tactic designed to be a decoy to German troops, drawing them away from the imminent assault in the Pas de Calais.

Hitler himself ordered a state of alarm declared for the Fifteenth Army in Belgium and France. The false perception had been fortuitously reinforced by an Abwehr agent's report from Stockholm, anticipating a second, cross-Channel attack against the Pas de Calais. Halted in its tracks, the First Panzer Division did not resume its course towards Normandy until 16 June.

On D-day morning, 6 June 1944, Garbo was authorised to signal that the invasion had begun. The emptily impressive communication was later rewarded with a confident (albeit late) response, 'I wish to stress in the clearest terms that your work over the last few weeks has made it possible for our command to be completely forewarned and prepared.' The Germans waited for ten days after D-day before they started withdrawing troops and transferring them to the real head of the invasion: Normandy. Brutus was still working away to maintain the smokescreen, alleging that the Allied landing in Normandy represented but a fraction of the total available forces and that a major attack against the coastline in the centre of the Channel was planned.

Such was the conviction generated in Germany's mind that the High Command's own intelligence estimated that the First US Army Group was 100 000-strong in southern England. In fact, there were virtually no troops there at all.

Early breaks into Abwehr hand ciphers by Oliver Strachey's section and Abwehr Enigma's subsequent fracture allowed the Allies to adopt and manage, wholesale, incoming German agents. Coupled with the maverick brilliance of Garbo and other agents, a massive, strategically crucial fraud was perpetrated on the enemy. Generous in his apparent triumph, the Führer authorised the Abwehr to confer the Iron Cross upon an overwhelmed and grateful Garbo. It had been a triumph of intelligence over desire and Garbo responded with humility and emotion, saying, 'This prize has been won not only by me but also by Carlos and my other comrades.' Not slow to catch on, the British mustered an honorary Membership of the Order of the British Empire. 'By God,' said Eisenhower, many years later, 'we fooled them, didn't we?'

In the run up to D-day, during 1943, the Allies used Enigma intelligence to avoid key convoys being destroyed and to outwit the huge tankers sent to refuel U-boats. Disastrously, in 1942, the Germans had sunk more tonnage than the Allies had been able to build and with the spring tide's rise in 1943, the U-boats multiplied daily in the Atlantic and the Arctic, doubling the monthly number of Allied casualties. A submarine feeding frenzy around two convoys in March 1943 sent ships in their dozens plummeting to the ocean bed.

By the end of the first quarter, the field began to level out. Shortages and rationing in Britain, where the weekly tea allowance was two ounces and just four ounces each of bacon, cheese and ham, increased the pressure to secure safe passages for vital supply ships. Dönitz had a clearly stated objective to make the Allies bleed and to sink more ships than they could build, a goal that commended him to Hitler. Over sixty submarines were prowling the Atlantic at that time, waiting to prey on unwary convoys and, with their superior surface speed, they could cover up to eighty more miles per day than the average merchant vessel. Twenty-six hungry submarines in a wolf pack were awaiting a convoy's arrival, one day in April. Instinctively, they seemed to know where to lie in wait. The U-boats had formed a patrol line but this was anticipated by Ultra intelligence, and the convoy, SC127, was ordered to change its course. Once again, disguised Enigma solutions prevented crucial deliveries being captured or destroyed. Enigma had diverted the Fates.

Ultra's survival depended on releasing red herrings for the enemy to swallow. Earlier in the Second World War, in 1941, the Allies' efficiency in sweeping up the ships remaining after *Bismarck* had been destroyed almost led to Ultra's discovery. Had that happened, the Germans would have been empowered to devastate the Allied navy, win the Battle of the Atlantic and possibly the war. Enigma red herrings, fabrications intended to protect the Ultra secret, were close to being netted on a number of occasions: notably during the invasion of Crete in May 1941; when the Allies captured *U-570* in August the same year; and when Allied destroyers located *U-559*.

A stroke of bad luck propelled *U-570* to surface one August morning in 1941, right under a British patrol plane's flight path. Depth charges, instrument damage and incoming south-Icelandic waters persuaded the submarine captain to give up the ghost, leaving the damaged craft to be towed back and despoiled at leisure. Aware of the incident from an Admiralty report, the Germans considered the implications from an intelligence point of view. 'If the enemy had found the Enigma undisturbed and all the key documents, current reading was possible' concluded a security review by the Germans' chief of naval communications, Admiral Martens. In a somewhat contradictory report, he nevertheless concluded that the British were not reading Enigma messages and that full security would be restored by the forthcoming new keys.

Idyllic Crete was the unlikely landscape for an Enigma-fuelled attempt to repel the German invasion. Upset by Hitler's cavalier carve-up in the Balkans, Mussolini had retaliated by invading Greece, which he did at the end of October 1940. The Italian fleet at Taranto was crushed in a famous Allied attack, leading Hitler to conclude that Mussolini's compatriots needed support if the route to Balkans oilfields was to be preserved. Mussolini's attempts to subjugate Greece had precipitated grave losses and he held back while the Germans battled through Yugoslavia and into Greece, where the under-resourced British forces tried vainly to confront them. Almost 51 000 British troops were evacuated and although their survival was near miraculous, the debacle represented a serious reverse. At this stage, Enigma dealt in significant intelligence about the enemy plan to take Crete, which could have served as the perfect base from which the Royal Air Force (RAF) could control access to the Balkans oilfields.

German General Kurt Student masterminded the opposition's plans to invade. His strategy was primarily airborne, mobilising close on 300 aircraft against the tiny island. Planning to hold Crete if possible, the Allies had in place over 40 000 men, but only a handful of functioning aircraft, due to the Luftwaffe's heavy bombardment beforehand. It was to be an uphill task for British commander General Freyburg, who arrived weary from the dispiriting combat in Greece and with only three weeks to prepare. Freyburg was told at the end of April 1941 to expect the invasion within days, between 5000 and 6000 troops and a flotilla of seaborne tanks. Privy to this Enigma foresight, Wavell decided to brief Freyburg on Ultra, eliciting a comment long afterwards that Freyburg had been advised about Hitler's plans through 'War Office intelligence and most secret intercept sources'. Two binding principles governed Ultra's use: the recipient was never to divulge the source and, second, never to act on Ultra information alone.

Late in April, the details about the German operation codenamed 'Mercury' began to filter through from Bletchley decrypts. Enemy forces were massing in Bulgaria and intercepted messages suggested that the likely target was Crete, a thesis confirmed early the next month. Enigma revealed, in a major strategic coup, the probable date by which the German preparations would finish and nothing less than the full operational battle plan. Crete's commander received numerous Ultra messages during the period, using a designated reference – Orange Leonard (OL). Towards the end of May, a note of strong concern sounded through the transmissions:

> Am worried about the inclusion in your special intelligence summaries of items of information which can only have been obtained from most delicate sources.

> Information from these sources is only to be included when there is operational need for it and only to those stations directly interested.

For the enemy stations were equally as interested as the Ultra-users, as intelligence of German monitoring activity revealed.

On 23 May, German military intelligence had intercepted a message announcing the intended time of an Allied attack, and a subsequent Allied message talked about the arrival of fighter planes, petrol and munitions. Enigma had revealed that the Germans' understanding was rather too close for comfort. It was hardly surprising that the enemy knew their attack, albeit successful, had been compromised, but it was a seemingly innocuous message arriving after the Allies had evacuated that almost blew the whistle on Ultra.

During the invasion's aftermath, there was a hunt for stray soldiers who had till then avoided detection. A famous saboteur's base was discovered in the Cretan hills, endorsing German suspicions that the British Secret Service had been stirring up dissent. Amidst the mainly routine orders and advice on dealing with parachute troops was a handwritten note for General Freyburg. It was the copy of the first page from an Ultra message talking about German troop positions and their plan of attack. 'According to a most reliable source', it began. Translated into German, it formed part of a bundle that was despatched to Berlin where, astonishingly, it passed without remark. US diplomats in Athens had been suspected of the leaks, even though their communications had been cut off before the invasion. Ultimately, the Germans blamed British agents left over from the mainland incursion for the security breach. A final German report on the battle drew a line under the incidents, concluding, 'The actual day of the attack on Crete was well known to the British through their efficient espionage system in Greece.' Enigma narrowly survived, unscathed.

CHAPTER TWENTY-TWO

Birthday presents

Enigma detectives trawled a fine catch of red herrings during the case: the red car, pink elephants, a brace of mistaken identities and a Scottish nobleman. They were to be expected in an operation that had left no stone unturned. I thought back to the tremendous expectation evoked by a frantic chase for the owner of a red car that might have been a getaway vehicle. The police, the media or both had over reacted, launching a 'national manhunt' to track down the unidentified intruder who had parked behind the mansion in a highly suspicious manner. The Enigma machine could have been concealed in crates, which one eagle-eyed sleuth had certified as being in the car's back seat. There were radio alerts on the hour (just in case the driver was deranged or dangerous) and postbox-red vehicles were fair game for local Enigma-spotters. In due course, the appalling realisation dawned on a harmless female pensioner. She had been on her way to Bletchley's local garden centre, with a load of empty seed trays stashed in her hatchback (hence the 'crates'), parking en route at the back of the mansion due to 'bad feet'. When Ouida Unger, a Bletchley Park volunteer in her eighties, 'turned herself in' to me, and amateur detectives' egos flopped like pancakes missing the pan. It was the first of four flounders.

Later in the Enigma mystery, Dave Barker's girlfriend was looking forward to a slap-up dinner on the town, to make up for a string of promises abandoned due to the investigation's demands. It was a Thursday and Dave had just eased out of his shiny uniform shoes. Reaching for a dark blazer to complement a vivid tie and crisp cotton shirt, he heard the phone ring in the hallway. He took the call, expecting to be asked if he were ready to collect his date. 'Dave,' said the familiar voice, 'I really need you to go out and sort this for me.' It was Chesterman, who was also about to change Barker's colleague, Mark Smyth's arrangements for a relaxed night in. Sighing inwardly, but resigned because it was par for the course, Barker 'blasted across town,' to rendezvous with Smyth and Richard North, a police constable on attachment. By the time they had collected the necessary warrants, got in touch with the head of the surveillance unit, 'took the crime squad boys out', and motored to Sandy in Bedfordshire, their mood had changed from frustration to excitement. It seemed that the moment of truth was at hand. In the squad car, the atmosphere crackled. A Milton Keynes coup was in the offing; perhaps they would catch the Master in the act. Police surveillance activity had homed in on a suspect and there was reason to believe that the Enigma machine was about to be fenced off to a third party. The goods had been tracked to a suburban destination, and Barker and co. were about to get Bletchley Park a result, sooner than anyone expected. And what a result! Promotions and pints all round! Barker smoothed his hair and straightened his tie as they reached the ordinary house and tiptoed up the unremarkable path. At around 22.30, they executed the warrant. There were angry exclamations and a wedge of light glared in Barker's face. In he stepped, to confront the confusion.

Right at the centre of the scene was a typewriter-size parcel, Enigma-shaped. Oddly, the box it contained had been covered in pink-and-blue paper, patterned with elephants. Was the paper to disguise the contents? The penny dropped. Barker recoiled in shock. He had barged in on a birthday party. The box contained a farm set and the furious occupants had been apprehended mid-festivities. Muted, polite questions confirmed that the toys had been a birthday present from grandparent to grandson. 'From the moment the door was opened, I knew that this was wrong,' said Barker. 'You always get a feeling right away.' The surveillance team had certainly been monitoring a likely suspect. A bulky rectangular box had been clearly seen being loaded into the back of a car and delivered to the address in Sandy. There was 'no way' the police could have ignored such potentially incriminating circumstances.

The next day, the tables were turned and the officers found themselves on the receiving end of a splenetic phone call. 'You've been bugging my line and following me, stay off my back,' hissed a sibilant male voice. The caller knew the drill, understood his rights. DC Barker set off to the misjudged target's house to explain the circumstances that had led to what seemed like reasonable grounds for suspicion, till the parcel betrayed them and delivered another humiliatingly red herring.

Digging around was DC Fulton's forte and had earned him his nickname, 'the Ferret'. He had been poring over lists of telephone numbers clustered around calls from suspect phone boxes to which the police had traced the calls. Information, a tip-off from a suspect, led the investigator to believe that the middleman's client might in fact, exist: an Enigma machine had been bought at auction for a person in Edinburgh. Putting the information strands together, the Ferret quickly ruled out one of two telephone numbers that might fit. The second warranted an express trip to the Highlands. Scenting a revelation that could unlock the mystery, Fulton marshalled his paperwork and sped north of the border. Scotland's scenic poetry was lost on the inveterate detective, neither gourmet Craster kippers nor Scottish high tea detained him. He arrived at the gates of discovery. Fulton stood amazed, like Carter discovering Tutankhamun's tomb. He had turned up at the address corresponding to the supposed client's telephone number and was agog before its mighty walls, an edifice that was nothing less than a Scottish fortress. A battering ram was unnecessary. The castle and the fantasy lifestyle belonged to a cultured antiques lover, a collector whose passion turned out to be early technology. Fulton was very keen on antiques too and the place was bedecked with intriguing and beautiful antiquities. The erstwhile Scottish lord dipped into fine cabinets that overflowed with academic precedents and records. Although Fulton put the owner's chances of locating relevant details about on a par with finding Enigma keys, the man had a photographic mind, informing and entertaining his surprised visitor with incisive eccentricity. The evidence dissipated. SIO Buckenham's proposed ambush and warrant were never activated. Another red herring for the platter.

Telephone traces featured prominently in solving the theft. Long before the work with the *Sunday Times* and the Trust's website, enquiries had traced someone who had used a telephone kiosk to call a mobile phone after a 'demand call' had been made. A telecoms security group had supplied the rundown of itemised billing that enabled police to make the correlation. Patterns showed that a mobile phone user had been in touch with the person in the telephone kiosk, or 'TK' in police parlance, and that the second person was in close proximity to the kiosk. On the face of it, someone had been making demand calls and then reporting back afterwards to the client or 'Master'. What remained was to establish a robust evidence trail and the team set about identifying the mobile phone user and the accomplice or controller. Powerful circumstantial information suggested that, at last, the endgame was in sight. At a first pass over description of the individuals identified, a contradiction arose. They were apparently fine, upstanding members of the local community and not the criminal type. 'From a nice family' and 'hardworking, conscientious', was how people described them, which gave rise to the question, why should they need £25 000 or want to jeopardise successful careers and lives? Chesterman and Buckenham had grave misgivings about pursuing the pair but all the evidence pointed to their being good strong suspects.

Jubilation was rising in the team and there was a fact-finding drive that preceded a move to arrest the suspicious couple. Behind closed doors, Buckenham and Chesterman had soul-searching discussions. Neither wanted to dampen their colleagues' enthusiasm, especially after a string of disappointments and blind alleys. As a precautionary measure, they asked

Trevor Fulton, the inventive and thorough detective constable from the Force Intelligence Bureau to give a view. Fulton had been to talk to one of the suspect's employers to check out an alibi, and a more orthodox or respectable corporation would have been hard to find. The employee had been given a glowing report and a clean bill of health. 'The intelligence is there,' Fulton the Ferret had said. 'I can't see any reason why you shouldn't go in.' As is standard practice, the case was reviewed, on this occasion by Detective Superintendent Steve Morrison of the Major Crime Department. Chesterman had been punctilious all along the line about weighing up policy decisions, which were also reviewed with Acting Assistant Chief Constable Ralph Perry.

Reluctantly, the senior policemen decided that 'The only way to bottom this out was to plan the arrest'. Such compelling evidence could not be ignored but, all the same, they agreed to adopt a 'softly, softly' approach to minimise any potential embarrassment for those concerned. Whatever it was that undermined their confidence, there was certainly reasonable suspicion to give grounds for a warrant. Throughout their enquiries, the senior policemen had been double-checking their information. The 'strike', as they referred to it, was going to happen the next week.

Detective Sergeant Gary Grewal was also uncomfortable about the suspects' profile and he had no difficulty in persuading his two seniors to sanction a final audit of the telephone numbers. All of the phone checks were done again and a strange thing happened. One of the calls did not exist. Its inclusion in the list had been a fluke – or an error on the part of the telecoms security adviser. On the first call, the mobile had been called immediately afterwards. The next call had not, as originally thought, been succeeded by a call to the mobile phone. There was a bug in the computer system or elsewhere. This news tended to fit with Chesterman and Buckenham's fears and led them to the conclusion that the person calling the mobile might not be the person they sought and that a false lead had been followed up. No one could be sure at this stage whether the person was still a suspect, but a likely scenario was that they were nevertheless a potential witness, having followed the caller into the telephone kiosk. Gremlins in the system corroborated the team leaders' fears but they did not exclude the possibility that the citizen could materially assist enquiries.

Frustratingly, the pair who had shared the call could offer not a shred of comfort to the investigation. They had been making arrangements for a community event. A telephone that ran out of credit had diverted the caller to the kiosk and although the caller had indeed closely followed 'our' caller in the sequence of numbers dialled, the middleman had not been identified because the person who followed him had parked in a lay-by till the booth was clear. The evidence evaporated and the investigation was back to square one. Community event! Not the catch they had hoped for but a red herring to add to the list.

A difficult meeting followed with the team, whose morale had plunged. Motivation was starting to be an issue for the exhausted police, twisting this way and that in a blind-alleyed maze that defied conventional tactics. 'We were not just managing the enquiry,' said Chesterman, who could take no pleasure in his vindicated instincts. 'We were managing people and their expectations.' None of them could then have predicted that their tormentor was about to dig his own grave.

CHAPTER TWENTY-THREE

Petty cash

Buried on the Bletchley Park website was a message that chance had more prospect of unearthing than reason. You would have had to be a detective to find it, even if you knew it was there ... somewhere. The technology unit's next attempt was, in my opinion, sufficiently blatant to bemuse regular visitors and attract national media comment. Might as well run a national poster campaign! Games of intrigue were something that our adversary relished and he had a sympathy and respect for historical context. I thought that we could use the attributes of the site to place a secret message that would be undetected when it was right in the open. I suggested to the police that they use a section of the Trust's website that is designed to show visitors how to get involved in helping Bletchley Park. Becoming a volunteer, making a gift-aided donation or leaving a legacy is covered in an area entitled, 'How to help.' I had introduced a column in the Bletchley Park Trust newsletter for Friends, which assisted former Bletchleyites to get in touch with colleagues and friends whom it might otherwise be difficult to trace. It had become a popular feature in *Bletchley Park News* despite carrying sad tidings from time to time when a great codebreaker's obituary was published. I suggested that we add the same dimension to the website. It was high time we did so anyhow, for the overseas alumni and their families, and it would give the police the opportunity to place a message there from Alice Fletcher.

It was probably just as well, I reflected, that the negotiator had totally missed the first police message detailing how the

£25 000 ransom money could be collected from its burial site in northern England. The website page had been obscure and could only have been found with specific instructions. 'How lucky,' I thought, 'otherwise the recovery would have been made under a blaze of popping flashlamps.'

Alice Fletcher was the Master's servant's protégé. Whether real or fictitious, brief notes of her virtual billet on the Buckingham Road running through Bletchley were posted in the new 'contact' section on the Trust's site, along with five other bona fide applicants who were hoping to hear from Bletchley Park contemporaries. Clicking on 'How to help' and looking at the 'Meeting Point' feature, the letter writer would find a reference to Alice. Since she had never been near Bletchley, the chance of another site visitor clicking through was miniscule. When the site was ready, I tested it out and it seemed very satisfactory. Nick Fielding had been asked to make these instructions clear and he did so in *The Times* personal column announcement of 10 November, concluding the brief advertisement with, 'Alice F. needs to make urgent contact. Please check "How to help, Meeting Point" for a message.' Neatly, the plea avoided any reference to Alice's surname or to the Bletchley Park website, thus staving off potential traffic.

When my mysterious correspondent clicked on Alice's name, he would be diverted to a page that held the graveyard site details. Well in advance of the Sunday deadline for the rotors' destruction, the page stated that the money would be in place until 16.30 that Friday.

Fielding and the police fully expected the letter writer to contact the journalist. A desire for media profile and the means to manipulate public perception of his truth would be strong temptation. Fielding might be more worldly-wise and less vulnerable than me but he would nevertheless be accompanied, at a discreet distance, by a plainclothes policeman. The police had explained their intention to plant a video at the designated spot, still holding fast to their objective of getting negotiators inexperienced in such matters out of the loop and putting

Transcam's man in the driving seat. 'What-ifs?' had been anticipated, one of them being that Fielding would be asked to display or count the money. At that stage, calculated the police, they would have to trust to providence that the middleman would opt to be put in contact with the benefactor's representative.

Friday dragged past without the collection point being visited or any communication sent to Nick Fielding. The police called off the operation at Friday teatime.

Once again, the Enigma recovery crew was pitched into an uncomprehending limbo. Why had there been no response to the compliant website missive? Had the letter writer been suspicious of the rendezvous that he himself had proposed? What would happen to the rotors if there were no communication before Sunday's midnight deadline? The post brought no news for the police or for Bletchley Park. Anxious hours ticked away. Stationed at my desk till early Monday morning, my hopes faded as the ultimatum hour receded without contact.

Had the rotors been destroyed? Two further letters for Nick Fielding, in duplicate, arrived in Monday's post. Even the clarified message on Bletchley Park's website had proved insufficiently clear for the negotiator to make his move, or at any rate, the one anticipated by the police.

> Thank you for the announcement. However, the message on the BP meeting point page is nebulous in its content. Have my client's terms and conditions for recovery been accepted by the police and the funds made available for recovery?

Time was of the essence, said the letter, and further delay would result in the rotors' destruction. The writer's client had refused 'to allow me to contact Christine Large because of doubts about her sincerity'. Furthermore, Fielding had not attended to the question about 'the Times lawyers (*sic*) opinion on the points of law raised by me because of my involvement in this affair'. Hard on the heels of this missive, posted on Friday, was Saturday's despatch. Nothing had been found when the middleman had visited the scene of the proposed money drop, which must have happened after the time set by the police. Eschewing his characteristic impatient dogma, the writer put forward his best impression, explaining that he had gone to great lengths to persuade the keeper to extend the deadline in order for instructions to be made clear. Evidently, the middleman's advocacy had succeeded. Sunday 26 November was set as the new deadline.

On the assumption that the Enigma pen pal had not fully understood the previous information (perhaps he took more joy from setting puzzles than from solving them), the police and the *Sunday Times* collaborated on another advertisement, prepared for insertion on 15 November. 'I.......!!!!!' it ran. 'Go to "meeting point". I am sure if you click with Alice, you will get the message. I'm happy to keep talking, Nick.' Alice Fletcher's 'open sesame' would reveal the secret website page, which had been slightly altered to tell the writer to contact Nick Fielding. Fielding, the police and I waited, intently. Alice's trap was about to be sprung.

'Hello, Alice asked me to call you,' came the voice, abruptly relegating the *Sunday Times* newsroom's mêlée. Fielding started in his seat but his voice was level. Mentally, he pictured himself opposite the prolific shadow. He leaned back pensively in his office chair, feet planted openly on the ground, arms receptive to the story and his head tilted quizzically to the side, cradling the phone, listening very hard.

'I must have a guarantee, either in writing or however the police intend to produce it, whatever they suggest is the best way forward, which will guarantee the points that were raised in the initial letter from my client.'

Fielding hesitantly referred to the Bletchley Park website, saying that as far as he was aware, there certainly was reference to the key points raised, including immunity from prosecution.

'We are all innocently involved,' said the voice, speaking in a warmer tone and more fluently than in his stilted near-monologue and messages for me.

'My interest,' said Fielding, calmly but faster than his natural conversational pace, 'is, I'm very very keen to know your side of things ...'

'That's fascinating, I can assure you,' was the gruff reply tinged with pride. The faintly northern, deep voice carried on, 'I can call back whenever you suggest. I'm at liberty to do so whatever the time of day or night ...'

As the man paused, Fielding fumbled for his mobile phone with alternate microchips. He had his own communication networks, depending on the caller.

'Where my client was also perturbed was the fact that *if* there had've been a benefactor involved that they weren't willing to accede to instructions in the letter that were given to Christine Large for the deposit of the *refund* to be made some time ago.' He was referring to the Friday night exhumation. 'Did it ...?' asked the caller.

'I think,' said Fielding, 'though I'm not really in the loop, they haven't told me what's going on ... that the police removed it at around four, four-thirty.'

'I did actually visit the site,' said the caller. He had been to Alice's grave and would, he confirmed, be willing to go through that procedure again but ... there would need to be a rethink about the point of deposit, because he was unsure 'whether that site would be secure'.

Fielding gave him a direct line number to his journalist's desk at the *Sunday Times* and the caller rang off. For the first time since the Abwehr Enigma had been stolen, the man who was the key to its return had broken cover.

'Phooh,' Fielding exhaled gently, saying under his breath, 'Unbelievable! Almost like a normal interview, quite mundane, really.' 'Normal' was not how people who knew Nick Baxter Fielding's credentials would describe his journalistic round. The sleuth from the *Sunday Times* Insight team had broken the David Shayler story, gaining the trust of the aggrieved ex-MI5 officer who committed a cardinal sin by revealing some 'trade secrets' because he had, he claimed, been unfairly dismissed.

The newspaper had published the story after financing many months of research and self-restraint, eschewing an early 'scoop'. David Tomlinson's book on MI6 was another coup. Behind the scenes, Fielding had explored dangerous territory around Benazir Bhutto, who, he concluded, had been set up and whose life continued to be endangered by rivalries and ideology. Fielding had a critical mindset and did not accept secret service methods or briefings at face value. Richard Caseby, Fielding's editor, respected his senior reporter's track record and gave his journalist the latitude to delve into long-term cases, till he had gently picked apart each investigative artichoke.

Screening out the hurly-burly newsroom, Nick Fielding drummed a pencil lightly on a pile of research and tried to distract his preoccupied mind. It was not an assignment for an ordinary journalist but Fielding had neither a conventional curriculum vitae nor run-of-the-mill attitudes. He could easily have had a career in intelligence but if ever he had had a 'background', he was giving away no secrets. Medium height, medium build and unobtrusively dressed − no obvious distinguishing brands − Fielding might have passed the same person half a dozen times in the street without it being remarked. Yet he had a very specific face. Sea-blue eyes were set wide open in an agreeably weathered landscape. His round smile was encircled by springy blond hair, short and neat except for the thinning top scrub that he intermittently attempted to batten down. Tranquil, cultured interests moderated the journalistic cut and thrust for Fielding, who collected Far Eastern silk prints and antique memorabilia redolent with human interest.

The pressure of routine deadlines would have been a welcome respite from the waiting room. 'You're growing roots, Nicholas. Coming for a bite of lunch?'

'Cheers! Not right now, mate,' said Fielding. 'Got a few calls to make. Catch up with you later.'

The second game started on cue. 'I've been trying Chesterman,' said Fielding, 'but he's not answering his phone. I'll try again later, sorry.' The journalist let his inquisitor know that he had got a telephone number for the man acting for the benefactor.

Taking down the details, the caller said he would let Fielding get in touch with the representative.

'His name is Gary Brent and my understanding is he works for a company called Transcam,' answered Fielding. 'I was told, I think it was several weeks ago, to put him in touch with you.'

'I'll speak with him,' stated the caller flatly, changing his mind. 'None of these calls are being recorded I trust? Or attempting to be traced?'

The reply from Fielding came cautiously, but not so the hesitation to find the honourable phrase would have been noticed. 'Not to my knowledge, not as far as I know – and I think it would be very difficult,' he said disingenuously.

'Well, it can be achieved, I can assure you,' affirmed the caller, a trifle pompously.

Nick Fielding laughed hesitantly. It would be better to seem subservient; the Enigma machine and a magnificent story could be at risk.

'Now then, the deposit of the funds, was that done under the terms of the agreement … no surveillance, no trickery?' came the query.

'I might possibly be delegated to do that,' said Fielding. He spoke hesitantly, seeking his interlocutor's tacit approval to continue and when he had it, continuing in a deferential manner that defined the new relationship: the caller was the client and Fielding had become his 'honest broker'.

They talked about recovering the rotors, which the caller said was a difficult point because the cash would not be exchanged at the same time. 'They're going to have to take my client's word on my behalf that the rotors would be returned after the funds have been recovered.'

Fielding suggested that some sort of assurance might be helpful and the caller did not demur, 'That can be arranged.'

The reminder of lack of respect from me and the police, their insubordination, threw a switch. 'They've had a goodwill gesture by the return of the carcase of the machine. I'll have to go now,' he said.

And Fielding hurried on, before the call was terminated, 'Call me at one tomorrow?'

He sat at the desk the next day, body turned away from Gerry McGowan, enclosing the space around the phone in a protective gesture, just in the way that Fielding defined the territory for his interviewees. Detective Inspector Gerry McGowan was a highly trained police hostage negotiator, alive to Fielding's capabilities and the ambiguous situation. He was perfectly cast to support the reporter and the operation now revolved around the hub in Wapping, the *Sunday Times*'s premises. 'We've got to look after Nick,' McGowan was given to understand. 'He's been a star in terms of co-operating with us and bringing new perspectives to the enquiry.' Fielding also happened to be a very decent man, a condition not endemic among investigative journalists who, in common with all news organisations impelled by driven proprietors, have a principal duty to produce copy that sells the medium, rendering most participants in 'stories' to commodity status.

McGowan updated with the mobile surveillance team, at the same time scanning the office and Nick, who leaned into the desk. It was after 13.00, and the rendezvous deadline had passed. Pager, mobile phone, phone on desk, monitor, Fielding, comms. unit, Chesterman, pager, ring-ring. Ring-ring. It was he! Calm, keep talking. Worry in head (Fielding): 'Will he ask why the money wasn't there? Will he want me to speak to the benefactor? Has he checked out Transcam? Keep calm, talking.'

McGowan tapped Fielding on the shoulder and mouthed, 'Is it him, is it him?'

Thumbs-up from Fielding, who turned away again. A line was being kept open to the ground team as, wished McGowan, 'The witching hour approaches.'

'In respect of my conversation of yesterday,' Fielding and McGowan heard, 'there are a couple of points raising concern. You said the funds had been deposited, but then you said that

Christine Large was not willing to negotiate depositing the funds without the rotors.'

It was a very delicate moment. The wrong hesitation, or an indiscretion and the match would be lost. 'I don't think I said that,' mumbled Fielding apologetically. 'Something was put in the ground at the correct place and left there till four-thirty.'

'Sorry the money's not here.' Chesterman was straight on to the camera, quiet and unconfrontational. 'The benefactor's not going to leave that amount of money buried in the ground, we'll provide the benefactor's contact details but I'm afraid we cannot provide the money – certain reassurances will need to be satisfied.' After the Thames Valley Police Technical Support Unit had arranged for the video to be filmed, it had, like the Enigma 'carcase', been wrapped in plastic and heavily bound with tape. Bletchley Park's website message had confirmed that the parcel was in place, but would be there for only forty-eight hours. Alice's resting place had been covered by covert surveillance, a signals interception unit and McGowan's personal team. Not that Fielding knew, or needed to know, the detail.

'Now, erm ... I don't know any more than that in terms of ... erm what was to be the next stage or anything else 'cos I was not made party to that.'

'Hmm, hrmph,' the caller wanted to believe, he cleared his throat ...

McGowan on open phone line to surveillance group; cars moving in, closing, closing; keep talking calm; right by target; see telephone kiosk, man inside. Strike, strike! Strike!!! 'You're under arrest.'

The payphone receiver spiralled upwards, suspended in its performance and twisted down heavily to the end of its tarnished metal coil. Dennis Yates turned, aghast, to confront the intruders. 'I was just trying to get the machine back,' he babbled. Mid-sentence, he had been hijacked in his telephone box. Fielding kept the lid on his delight. The job was up and the secret was out.

CHAPTER TWENTY-FOUR

Hush! Hush!

Thousands of people were keeping the Bletchley secret in the 1960s. Each island of knowledge had grown up on a bedrock of grave instruction and peer pressure to guard the silence. In 1946, Morag Maclennan was a member of the task force charged with concealing the fact that Bletchley Park had ever existed. She and her group combed through every hut and building, seeking and destroying the evidence that would betray Bletchley's secret. 'It was part of the job,' she said. 'We were finishing off what we had set out to do. The prime minister had ordered it and we didn't think to question.' Intercepts and decrypts were prised out of the chilly nooks and crannies they had been plugging. Then they were burned.

'When I joined the Government Code and Cypher School – GC&CS – in 1938,' said Charles Collins during a visit to Bletchley in 2001,

> I was instructed in a simple rule of conduct in relation to the work I was about to start – a rule to which I adhered throughout my forty years of service, and to which I have adhered ever since, at least until now. It was, 'Never say anything.' I still find it hard to adjust mentally to today's climate in which everyone tells everything. Or nearly.

In 1986, Alan Stripp, who co-edited *Codebreakers* with Professor Sir Harry Hinsley and wrote lucidly on how the Enigma machine works, received a letter from Air Vice Marshal Dennis Allison. Dr (now Professor) Christopher Andrew was proposing to publish an article on Japanese code systems by Stripp in the *Intelligence and National Security Journal*. At Stripp's request, Dr Andrew had submitted the piece to the Secretary of the Defence Press and Broadcasting Committee (DPCB) for consideration under the D-notice rules. Despite, 'some deletions and amendments being required, Allison believed that 'the proper course was for you to submit any proposed publication to the Ministry of Defence, *in accordance with the special undertaking which you signed many years ago* (no italics in original)'. The air vice marshal asked Stripp to consider, 'not only the direct damage to security but also the knock-on effects' of the proposed action. Allison wrote,

> each time a person like yourself, of obviously deep knowledge, publishes inside information about the inner secrets of our work, there is more temptation and more excuse for others to follow suit. We do not expect outsiders to show any great sense of responsibility in what they publish, but, in your case, I ask that you honour the obligation you freely undertook ... and withdraw ... your article.

Stripp refuted Allison's logic in a closely argued manuscript letter over three pages in length. He cited numerous, published authorities, including Professor Sir Harry Hinsley, pointed out that, of the 8 per cent of his article content that the DPBC Secretary had asked to be deleted, more than half related to well-known phenomena and rationalised that 'Excessive security breeds not good security, but leaks.' Stripp was far from unique in having received such a letter (as his subsequent correspondence acknowledges), for it was modelled on the exemplary text sent by a former GCHQ director, to the late Gordon Welchman, in 1985.

The caution was perhaps understandable, especially in the post-war period when, it has been said, redundant Enigma and other cipher machines were recycled to suspect nations in order that their traffic would be easier to read! A former deputy director of the USA's NSA commented recently on the different priorities set by Britain and America in releasing sensitive information.

> We Americans are happy to give the principles and policy behind intelligence agencies a public airing, whereas you Brits released an astonishing amount of technical detail early enough to catch us by surprise.

During the Second World War, regulations for the use and distribution of special intelligence were clearly established in writing. 'Special intelligence' was, 'highly secret information obtained by intercepting and reading enemy messages which have been enciphered in cryptographic systems of a high-security classification'. 'The extreme importance of Special Intelligence as a source of reliable information concerning enemy activities and intentions' had been proved repeatedly. All documents or messages transmitting Special Intelligence would contain the code word 'Ultra', buried and cryptographed as part of the text. The regulations governed authorised recipients, personnel channels and ciphers for Ultra, the form and content for briefings, how security surrounding it physically would operate and the emergency action to be taken should the situation warrant it. The regulations conclude with an exhortation: 'The meaning of the code word Ultra shall not be disclosed to any person not authorised to receive Ultra.'

Bob Watson, a Bletchley local who was apprenticed to Bletchley Park's builder, Captain Hubert Faulkner, allows a smile to flit across his face when the subject of Bletchley's secrets comes around. Bob remembers one day, when the bonfires were blazing and a staffer was putting boxes of photographs and documents beyond history's reach. 'It was coming up to lunchtime,' Bob said,

> and I said to him, 'Go on, you have a break, I'll look after this for you for a while. And he went off to have his bait and his baccy and I was stood there, feeding the fire. There was this box of photographs with pictures of Hitler and his high-ups

and I thought, well, who will care? And I just kept a few souvenirs.

'I wasn't the only one,' Bob winked. Bob disposed of his Bletchley trophies long ago and is a regular visitor to Bletchley Park, where, without any malice, he likes to remind the people who latched on to Bletchley after the war that some of the site's secrets still elude them. 'There was this chappy, pompous 'e was, prattlin' on about this hut and that, like he was the bee's knees. And do you know,' Bob said gleefully, 'he got it wrong and he's still getting it wrong because he thinks he knows it all. Wasn't there in wartime, right enough.' Bob's memories of building Bletchley's wooden huts date back to the days when there was a sudden shortage of coffins in the locality due to an 'all hands on deck' call for labour and materials at the Park. 'A little bit of my soul will be buried at Bletchley, I dare say,' said Bob, 'and maybe some of my secrets, too.'

New recruits to Bletchley Park had a variable impression of the secrecy strictures. Before the war, Captain Ridley's unlikely shooting party might easily have raised question marks, including as it did women, and its image being confounded by a notable lack of shooting, for which it was the wrong season. Barbara Abernethy, now Eachus, said, 'When you think about it coolly, it was a ridiculous cover. Whoever would have believed in a shooting party of which I was a member, all youthful spirits and high heels?' Some Bletchleyites recall being asked to sign the Official Secrets Act, but many do not. Others were left with the distinct impression that, as Sarah Baring testifies, 'If we let drop just a hint of what we were doing, during the war or afterwards, we would be shot!' Whatever the method, it was effective in maintaining an unprecedented information blackout so strong that even today, some Bletchley graduates will not speak of their wartime experiences. Certain technical and mathematical information is still judged by GCHQ to be too potentially dangerous to release, and authors of documents written in wartime have found it difficult – and occasionally impossible – to persuade the security services to allow them access to their work.

Around Bletchley and in the neighbourhood, there was a general understanding that it was a government communications base, '… but,' said Barbara Eachus, 'people left it at that. They knew when not to ask and anyhow, you realised that letting the cat out of the bag could very easily put at risk someone you knew.' The 'hush-hush' place's veil of secrecy stayed intact.

'One did know,' said Robert Baker, 'if anything useful came out. We were aware of Peenemünde (a German rocket-development centre) but we also realised that our side couldn't do anything about it because no amount of bombing would help – it would damage vital runways.' Bob Baker, who was to spend his war in Hut 6, was among the first batches of what he calls 'ordinary civilians' recruited by the Foreign Office in 1940. Bob had been working at a Lloyd's bank branch in central London. He deduced that his recruitment came about because 'My manager was friendly with the manager of the bank who was pally with someone at the Foreign Office. I had been turned down by the Forces because of asthma and my manager said, "We're looking for someone, you might do." I think that my numeracy had quite impressed him.' When Bob Baker got to Bletchley, there were, he said, 'two or three more bank blokes. The rest were mostly public school chaps or ladies from finishing colleges.' Baker went straight into the control section in Hut 6, 'with the intercepting stations and the crib boys.' Baker's recollection of secrecy gently chides purveyors of the received wisdom.

'In Hut 6, the chaps gave us titbits. For instance, we knew when the Germans were watching us and probing Enigma – they tried it on too, for example, sending empty ships from Italy to Malta to test whether we knew which ships were worth sinking.'

Bletchley's marginally imperfect security was infinitely better than the enemy's. 'The Germans were so naïve about the security,' said Baker. 'One chap used to broadcast the same thing every morning.'

Baker's task in the control room was to keep track of radio frequencies and call signs.

> When the Germans changed the system to new frequencies, we were rather left in the air. They altered every frequency and every operator's call sign. All of our outstations were put on intercepting every message because all forty-two frequencies had utterly disappeared. Our interceptors recognised the handwriting in Morse and they used to say when a call sign had been discovered on some frequency. I kept this information in a card index that became quite a reference library of what the call sign was and what the frequency had previously been. It was all trial and error and I happened to strike on a fortuitous discovery.

Baker had latched on to a typically systematic German procedure: they had decided to use a call sign frequency book, allocating one page for each colour for each day. Once Baker had found a 'red' message, he looked up the page number of the call sign and, 'those gave you the clue of what colour you were on'. Baker's intuitive leap earned him a trip round the outstations, to the War Office Y Group at Beaumont, Chicksands Priory, Forest Moor near Harrogate, Harpenden and to other Y Stations. 'Incidentally,' he muses, 'there wasn't a single woman on any of those intercepting stations.' Far from keeping quiet his achievement, Baker's mission was to persuade the duty officers to serialise the call sign in each message. 'Most people did believe that Bletchley Park was a head office for our own secret transmissions.'

Inside Hut 6, information did flow a little more freely than previously suggested. 'One night,' said Baker,

> an important message came in from Kesselring and it was flashed right across every station in Europe. We went head over heels because we considered, coming from one of Hitler's top generals, it must be important.

It turned out to be a message from Kesselring saying he had left his eyeglass at one of the stations he had visited and the general was requesting its return. On another occasion, the Hut 6 cryptanalysts had been working all night to break the Africa code. They were successful and a message was got to General Montgomery. Monty made it pointedly known that their hard and good work had been irrelevant, because he found it on his desk after he had conducted another 'brilliant' engagement. However, he benefited from their work in other timely and significant ways. It had been an abortive attempt to get the message through, 'And,' said Baker, 'Monty had been the lucky one, though he didn't appreciate it. Imagine fighting an enemy on whose advance intentions you have every bit of information. But it was well known that Monty resented Eisenhower being the boss and that was reflected in some of our general's messages.' According to Baker an 'incredible' amount of information went out from Hut 6 and within its walls, secrecy was respected, but the hut's occupants were not enslaved to it.

'The original crowd of cryptanalysts became a bit of a mutual admiration society – understandably, you might say,' said Baker. 'They issued a weekly broadsheet – can you believe it? – in Hut 6 giving details like, "So-and-so has discovered this crib, A. N. Other has worked out a menu." It was full of top-secret titbits and quite insufferable.' Bob Baker and his team decided to get their point across by retaliating, with a Hut 6 Control Room newsletter. 'Some of the content,' Baker remembers, 'was a bit undignified. Unfortunately, at least one copy "got out" and went right to the top. Strangely enough, there was not another word out of the cryptanalysts and their newsletter ceased publication.'

After the Second World War, in theory at least, nobody who had been at Bletchley Park was allowed to go near enemy-occupied territory. The culture of security that had governed Bletchley's past maintained an iron grip on its post-war present. True stories abound, like the ex-Wren who was terrified she might 'talk' under anaesthesia and took a friend along to ensure that she did not. Precisely what the mystified friend would have done in the case of unwitting revelations, makes the mind boggle. Until the mid-1970s, when the truth started to come

out in a book by Wintherbotham, Bletchley's past remained an enigma. Professor Sir Harry Hinsley's monumental *History of British Intelligence in the Second World War* was published in five volumes between 1979 and 1990 and remains the single most authoritative source on Bletchley. Its author, after all, had been an insider. 'Thirty years after the war,' said Bob Baker, 'I'd be in family discussions and not able to say anything. Imagine that.'

CHAPTER TWENTY-FIVE

Knave in chains

I was under strict instructions not to say why I was leaving my husband and friends in the lurch. A ticket for the performance of a controversial production of *Don Giovanni* at Milton Keynes Theatre lingered wistfully in my briefcase. It was Friday 17 November 2000, and a man had been arrested in connection with the theft of the Second World War Enigma cipher machine. DCI Chesterman had phoned me on my mobile very shortly after the operational 'strike' to confirm that they had their suspect. 'Christine?' There was a lift in his voice. 'I've got some news I think you'll be pleased about.'

The net result was the unexpected pleasure of an unscheduled visit to Bletchley Police Station. 'Go to jail. Do not pass "Go". Do not collect £25 000,' I thought, not really minding, for once, about the cultural deprivation. Bletchley Police Station has the architectural grimness of the Blocks on Bletchley Park, but none of their atmosphere or charm. It sits hunched on the side of the thoroughfare dividing Bletchley Park from Bletchley Station and on the station side. Station and police station share a similar, brutal approach to building. I had once spoken with Bob Hill, then director of property at Railtrack, about turning over the station to a wartime theme that would complement its notorious neighbour. 'Well, we wouldn't have to change much,' Hill had wryly commented.

In the late afternoon sun, lengthening shadows hastened the police station's retreat from the roadside. A concrete canopy hovered over the inconveniently shallow steps leading up to the main doors, which were glass but blackly reflected outdoors. I expected at any moment that a wooden panel would slide open, as in an old-fashioned post room and I would be asked for my credentials, but no one came. I walked around to the back of the police station, my shoe heels sinking in the marshmallow turf that lay like a neat green collar round the front courtyard's lumpen concrete slabs. Through the high, dark, solid-wood gates, I could see police cars and vans, stationed higgledy-piggeldy in the curved car park, as if in a mouth whose dental care was long overdue. I telephoned Chesterman from the mobile and he came out through the back-steps door, silhouetted against the light. As I approached, I saw a great big quiet smile illuminating his features. 'We seem to be making progress,' he said, mindful of professional etiquette. 'I hope you don't mind giving us another statement. It could take a little while.'

Copious notice boards in the corridors advertised crime reduction statistics difficult to absorb without losing track of my guide. I was led to an office indistinguishable from many others in the building: hard floors and functional plastic tables; semi-upholstered chairs whose legs screeched on the tiles due to missing rubber stops. Paul Allen, 'known as Porky to my mates' he confessed, had been drafted in to prepare a comprehensive account of events. It would knot together the existing strands that had so far been captured in the string of my sporadic testimony. 'The boss thought it would be a good idea if I tackled this one,' said Allen. 'Hope you don't mind. I've been involved behind the scenes but we hadn't met before. Cup of tea?'

Allen took me right back to the basics, taking great care with the sequence of events and my reaction to them. Punctuating the exercise with vended tea, which he cheerfully offered and brought from time to time, Allen set out what was to become the prosecution's stall. He and I cloistered ourselves in the corner of the room away from the door, which opened onto a large utilitarian table staked out in the narrow rectangle.

'Now, I don't want to put words in to your mouth, so could you just play that back to me? You had been feeling under stress and you had some sort of medical appointment?'

'Yes, osteopathy,' I said.

'What's that when it's at home? Do they use needles?'

Oh dear, I didn't think my osteopath Jonathan would be impressed. My osteopath, so elder daughter Sofy had informed me, was the younger brother of a rather successful 'rock' star – 'your generation, not mine'. Talented as Jonathan Le Bon was, though, and tolerant of the fact that I usually only visited him in case of crisis, I didn't see why a judge would be interested in the techniques of cranial osteopathy.

'The point is that you personally were being blackmailed. You suffered serious stress. It affected your health,' Allen spelled it out.

'Yes, but I didn't take time off work.'

The patient constable sighed.

Over four hours later, I left Bletchley Police Station with a lighter mind. Try as I might, I hadn't been able to translate the statement into regular English; it was pure 'plod-speak'. But the courts, if it came to that, must be used to the stilted language and laboured description. I caught a train from Bletchley to Milton Keynes and took a taxi from outside the station to the theatre; both short rides. 'At last,' hissed my friends as I slipped into the theatre for *Don Giovanni*'s last agony. I missed the opera's conclusion, too. I had fallen into an exhausted sleep, but fortunately I did not snore.

Bletchley Police Station had hosted as many secret visitors that night as a merchant bank insulating clients from bidders. Nick Fielding from the *Sunday Times* was depositing his account of the incidents leading up to the arrest. Down in the cells, Dennis Yates had been waiting interrogation, dazed by the arrest and perplexed as to how it had come about.

Dave Barker was strongly built, with a firm jaw that invited no challenge. His bright blue eyes, either side of a pugnacious nose, glittered in anticipation. 'At last,' he thought. 'The bastard's given us so much trouble, been just so smart. Might stop being pleased with himself now that he's been nicked in the act.' He worked hard to banish a sneer from his face and suppressed his full mouth into an unreadable professional expression. Barker ran his workmanlike hands through lightly gelled blond hair and pushed his unruly fringe aside. He twisted a sporty metal watch round his wrist, positioning the dial on the inside of his wrist so that he could surreptitiously monitor the time. 'Right then!' He braced himself up to his 6 feet 1 inch and went downstairs to the anonymous interview room.

Dennis Yates uncoiled to his full height, bearing over Barker even when stooped, as he was. Stubble besmirched his thin chin and he was unkempt, apart from a visibly expensive Rolex watch. A grey anorak clung to his narrow shoulders. His voice, in contrast, was manicured and deep. Barker did not doubt that he was dealing with an educated man. 'I've got to get him to talk,' Barker thought. He had been on duty, 'since sparrowfart' but, despite the dawn start, no one but no one was going to deny him the pleasure of this first interview.

'No, thank you, there'll be no need for a solicitor,' said Dennis Yates quietly.

'Sounds very confident, but in his face he's a worried man,' thought Barker. They were seated level in the interview room, across a Formica table-top. Barker strove to dissipate the deep creases disfiguring Yates's Grecian forehead. 'Mr Yates, I'm sure that you know where we are and why,' said Barker. 'I won't insult your intelligence, but let me know if I've been unclear or if I can help with any further information.' Barker explained what the Derbyshire search team had found in Yates's home and assured him that every care had been taken not to distress his two teenage daughters, mother-in-law and wife. Yates began to talk, and he talked for almost an hour and a half.

Trevor Fulton's methods were different and he knew it. He had to get results. While he had no quarrel with the boys who ran policy books, kept their noses clean and ascended the good ladder of corporate behaviour, Fulton had a different mandate. 'Yes,' he knew he was accountable, 'but he did not have to account for every step in the solution'. Already a breed apart, by virtue of being a Geordie, a plain-speaking northern type who used the musical accent to disguise his incisiveness, Fulton was reckoned to be a force within the Force. He checked everyone out, 'friend' or foe, he looked at them in the round, he formed his own opinion and he took no bullshit.

Till Yates had been arrested, there was no real thread of evidence; it kept snapping and unravelling. The man had a high-rolling lifestyle for a discharged bankrupt, though nothing was in his name and he was a seasoned dealer in technical equipment and memorabilia. Among Bletchley Park's special interest groups is the Radio Society of Great Britain. It turned out that Yates was a member – the only one in their long history they had ever considered blackballing – excluding from the club – because, they believed, he had exploited his membership to acquire goods traded on at an inflated profit. David Hamer had turned up an email from July 2000, signed only with 'Dennis'. Originally, 'Dennis' had asked Hamer's advice on pricing a minor item – a cipher machine manual – but then went on to tell Hamer that he had a large collection, which Fulton was about to discover, in storage in a barn. The hoard included cipher machines, radios and the like and Dennis said he would get back to Dr Hamer when he had found time to sort and catalogue it all. There had been no mention made of the Abwehr machine, 'but,' said Hamer, 'he did say that he had what appeared to be a Swiss "K" Enigma and a Type X, a sort of British equivalent, among his collection.'

After the arrest, Fulton had sped up from Surbiton to do the briefing for the Derbyshire boys who had helped with day-to-day surveillance but according to Peter Spindler they did not major in the arrest. 'Perhaps it would have screwed up their weekend and their overtime,' mused Fulton, irreverently. In the end, it was Gerry McGowan and his crew who 'pelted' from

Surbiton to Derbyshire to catch Yates 'in flagrante', verbally speaking. Two police officers and a panda car had, after pressing, been loaned by the Derbyshire and Nottinghamshire police, but that was a drop in the ocean compared to the National Crime Squad (Gerry's 'lot'), National Criminal Intelligence Service and Thames Valley Police. Following the arrest, said Simon Chesterman, 'Derbyshire were more than helpful and assigned a tremendous amount of resources to the task.'

Fulton and his partner Dickinson had got the warrant for the search and they were on the verge of implementing it. A red brick wall climbed the road round the premises in long steps, curving round the corner up the hill. Parallel to the road was an ample conservatory. It had broad and high glass, white-framed windows, arched roundly at the apex, with a side view over rolling paddocks whence two curious fillies peered from their blankets at Dickinson and Fulton. They arrived at a white metal gate opening from the road up the drive to a gleaming, massive white house, resplendent with its lawns, its ten-horse stables, its dogs and its Jaguars. Locals called it 'the house on the hill'. It had been built in the 1890s and extended. Around the new-built stable block, horseboxes fanned out. The warm brick and timber outbuildings guarded as yet secret treasures. Fulton knew that they had to secure the evidence, which would be a challenge, given the vast estate. 'Touch nothing, do nothing, control the movement within the house, don't say the husband has been arrested,' he intoned under his breath.

Mrs Yates, a petite, attractive woman with harshly made-up, doll-like features, opened the door and burst into tears. The unexpected visitors gradually reduced the hysteria to intermittent sobs, largely unheard by Yates's selectively deaf mother-in-law. Mrs Yates rubbed her brown eyes, pushed her chin-length, damp auburn waves behind her ears and blew her nose. Life had to go on. There were dogs to be fed, the birds were cheeping from their bell-shaped brass cage, people needed to go to the loo and the house was populated by a nest of ruffled females. Tim, being the detective sergeant and Fulton's line supervisor, held the fort.

The policemen could not be sure whether the women were part of the plot, onlookers or innocent bystanders. Fulton the ferret intended to find out. Something told him that Yates's wife was not au fait, not 'in the know'. She struck him as the type that was 'naïve and would leave the decisions up to the man of the house', though protective of her family and her husband's image. Valerie Yates crossed the soft red carpet decorated with urns and flowers, brushed past the gleaming coal scuttle and bronze fire set and straightened out the plush pink velvet curtains. Pink seemed to be a theme in the house. She made for the kitchen and Dickinson followed her into a farmhouse environment. One wall was ablaze with coloured rosettes won by their horses and the room was a gallery of family pictures and photographs. Quality leather boots had been kicked off into a corner. Mrs Yates put the kettle on.

Apart from the wide flat-screen television, antiques were disported in the abode's every vista. The spacious, walk-in drawing room was an open book. Fulton was searching for enclosure, not openness. If Yates had not ensnared his immediate entourage in his dealings, he would have planned and executed them in solitary. 'Where is Yates's den?' he queried. He noticed a new-looking upright electronic organ and, in a side room, a Wurlitzer jukebox. Then he came across a staircase, leading to a room the size of a large wooden cupboard. There was one way in and only the same way out. The policeman spied a calendar, ripe with voluptuous female nudes, that caressed the door. The dingy cul-de-sac was not the product of a meticulous owner. Dusty and untidy, there was an absence of the special edition books paraded elsewhere in the stately house. 'Could the coding wheels be here?' Fulton mused. A big, old-fashioned rolltop desk dominated the unloved space. Above it was a window, refreshing the eyes with a panorama of fertile hills. An old wooden radio sat atop it, alongside what Fulton called 'a real "His Master's Voice" funnelled speaker'. Underneath were rows of small wooden compartments stuffed with papers, horizontally and vertically. Black discs and old-fashioned records in brown paper sleeves were stacked on the writing tray. Beside them squatted a wireless radio encyclopaedia. Auction catalogues sprawled on the floor and a round brass clock's quiet tick measured the dishevelled space. A preformed plastic computer squatting on a cheap do-it-yourself table was quite out of character. Like a camera, Fulton's mind clicked on the room's frames, mentally logging them. It was not going to be a two-minute search for the incoming team and Yates's custody carried a time restraint. Fulton sat at the desk, breathing slowly, looking intently, sending deep X-rays through the reluctant furniture, taking in the story whose key, he felt sure, was buried in this enclave. It would be four or five hours till the Milton Keynes search team arrived.

'Yes! Yes!' exulted Fulton. Secreted under the bureau cover they had discovered and seized a document classified as 'TF1'. Yates had left an account of his role in the negotiations actually hidden in the rolltop desk. 'It's like having had sex in the room,' he admitted to himself, very privately. The members of the search units did not discuss their major find. They went to the local police station, having had an understated word with the two senior officers there, and they photocopied the document, destined for high-ranking officers and to assist with the interrogation underway. Fulton studied Yates's direction to Alice Fletcher's earthly memorial.

Barker explained to Mr Yates that he would be locked up for the night, following which the procedure would be an interview first thing. They would carry on where they had left off. Barker turned off the tape and wrapped up for the day. 'I want my solicitor here,' insisted Dennis Yates.

CHAPTER TWENTY-SIX

Stuff and nonsense

History buffs in English-speaking lands were reaching for their lawyers at news of a film that threatened to hijack Enigma's history. In 1939, a village once known as 'the largest in England' had gone to war and sixty years later, in 1999, they set off on the warpath once more. Their new objective was to scuttle a Hollywood invention called *U571*.

Wartime Horsforth and Bletchley Park at full capacity had around the same number of people – 12 000. A leafy-streeted bastion of Yorkshire in middle England, Horsforth was remote from any front line or conflict but its sons had served in the First World War and Horsforth was intent on making its contribution. By 1941, with most of its able-bodied men conscripted, Horsforth was conscious of the U-boat war's impact, felt not least in the shortages of essential supplies and the country's dependence on massive imports to support the war effort. For the first time, that spring, Horsforth recoiled to the Luftwaffe's heavy drone across its skies and the imminent devastation of a nearby city centre. Village folk debated what more they could do to turn the tide in the maritime battles against Dönitz's wolf packs, for victory was slipping from the Allies' grip. They had melted down park railings to bolster production lines and adopted the latest camouflage tactics. Finally, Horsforth decide to follow the example set by its bombed neighbour Leeds and resolved to sponsor a warship.

Lacking Leeds's deep pockets, the good citizens alighted on a more modest prospect than an aircraft carrier and selected a corvette called *Aubretia*. The ship's breathtaking cost in today's terms would be around £2.5 million. The actual target was £120 000, which represented £10 for every village inhabitant of all ages. The average weekly wage was £3, which underlined how astronomic was the challenge.

Horsforth declared 'Warship Week' and set about its Herculean task with good cheer. Dances, exhibitions, tournaments and fundraising events proliferated. There were prayers to speed the quest on its way. Villagers sold their savings stamps and war bonds and incredibly, three days after starting the campaign, the money was in the bank. Brenda Cameron clearly remembers taking money to school to buy a warship. 'My father was in the RAF and my mother could only give me a handful of coppers. I was just six years of age and really thought that my shilling or so was going to pay for part of the ship.' Yet the money mounted up and Horsforth did not stop there, for the townsfolk went on to more than double their target. A telegram was despatched to the Admiralty by Horsforth council chairman Harry Willcock. It was admirably succinct, 'HMS *Aubretia* bow't and paid for, lad. What's tha want next?'

Supporters anxious for news of the corvette's progress and deeds were to be denied satisfaction for many years. Not until a documentary on Bletchley Park in 1999 was Horsforth alerted to *Aubretia's* important wartime role: facilitating HMS *Bulldog's* valiant and valuable attack on submarine *U-110*. *Aubretia* had participated in the Enigma breakthrough in the North Atlantic during May 1941. Horsforth's generosity had helped change the course of history.

Aubretia's role in the first significant wartime Enigma capture was a matter for pride. Pleasure was quickly replaced by fury when Horsforth's villages heard that a film was being made about the valorous feats – supplanting the British crew with Americans, transferring events from the North Atlantic to the Mediterranean and generally corrupting the story. The infamous *U571* was about to be released internationally. Horsforth went on the offensive; Hollywood had hijacked Enigma but the village was not going to relinquish its history without a fight. A first salvo was fired off to then US President Bill Clinton, who replied personally to local MP Paul Truswell, 'The citizens of Horsforth can take heart in having raised the funds to purchase that corvette. The Royal Navy action undoubtedly saved thousands of Allied lives and serves as an inspiration for future generations.' Prime Minister Tony Blair made a statement in the House of Commons, recorded in Hansard. 'It is a travesty of history,' said the Secretary of State for Culture, Media and Sport, Chris Smith, and he repeated the assertion in newspaper articles.

Reporters were encouraging me to make outrageous statements. It was true that many Bletchley Park alumni were extremely upset by the synopsis in reviews that presaged the film. There was a certain amount of surprise at the fact that Sub-Lieutenant David Balme, a distinguished naval officer who had been at the centre of that wartime Enigma engagement, had acted as adviser to the film. Might he have been dazzled by Hollywood's lure? America had not even entered the war when *U-110* was relieved of its crown jewels. I researched the film's content and reviews at top speed, managing to see a trailer. Actor Harvey Keitel headed the strong cast and the action scenes were spectacular. 'Submarine *Star Wars*' I concluded, but the danger lay in the medium's power to supersede reality with fiction. Welcoming the heightened interest in wartime achievements and their subsequent impact, I tried to put the facts straight – and announced that Bletchley Park would shortly be opening a 'Not *U571*' exhibition, to redress the balance. Several weeks later, as colleagues and I laid plans to relocate the full-size central section of a submarine, complete with conning tower, from the *Enigma* film set at Elstree, to Bletchley Park, I enjoyed the delicious irony of using a prop from one film as the centrepiece of an exhibit to undermine the myths propagated in another.

'It is, in effect, the second time this year that the British have been robbed of cherished evidence of their wartime Enigma exploit,' wrote Warren Hoge in the *New York Times*. 'The thriller movie *U571* was based on the capture of the Nazi cipher device, but the filmmakers stripped the captors of their British identities. The naval heroes in the Hollywood version are Americans.'

Sixty years after Warship Week and in response to the Hollywood controversy, Horsforth mustered its resources to dedicate a plaque on a stone plinth to *Aubretia*'s memory. Six original crew members were guests of honour, including retired judge Sir Barry Sheene, who was the twenty-two-year-old lieutenant officer of the watch on the corvette's bridge when *U-110* was captured. Sir Barry said that he and David Balme 'went to see that terrible American film *U571*, in which they claimed to have seized the Enigma machine. What rubbish.' As Horsforth celebrated with a brass band, pipes and a parade, Brenda Cameron, who still lives in Horsforth said, 'That little ship is still in my thoughts', and she looked over to her garden planted with aubretia.

CHAPTER TWENTY-SEVEN

Alice's evidence

From Bletchley Police Station, the view was grey. 'Even the sensation of the name in the mouth was unpleasant, stranded somewhere between blanching and retching,' thinks the lead character in Robert Harris's novel. Yates's statement mapped out a featureless terrain relieved by colourful mirages. It was late in the evening, but he wanted to travel the extra mile in the journey that so far, lacked a destination. 'I want to speak to my solicitor.' A call was placed to a Mr Booth at a London number.

Dave Barker was instructed to meet Mr Booth, who had suggested a northerly rendezvous up the M1. Newport Pagnell Service Station was the compromise arrangement. Barker stepped up to the sleepy electronic glass doors and surveyed the institutional entrance hall. Arcade machines winked and chinked to the left. Refugees from a girls' night out tittered vacantly by the lavatory entrance, which was bedecked with permanent cleaning signs. Obvious by its invisibility was the surveillance team in place to observe the exchange, should it later be necessary to identify the rotor bearer. Up two steps and avoiding the motor services insurance man were an implausibly expanded corner-shop newsagent and the café. Barker's eyes switched back to the newspapers, where a middle-aged man was pretending to survey the available titles. Under his arm was a package. 'Mr Booth?' Barker took Booth for a coffee through the neon food court whose bright lighting failed to disguise the inflated prices. They took refuge near the long, roadside plate-glass windows on a carpet island surrounded by littered linoleum.

Booth's gaze drifted to the pantechnicon convoys. He did not speak, but pulled out a bubble-wrapped parcel about the size of a pineapple, and pushed it with the flat of his hand across the coffee-stained table. 'Mr Yates instructed me to give you this, which was in safe keeping with a third party.'

'Thanks,' said Richard Egan, who had joined Barker to oversee the handover. Barker and Egan took their prize back to Bletchley, where it was immediately despatched for forensics. They couldn't disclose what was inside the package, but they were sure it was the Enigma rotors. Yates was bound to try to use them in mitigation. He had made a great play of the 'fact' he had intended to deposit the rotors for collection from a roadside salt bin in Hollington, had he not been 'interrupted'.

'You had Enigma from the beginning. You're lying!' growled Barker as he opened up the noon interview shift. Now they had the rotors back in safe keeping, the heat could be turned up. 'Did you steal it? Yes, admit it, you did. And someone inside Bletchley Park orchestrated the theft!'

The police had Yates's account of his part in the Enigma affair. Truth would start to emerge but time was running out and Yates couldn't be held indefinitely.

There was an unexpected telephone call to the police station. 'How can I help?' said Dean Faulkner from the custody gang.

'Tell Yates to swallow the bullet for Queen and country,' came the reply.

Paul Allen, Trevor Fulton, Dave Barker and Mark Smyth beat a path to the offending caller's door in Huddersfield. In the corner squatted one of life's lost souls. He didn't seem surprised or shocked at the visit; in fact, he hardly registered it at all. 'Lads,' said Fulton, 'Another crank. Let's go and get in the beers.' They crashed down exhaustedly at three in the morning and jarred the dawn chorus at six.

Nick Fielding had been in agitated conversation with me on Saturday afternoon and through the evening. 'I can't believe it,' he said. 'We had this all agreed with Richard Caseby. The police had our complete co-operation in return for the exclusive to break the full story. They're ratting on their deal.' The journalist and I had a long discussion about the deal that Buckenham and Caseby had shaken hands on.

I asked if Nick had put anything in writing, assuming that the answer was 'No'. I agreed to talk to Buckenham, though I was not optimistic about the outcome. The SIO was playing off his own agenda and Nick and I speculated whether it was about procedure or for other reasons. Timing the charges against Yates was the critical issue.

I did some checking. The National Crime Squad (NCS) had, said one operative, advised Buckenham that it was not necessary to charge Yates straight away; in fact it would be a positive advantage not to, because it would allow more time for questioning. According to NCS, there was no need to go firm until the Monday. Thames Valley Police would take the decision about when to lay the charge. There were constraints on how long he could be held – even with an extension – without a charge being made and, once the case had been formalised, there would be immediate restrictions on what the media could publish. The case would go *sub judice*, for fear of prejudicing the trial outcome and there would be no exceptions, not even for those closely involved.

'The problem is, Christine, if we let Nick run the full story, we could quite easily lose the case. It's happened before,' said Dave Buckenham. The charging of prisoners is governed by law encapsulated in the Police and Criminal Evidence Act (1984), PACE in shorthand. As soon as there is sufficient evidence to charge, the law is quite clear that an offender must be brought before the custody officer and either formally charged or released. Infringing the rule could cost the prosecution the case on an 'abuse of process' argument. 'I know you'll understand.'

I said that I understood, but I was still puzzled and felt sorry for Nick Fielding, after his exceptional performance. I asked when exactly Dave Buckenham was planning to lay the charge. I knew that the first editions rolled early off the presses.

'A man has been arrested in connection with the theft of the World War Two Enigma code breaking machine,' stated the unusually circumspect *Milton Keynes on Sunday*. The reporting restrictions had already taken a grip. 'Enigma: man held by police'. It pictured Buckenham across its front cover in the wake of a hastily convened press conference. Calling the arrest a 'dramatic swoop', Steve Larner confirmed that the man, whom he did not name, had been detained by detectives from the National Crime Squad, National Criminal Intelligence Service and Thames Valley Police on the Friday afternoon previous. (The man had actually been detained by detectives from the National Crime Squad.) Larner said that 'the ransom, put up by a giant telecoms company, was not exchanged and that delicate negotiations were actually taking place via a go-between at the national newspaper when the police swooped.' He reported me as being 'pleased there had been a major development after so long,' but, I had said, 'the final chapter has yet to be written.' In the *Sunday Telegraph*, a reporter new to the case declared that, 'Detectives were celebrating their own codebreaking skills yesterday after a complex sting operation led to a man being charged.'

Nevertheless, Nick Fielding of the *Sunday Times* carried the reporting honours. Yates had been charged around seven in the evening but the paper had got its early edition away. The front-page splash unfurled a fully triumphant account of their reporter's intrepid adventure. 'How the *Sunday Times* cracked the Enigma code' trumpeted the headline. NCS knew that the newspaper had got its story, but not what had been promised and considered 'that Thames Valley Police had gone back on the deal. The charging could have waited at least till Monday,' thought a source (probably wrongly). Notwithstanding, even the second edition survived the judicial restrictions and libel lawyers' scrutiny relatively intact, concluding with the comment,

For the first time since the Enigma machine had been stolen, the letter writer had broken cover and spoken directly to someone. Although he had left messages on my answering machine, he had never engaged in a conversation with anyone.

Yates was very shortly to become a great deal more locquacious.

Valerie Yates hovered behind the fencing of their three-storey Georgian mansion and tearfully confessed in Monday morning's *Daily Mirror*, 'I wouldn't believe this could have happened to us. I can't understand what's going on. He's always been interested in the military and that kind of thing but we had no idea about this.' Mrs Yates's weekend had been rudely interrupted and she was about to take her husband some fresh clothes for the hearing on Monday. The *Mirror* revelled in describing the 'former cattle farmer's' estate, where the family had lived for seventeen years. The house was in No Man's Lane, 'surrounded by four acres of grounds including paddocks and stables ... one of the most expensive properties around' in Sandiacre, Derbyshire. Digging among talkative neighbours, reporter Rod Chattor had discovered that Yates had told locals that 'he has been a pop star and a gold dealer'.

'We'd all sat around on the news when Enigma was stolen and I couldn't believe when the police arrested him,' said Valerie Yates in *The Express*. It would have been very surprising indeed if an avid collector such as Yates had not been aware of Enigma's disappearance and value.

Cameras were winking expectantly by the concrete steps of Milton Keynes Magistrates Courts, a clean-cut building fronting the city's business boulevard. 'Would you mind just walking up there again, Christine?' asked the Central Television cameraman. 'We didn't quite catch that.'

I had been escorted to the court by Mac Hobley and Bletchley Park volunteer Dave Whitchurch, who had been keeping a scrapbook on the Enigma affair. A preoccupied frown creased my brow. The solicitor from the Crown Prosecution Service, who was due to advance the case for denying Yates bail, was running late and it was likely that the brief had been allocated at the last minute. Bletchley Park's contingent squeezed in the few remaining seats at the back of the court. The press benches were packed and the journalists were animated. Yates's solicitor came and went and came and went again, but Yates did not come. Mac Hobley and I speculated about the delay. Then, at the last moment, two women slid themselves into the seats next to me.

'Are you all right, muther?' asked the younger of the two in a loud flat voice.

The woman, probably in her forties, had a round face with curtains of dye-streaked dark hair dropping by pencilled eyebrows, under which shone dabs of highlighter. Valerie Yates, for it was she, looked strained. She had dark eyes, tending to hooded at the outer corners, and a blunt nose. Her lips were pulled tensely over white teeth and her head sat back in a tortoise-like cradle on her neck. A warm jacket's pointed collar lay over a generous gold neck chain that contrasted with her black sweater. 'Muther' affected to be deaf and they clearly had no idea who their neighbours were. 'Court rise for their worships,' intoned the clerk. Everyone got dutifully to their feet and the press gallery exchanged visual bets.

A chill silence descended as Yates entered the Perspex-encased witness box. Anonymity shed its veil. This scene, the hijack's next act, was intensely close and personal. It was the first time I had seen the middleman but he would not confront me by looking. He simply stared ahead, disguising his heart in a cool grey suit and maintaining a subservient pose under the judges' eyes. He answered only to confirm his name, address and date of birth. Yates's solicitor displayed an intimate knowledge of his material, he was in control.

'Wouldn't surprise me if their barrister offers to do this for free, just for the publicity,' whispered Mac.

'And would you be prepared to stand bail in the sum of £25 000?' the defence solicitor was asking Mrs Yates.

'Of course,' she replied.

'Would you be prepared to go further than that, say to £100 000? Think about it carefully, Mrs Yates. You might be putting your house at risk.'

'Yes, I would be prepared to do that; even more,' said Valerie Yates.

Then it was Dennis Yates's mother-in-law's turn. Yates had been described to the court as an unemployed father of three. The manor house was in his wife's and mother-in-law's names. The police had also located £23 000 in cash in the house, said to be, 'insurance money from a claim on a stolen car'. Valerie Yates's mother was being asked the same questions put to her daughter. 'And would you,' the solicitor put it to her and paused for effect, 'be prepared to put up £100 000 in bail?' There was attentive silence.

'Oh, no. Definitely not,' said mother Yates. The press gallery collapsed in muffled hilarity.

Yates was charged with blackmail and with handling the stolen Enigma machine but he was released without any order for bail, or needing to surrender his passport. Yates staged his encore on the steps of the court, dramatically declaring his innocence and denouncing the police, who, he said, 'have acted abysmally'.

All I did was broker the return of the machine and the rotors to Bletchley Park. I had no intention of taking any reward in return for the machine or the rotors. I was innocently involved and the circumstances of this will be made clear. I was brokering for a client of mine who is not resident in this country but he is in high office. It may be that we learn eventually who this gentleman is.

Yates turned lugubriously to the cameras and claimed that the rotors had been delivered back. 'The person involved in the theft of the machine is known to the police but they are not in a position to arrest him. I know who it is but I am not going to say.' He and his women stalked round to the back of the court and reappeared minutes later, disdaining further conversation in a streak of bright red Jaguar.

Yates had been given unconditional bail and was due to appear again on 15 January 2001. 'And a very merry Christmas to you,' muttered an incredulous Mac Hobley.

To the uninformed reader, the next morning's press celebrated an innocent scapegoat. 'I was only returning machine,' said the accused to his local daily, the *Derby Evening Telegraph*.

Adam Fresco's report in *The Times*, however, reflected an interesting use of language. 'I had no intention of taking any reward for the repatriation of the machine,' said the accused. Asked why he did not go straight to the police, Yates explained that it would have meant involving his client: 'He is a man of high office and it would have embarrassed him.'

To my mind, Yates's self-vindication was based on a tenuous argument that whoever was behind G312's theft, had persuaded the client Yates claimed to have into parting with £25 000 for it and Yates had been engaged to retrieve his alleged client's money. If the transaction had been honestly conducted, I thought, there would be no *mens rea*, no criminal intention and therefore, no guilt. The conduct made this difficult to believe, but could it be proven in law?

Although 15 January was the date for the hearing that would commit to a date in the Crown Court, the defence engaged in a series of tactics to delay the evil day. At the very last moment, Yates's solicitor tried to get the case moved to Derbyshire, onto home ground, because, he argued, the jury would be unbiased. Eventually, the examining magistrate decided that there had been enough prevarication and cost. A date was set. The case was due to come to court the same day as the *Enigma* film premièred in London.

CHAPTER TWENTY-EIGHT

Magic watch

Film history was made by the USA's National Cryptologic Museum Foundation when in May 2000 it recorded a group of US alumni from Bletchley talking at an open meeting about their experiences. *The American Experience at Bletchley Park* was the Foundation's first film and the interplay between participants brings alive the Ultra-Magic relationship. 'Never before had sovereign states revealed their vital intelligence methods and results even to their closest allies,' wrote Bradley F. Smith in *The Ultra-Magic Deals*. The consequences of this secret alliance about secrets was more far-reaching than either nation had imagined, for, says Bradley Smith,

> They also knew that each side had learned too much about the other's highly secret activities to make possible a return to the earlier condition of total independence in which a constant cryptanalytic war prevailed of all against all.

'These days, almost every time there is a war theme in television programs, at least in Europe, it turns out that Bletchley is in there,' said Major-General John Morrison, National Cryptologic Museum Foundation chairman and a former director of the US National Security Agency, introducing the reluctant movie stars to their audience.

British-born Barbara Abernethy was an early starter in the cryptanalytic field. An administrator in the British Foreign Office in 1937, she 'had German, French and Flemish — a pretty limited language', and after joining the advance party to ascertain

Bletchley's suitability for its wartime purposes, Miss Abernethy was mystified by her transfer to BP's Italian section where, she said, 'I learned *buon giorno.*' Barbara Abernethy continued in administration and over the war, she got to know about all the Americans despatched to Bletchley Park under the Ultra-Magic arrangements. Her future husband Dr Joe Eachus was one of them. Joe Eachus came from Op 20 G and his function was to select the intelligence to be sent back to the US Navy. All three services were represented at Bletchley but the navy élite came in for a certain amount of special treatment and there was a jibe that a communications liaison person, Geoffrey Tandy, had to be appointed at BP to communicate efficiently with the US naval section. (Tandy himself had been recruited due to a misunderstanding. He knew about cryptogams, but these turned out to be algae rather than ciphers. However, he did advise most effectively on how to preserve documents damaged by seawater.) 'The navy was a separate body,' said Selmer Norland, tongue-in-cheek. 'We did have a liaison near to Hut 3 so we had some way of getting in touch with the navy without ...' he paused for effect, '... going back to Washington!'

Selection for Bletchley had seemed haphazard to American initiates. Bob Button signed a bulletin board in the regular army's signals intelligence service quarters and does not remember seeing other names besides his. He was sent to Grosvenor Square in London's Mayfair district for an induction course and found himself at Bletchley in the summer of 1943. Walter Sharp, a US army mathematician, was questioned about his aptitude. 'What do you know?' asked his interlocutor in a southern drawl.

'I've been to pre-radar school,' replied Walt.

'Today we don't need no radar. Today we got cooks, truck drivers and cryptographers.' Sharp chose the lesser of the evils and became a cryptanalyst, serving at Bletchley between 1943 and 1946.

Selmer Norland had been teaching German in a southern Minnesota high school. After a Morse aptitude and 'wire' tests, he raised his eyes to the blackboard, Chalked up was the day's priority: cryptography. 'I don't remember that I ever heard the word before, so I asked, "What's cryptography?" and the officer said, "Well, I don't know. It's censoring mail, I think."'

The Americans' induction and training for Bletchley ill-prepared them for the voyage of discovery ahead. 'Paul Whittaker and I were two members of the first shipment of Arlington Hall people to be integrated at Bletchley Park,' said Selmer Norland.

> Paul had a PhD in German from Munich and apparently the Brits were concerned whether I had enough German. I had a degree with a major in history and a minor in German. I'd taught high-school German for three years. While I couldn't discourse the finer points of Goethe and Schiller, we didn't see much of that in the Enigma traffic.

'My first problem at Bletchley was the language,' said cryptanalyst Arthur Levenson.

> I went to a room and was stationed between Major Babbage, a Cambridge mathematician who mumbled to me in incomprehensibly 'refeened' language. The other side of me was a Scottish chess champion, Dr Aitken. He spoke a foreign language and 'Brooklyn' was impossible for them.

Levenson, his wife Marjorie (Midge) and Bobby Hooper (Osborn at BP), met me in April 2002 at a resolutely English hostelry in London called 'Grumbles'. Levenson expounded on his discussion with American former veterans of Bletchley. They all agreed about the impenetrable language, 'though,' joked Levenson, 'we never had any serious "grumbles" and somehow we grunted our way to comprehension.' Abbreviations were the most difficult, according to Selmer Norland. The British kept files, maintained by Trevor Jones, on these and many linguistic variations, all recorded in context.

Midhill Farm Station was the venue for preliminary training recalled by Walter Sharp. Cryptology classes were held for signal corps army people.

> We got as far as simple substitution, playfair and we fiddled with the Hagelin machine – it was very introductory.

When you hit Britain, there were three days of class and then on to Enigma. It was like going from kindergarden to graduate school in a very short time.

Nevertheless, those who received their Enigma training at the hands of John Herivel were mightily impressed. 'John was a very nice, Irish mathematician,' said Art Levenson, 'who achieved immortality through his "Herivel tip".'

Messrs Levenson, Sharp and Norland were involved in a project about one of three radio intelligence companies coming from Arlington Hall. They each rejoiced in their unusual assignments. 'At the risk of inviting controversy,' said Norland, 'I had the best job of anybody at Bletchley Park. There is nothing like taking the end product.' Norland was in Hut 3, taking messages for emendation and translation. However, Art Levenson 'went to Hut 6 where the good jobs were. Each of us was assigned a key or two of which we were guardians and we had to ensure we had the right cribs.'

Bletchley Park notions of Americans, 'probably came from the movies', said Selmer Norland, and there was equal initial apprehension on the US side. British-born Barbara Abernethy was advised 'to draw the curtains. The Americans are coming.' She disingenuously describes her job after the 'shooting party' days as: 'to go in with a great cask of sherry, which I could hardly carry. No doubt it was to "soften them up". It seemed to work!' Any reservations between the nationalities rapidly dissolved. 'We were treated royally,' said Norland,

and given every opportunity to learn the ropes. I tried to abbreviate by writing, 'from the 17th thru 21st instead of, 'from the 17th to the 21st inclusive', and to sneak in American spelling – it seemed a shame to have extra letters in words like 'labor' – but they never let a single one of those Americanisms survive.

'The English stereotype was very stuffy, no humour, they didn't speak till introduced,' said Art Levenson. 'I didn't find any

Englishman like that at all. They fed us when food was rationed. We went to their homes.'

Bob Button's experience in 1942 bears this out.

Christmas was coming and the British Red Cross was looking for families that could entertain we 'poor Americans'. The word came that they could take three up in Barnes, a grand district in south-west London. Off we went to Castlenau. Well, I found out later that the family had scrimped, begged and borrowed from friends. The table was groaning with fine food, including a turkey. You wouldn't have believed there was rationing.

Decima, one of the young ladies there, was asked to sing and agreed – provided someone would play the piano. Button, with a musical gift and ear for transposition, stepped forward. The strains of 'You made me love you' rose over the whining air-raid sirens, whose intrusion the assembled party, led by Decima, chose to ignore. The pair saw one another from time to time, and on D-day a package for Decima somersaulted through the letter box. There was a ring, without any words. 'Must be from your American,' said her family. Indeed it was and, said Button, 'This was an Enigma marriage.' The gallant Joe Eachus claims that his greatest discovery at Bletchley was Barbara, who exchanged her Abernethy for a partnership of Eachi. Both couples still reside in the USA.

British gastronomy was somewhat constrained on occasions. Selmer Norland 'learned to eat very gingerly because of the lead shot peppered through the rabbits'. The advent of the US camp at Little Brickhill, a village near Bletchley, turned the culinary tables. 'The Brits appreciated a lot of things, said Walter Sharp. 'After dinner at our camp, one of the Brits went to the bathroom and when he got back, I asked him what he thought of the fare. "Great," he said. "That was the softest toilet paper in four years."'

A letter from Hut 6 director Stuart Milner-Barry to William P. Bundy, a major in the US signal army corps at the end of the war, underlined the strengths and characteristics of the Ultra-Magic alliance. 'After taking over as director of Hut 6 I was informed by the Director that a large body of Americans was bearing down on us, I viewed the prospect with some consternation ...' Milner-Barry was not aware that he imminently needed recruits, but he soon changed his mind, writing, 'It was one of the luckiest things that happened to Hut 6 and one of the nicest things that has happened to me personally.' Like many of the British, Milner-Barry had had preconceived notions about the Americans and assumed that the United States had to show the world it was best at everything. 'The best of your men were quite first-rate,' he wrote, in glowing understatement.

> That is shown by the number of key positions they occupied but I never met any men less anxious to claim the credit to which they were entitled. I speak for the hut as a whole – to work with so friendly and likeable a crowd of men is one of the things that has made Hut 6 a unique experience for me.

This positive outcome might not have been predicted from the early Anglo-American rounders game at Bletchley, when each side consoled the other on having lost and vowed not to have a rematch. They had been playing by different rules. Gamesmanship was endemic in the Enigma crew. Milner-Barry was chess correspondent for *The Times*, Hugh Alexander a national chess champion and Jack Good, Cambridge champion. They challenged Oxford University to a match, with the understatement, 'We have the best chess players in England and we want to challenge you.' So it was they went to Balliol. 'It was the finest silver and the finest china I ever ate off, but the food was awful,' ruminated Levenson. 'As a matter of fact, we were quite lucky to win. The victories came on the lower boards. There was no return match!' Levenson said.

Although the Americans at Bletchley concurred that 'there must have been "British-eyes only" material', they did not have the impression of being excluded. Norland could, 'go in any door in Hut 3 but I didn't dare go into Hut 6'. Joe Eachus, who was acquainted with Turing, was a rare exception to the 'no travel' rule and on one occasion showed 'The Prof' around Washington, commonly known as 'DC'. The street-naming protocol intrigued Turing. Eachus explained that the roads were named in alphabetical order, words of one syllable. When they had reached the twenty-sixth street, they started the alphabet over again, with two-syllable names. 'That's great,' Eachus reports Turing saying, 'and what do you do when you get to 26 with the numbered streets?' 'Then he realised what he had said,' Eachus smiled, 'and after a brief pause he went on enigmatically, "Well, I guess you could go to 6, 26."'

Art Levenson remembers that Turing was a very good long-distance runner who rode an old bike to work. One tooth of its sprocket wheel was bent and one link on the chain was defective. Whenever that link came over that tooth, the chain would come off, followed by the rider. Turing's method of repairing the anomaly was to count the number of teeth on the wheel and the links in the chain. Realising that they were relatively prime numbers and did not have any factors in common, he instantly knew that they would only come together at the product of the two numbers. Turing rode along counting and when he came to that number, he just moved on the chain. It never fell off when he was riding it.

Thus the Americans and British learned to cherish one another's individuality and quirks, which were a very human consolation and distraction in the teeth of the vicious problems confronting the Ultra-Magic team in the Second World War. 'It was a problem-solving game,' said Joe Eachus. 'A great deal depended on being able to read what the Germans were about to do.'

'It's very hard to make a machine foolproof,' said Art Levenson. 'The fools are much smarter than the foolproofers – they think things you would never believe.' Levenson was sure that the German 'COMSEC' (communications security) people 'dismissed any suggestion their machine could be broken.' The Germans were convinced that the Allies did not have the resources, even if they had the theoretical technique. It was also, said Levenson,

'The cryptographer's arrogance. There was an attitude, "I created that cipher." And the author couldn't believe it was vulnerable.'

Allied codes and ciphers were broken by the enemy, as Levenson acknowledges. 'They did succeed, on Hagelin particularly and when they sent "depths", we saw intercepts with the plaintexts written in.'

As the war advanced, there were signs of the impending changes that could doom Ultra-Magic codebreaking attempts. 'We were all frightened,' said Levenson, 'because we were hanging on by the skin of our teeth. In fact after D-day, on the Fish (cipher system), they began to change the keys daily instead of monthly.'

Walter Sharp admitted that 'Getting near the end of the war, there was a great fear that the Germans would make a change that would put us out of business. I guess that happened all during the war.'

An echelon higher than even the Enigma traffic was the communications from Berlin to the supreme commanders, including Von Rundstedt. These messages were long and strategic, whereas Enigma was more tactical. Pressure was on at Bletchley to build more Colossi, Colossus being, said Levenson, 'in a sense, the first digital computer and it was very vital in breaking the Fish machine, called "Tunny".' Bletchley needed four or five more of the Colossus, which was composed of 400 vacuum tubes and other high-priority materials. Levenson recalls that word got through to Churchill, whose great faith in cryptography was again rewarded. It is intriguing to speculate on what might have happened had not Allied Enigma breaks truncated the war.

'When Op 20 G got the four-wheel Enigma problem, the Brits mostly stopped working on U-boats,' said Joe Eachus.

The air force used three-wheel Enigma and the British were really good at breaking that. They knew when and where the German Air Force would be attacking England and they would be there with not many planes to meet them.

'On the Enigma,' said Walter Sharp,

> there's something at the end called an *umkerwahlze* – it means turnaround or something of that sort – and the Germans had a pluggable *umkerwahlze*. Two days before the end of the war the Germans said, 'On such-and-such a date we will begin using the pluggable turnaround.'

Sharp took the message next door to the control room where he found Bundy, Nigel Forward and others. 'Forward jumped about 20 feet in the air.' The war was almost over and the news did not make a bit of difference, 'but that was the only message I ever read completely,' said Sharp.

Sharp had worked on part of the Enigma problem. Next door had been George Hurley and Bill Bundy, his commanding officers, putting cribs against messages to devolve possible 'clicks' between ciphertext and plaintext. Then the 'menus' were sent to the bombes to turn up potential 'hits'. These 'hits' came out to another section and they tried to prove whether it was a hit that would go on and be capable of breaking further messages, for some of the hits were spurious. After the decoding room, a technical translator such as Selmer Norland would take charge and the intelligence would be passed on 'to some general, somewhere'. 'We were part of a very important organisation,' said Sharp, 'though we had no idea where the war was going.'

Being a translator, Selmer Norland had the satisfaction of finalising the message jigsaws. 'You'll never know, unless you've done it, how interesting it is to pick up a message … "The Führer has directed … Signed, Adolf Hitler." That was a real thrill.'

By talking about present-day Bletchley Park, the international intelligence, cryptography, computing, communications and political communities go to the root of the Ultra-Magic relationship on which so much hope and experience is founded. As a report said, many years after the Second World War, there is no sense in US COMINT (communications intelligence) without understanding the British contribution in the shape of Bletchley Park. Yet Ultra-Magic was, and is, much more than an agreement on paper – it is an understanding between peoples and a treatment of their common fears, aspirations and beliefs. Bletchley Park opened the door to its British and American recruits for further involvement and employment in a vital activity that is at least equally important today. 'It was a barrelful of experiences,' said Art Levenson, and for Joe Eachus, 'My belief is that through our activities at Bletchley Park, we were able to shorten the war appreciably.'

One cannot help but wonder what advances the Allies might have made, had not Bletchley's technology and records, so we have been told, been destroyed. 'In a time of war,' said Winston Churchill, 'the truth is so precious that it must be attended by a bodyguard of lies.'

CHAPTER TWENTY-NINE

A tangled tale

Lies or half-truths were what Dennis Yates had been feeding journalists (or so police thought) to get them on side before the moving feast of a trial. It came as some relief that the excitement of the film based on Robert Harris's novel *Enigma*, being premièred in London, was not overshadowed by a court appearance in Aylesbury. The Yates trial had been inexplicably postponed yet again, and a day of legal argument was set for 26 September (which stuck in my mind because it is my younger sister's birthday). The defendant's attempts to have the trial transferred to Derbyshire and changed every which way to make it as inconvenient, time-consuming and stressful as possible for the prosecution had been brought to a close by Judge Daniel Rodwell, QC, a man with definite opinions.

Aylesbury is a place where I had had occasional meetings, or travelled through en route to London when the usual M1 exits from Milton Keynes were blocked. I took especial care to contact the Crown Prosecution Witness assistance department specified on the papers that had required my attendance right from the beginning of proceedings. As I discovered on the Wednesday morning, an hour in advance dissolves into ten minutes late when the car park on a map has disappeared under a new building. Aylesbury had never struck me as so busy or such a through route until that morning.

Jettisoning the car in an approximately local multistorey, I went hotfoot to the market square. The cameras had got there inhospitably early and I swallowed my tension to greet a

scattering of resigned faces. 'We don't expect a great deal of action today,' said Central Television's Simon Garrett. 'The police say it will be at least a six-day event, maybe more.' An unsociable curse was confined to my head as I thought about my groaning in-tray. 'Would anyone like a coffee?' I asked, quickly rejecting the idea as I glanced at my watch and the court's forbidding façade.

Imposing, light-green doors studded with thick metal bolts dominated the market square. A huddle of traders dispensed bargain goods and foods. From a converted caravan opposite the court's entrance, hotly indistinguishable drinks were being doled out with good cheer in a vain attempt to compensate for the poor amenities. Apart from the handful of journalists stamping their feet to disperse the chilly breath that hung in the air, there was no passing traffic. In front of me rose a wall of silence. Up the bleak concrete steps, contained either side by black railings rigid as sentinels, I rushed. The portals loomed and a viewing panel immovable from the outside offered no clue. It looked like the entrance to a vacated Gothic prison. I twisted the handle left and right. One door lumbered open just enough for me to slip inside and I was engulfed. My eyes blinked to adjust to the Dickensian gloom. I heard a voice before its owner became visible to carry out a cursory security check. The incongruous electronic scanner hummed inattentively.

To the left was a broad wooden staircase whose rich tone had diminished through neglect and down to the right, a dark wooden door lay confused in shadow. The grand staircase's destination was concealed and I climbed hurriedly, suddenly surfacing in an open space like a diver coming up for air. To the top of the stairs at the left sat a solid wooden desk manned by an attendant in uniform. Above soared a once-magnificent rectangular room, warmly panelled in wood. A carpet divided a series of upholstered benches either side of the desk and, as I handed over my papers for inspection, all faces were turned towards two high doors in the wall opposite. I looked at the people's unreadable backs.

'They're running late,' said the officer, 'Perhaps you'd like to get a coffee?'

I certainly did, though the canteen wasn't apparent.

'Afraid we don't have one here, but you can nip out to the market square, there's a stall doing takeaway.'

Instead I opted to run over the copy of my 'witness statement', a document comprising all the sworn testimony that I had given during the investigation. Moving along the wooden balustrade that defined the staircase's well, I felt the room switch to 'animation'. Simon Chesterman and Dave Buckenham turned round and got up to greet me. Near the entrance to the courtroom on the benches to the left was a group of three, two men and a woman, laughing confidently. I sat down with Simon and Dave, dropped my briefcase to the bench, glanced across to the three whose conversation stood out from the hushed murmur and froze. My gaze flicked back and forth. Chesterman and Buckenham exchanged glances. Simon told me that Aylesbury is a very old-fashioned court, there wasn't another of this type in use in the area. They didn't have the usual facilities and there weren't separate rooms for prosecution and defence. There was no enclosed witness box as there had been in Milton Keynes court and, innocent until proved otherwise, over in the corner, his solicitor and wife were rooting for Dennis Yates.

A briskly pleasant middle-aged woman with an air of practised do-gooding introduced herself. 'Crown Prosecution Service, CPS, witness support service.' The official was sorry that the CPS hadn't been able to be in touch sooner and wondered, did I get the map? I explained about the car park. She didn't know why they sent that out-of-date photocopy, she had given them these new ones. Here it was, for when I parked on the other days. Sorry for the inconvenience. Now, as I knew, she chattered on, they were expecting mainly legal arguments today and I might be called into court later on. If I did take the witness stand, I would be asked to do a swearing, that is, to repeat a pledge. Was I familiar with it? I remembered as a student bringing a case against a driver who had knocked me down on a zebra crossing.

The outcome should have been cut-and-dried, I thought, until the moment when I was asked to swear an oath invoking the Christian church and more besides. Feeling teenage unease with the moral commitment, I had asked for the secular version, then insisted on it although the court had some difficulty in producing the alternative pledge. I wouldn't be repeating the mistake. 'Yes, thank you, I know what's involved,' I said.

The morning wore down and, bolstered by takeaway coffee, I worked through my papers, deprived of a mobile phone through etiquette and inhibition. Chesterman, Buckenham, their officers and legal representatives were permitted to sit through the intermittent proceedings in court, whereas I, as a witness, was not. Defence and prosecution barristers were called for discussions in chambers with the judge. Yates's small cluster grew intense. By now, I was browsing through Chesterman's newspaper, which happened to be *The Times*. I had made a few trips down to the entrance, where the mobile phone signal reception was thin, but going outside would have entailed fresh security checks and being caught out on camera. Each time I turned my back on the benches across the carpeted aisle, I felt a cool stare follow me down the stairs. I walked more slowly than usual, soberly dressed in a long-skirted black suit whose fine white-striped grid and white school shirt (one of Sofy's old ones) softened the effect. My face was as neutral as can be for one that is accustomed to being expressive.

Yates's prehensile fingers were agitating the tie knot at his collar and his wife hovered nervously at the perimeter of the group. His barrister addressed him and their urgent huddle defied the room. The pair's conversation was a rumble, lacking the confident edge that had penetrated the earlier part of the morning.

On the other side, Dave Buckenham was explaining that there was a negotiation underway. 'Nothing is certain yet, but they've lost the legal arguments. The judge has swept them away. Our man was brilliant.' 'Our man' was a barrister from a prestigious set of chambers, chiefly skilled in forensic dissection. He had respectfully pared away the defence's chaff, revealing that the kernel of their arguments was insubstantial. Mr Justice Rodwell, being very focused on using the court's time effectively and minimising the already considerable strain on the public purse, had continued in session beyond the lunchtime break. 'We won't have long,' said Dave Buckenham. 'Let's nip across to the caff in the local department store. I can brief you then.'

Simon, Dave and I nodded to the reporters busy padding out the lunchtime broadcast and hurried through the improving day and gathering shoppers to Aylesbury's superior shopping quarter. We walked via the local multistorey, where Chesterman and I recharged our cars' parking permits. A perfume-counter waft confirmed our arrival in the store and we wove through the ground floor, avoiding consumer products demonstrations. At the bottom of the ubiquitous escalators, there came a cry of recognition.

'Hey, Dave, fancy seeing you back on your old patch!'

'I'll catch up with you in a minute!' said Buckenham, though he did not reappear for the entire remaining lunch.

'We've got twenty minutes,' said Chesterman. 'Let's grab something at this counter.'

The food queue was shuffling forward, so we opted for coffee and a quiet table against the far wall, artfully separated by wooden latticework. 'The position is that the barristers are working on a plea bargain.'

'Involving what exactly?' I asked.

'Yates has been charged with handling and with blackmail. It's possible that if he pleads guilty to the one charge, the other will be taken into account,' replied Chesterman.

'Meaning what?'

'Meaning that the defence has realised the strength of our case and they're throwing in the towel. But we'll see what transpires when we get back.'

Preparations for the prosecution had been exhaustive. Buckenham and his team had double- and triple-checked statements. They wanted to avoid being tripped up on a careless detail or a technicality. Fulton and Dickinson's 'threads of intelligence' had been meticulously woven into evidence, plotting the departures and arrivals of mailings and mapping telephone calls: Grendon, Kensworth, Isley Walton, Newhall Post Office, from which Paxman's parcel had issued forth, Melbourne and finally, Litchborough.

Back at the court's gates an air of expectation hovered. Journalists had deduced from the comings and goings and the slightly disrupted routine that a decision of some sort was in the offing. 'Wish I knew,' I replied, as I disappeared into the strongroom as fast as the reinforced doors would grind on their weighty hinges. The Crown Prosecution solicitor was intent on a discussion with their counsel and Dave Buckenham. Yates, his wife and their advisers were seated in a huddle. The accused man framed his face with his hands and rested his elbows on his knees, swaying forwards. Valerie Yates looked bemused and a little crushed. The court environment was austere and unforgiving and, to an onlooker, she seemed to be cast adrift on an alien tide.

'Looks to be going our way,' said Dave Buckenham. 'Yates has been brought around to thinking that he should plead guilty to the handling. If he maintains that he's innocent and loses, which he will, the sentence could be much more severe.'

'It's a bit complicated,' said Chesterman, 'but what that means in practice, as our counsel has explained to me, is that the blackmail allegation would not be tried, so it would lie on the record and be taken account of in the sentencing.'

What was the thinking behind this arrangement, I enquired.

Chesterman said that it would save the public purse the cost and time of an expensive trial. If Yates pleaded guilty to the handling, the alleged blackmail would be implicit.

It would go without saying, but it wouldn't be said? I wondered.

'Correct,' said Buckenham, 'but all the circumstances of the alleged blackmail will be read out in court, put on the record and the full story will come out.'

I heard the words, they were the experts, but I wasn't clear how the lawyer expected to get the full, I meant 'the works', story out if the case folded suddenly?

Buckenham shuffled his papers and muttered that 'we would have to see if the prospect of a conviction followed by a sentence might have some,' he hesitated, '... effect'.

To me, it seemed like a done deal. The prosecution could insist on pursuing the blackmail charge, but why would they risk irritating the judge unless the pursuit would unearth the hare that had been avoiding capture from the outset: the person who set up the middleman? I sat to the side as discrete groups conferred with one another, occasionally interacting with court officials or disappearing to the courtroom. Leafing through my diary, I wondered if the Bletchley Park Trust Board meeting for which I had given my apologies would have concluded and whether there was a rush hour in Aylesbury that would delay my getting back for a 17.30 meeting on town planning in Milton Keynes.

'... and so what we need to do now, Christine,' Simon was saying.

'Pardon? Sorry, miles away,' I stuttered.

Chesterman sat down on the bench opposite. 'He's pleading guilty. It's over. We need to agree what we're going to do about the press. I've asked our senior press officer to come over and advise us. Of course,' he continued, 'we can't be sure until we actually get in to court. It's caught us by surprise. We didn't expect them to give in so quickly.'

Everyone had been caught by surprise; 'on the hop,' as Dave Buckenham put it. Not least the media, apart from Central Television and Three Counties Radio, for after the early-morning broadcast caucus, the journalists had retired to concentrate on more imminent news. In the absence of the senior police press officer, who had been very rulebook-orientated on previous acquaintance, a junior novice had been substituted. It was his first big opportunity, he had just started and he did not know which way to turn. Barely concealed incipient panic was making him incoherent and he mopped the sweat beads adhering his straight black hair to his temples. I was saying that the media that had waited months for a conclusion were miles away. The obituary had come too early. Of course, it was possible that by the next day they would be diverted by another story, but that would be no worse than the result the press officer would get that night. In my opinion, no one had had time to get their stories together, the news would be bumping into drive time bulletins and the press people needed to get their copy filed. I suggested we make a brief statement that evening and hold a news conference the next day. I thought it warranted that.

'Seems sensible to me,' murmured Chesterman.

'I'll buy that too,' said Buckenham. The press officer closed his eyes in relief.

'By the way,' I said, 'if the case does wrap up, is there another way out of here, otherwise we'll be pursued for interviews?'

'I'll check it out,' said the press officer.

The clerk of the court had gone in and the court was about to resume. I enquired of an usher whether I would be allowed in. 'Oh, yes, the press are going in over there.' The usher gestured to a narrow staircase at the far right of the reception hall, behind the principal stairwell. Chesterman and Buckenham had gone through at ground-floor level and, apart from the desk official, the reception hall had drained of people. I creaked up the steps and perched on a folding seat by the door with several spaces between me and the scattering of journalists. Central's Simon Garrett gave a broad grin and winked, as well he might, for he had already put together a film with interviews from Nick Fielding and others including me and it would either be scrapped or virtually ready for broadcast should there be a sudden turn of events.

It was the first time I had seen inside the courtroom and some of its details were lost on me as the judge had already started speaking. A narrow public gallery overlooked the scene from its left and right, with a deeply alcoved terrace at the back. If I half-stood, I could see the top of Yates's thinning hair and an array of unrecognisable officers and lawyers. Mr Justice Rodwell presided crisply from behind a traditional wood bench, solid and solemn with the insignia of justice. I withdrew into my seat. Rodwell was reading from a script. His tone was descriptive, not judgemental and he was setting out the known facts of the Enigma machine's theft, handling and the blackmail attempt. I retreated as far as I could go in my seat and listened, like a rabbit caught in headlights.

Mr Justice Rodwell read as if it were an incantation from the document TF1 first discovered by Trevor Fulton. Yates's account cast a new light on the reason for the Enigma theft. The judge ran through all the letters and the phone calls. He made it clear that some of the evidence available to the court had not been produced, it not being in the public interest to do so. I was hearing for the first time in public that the Abwehr Enigma machine had been stolen to damage my career and to discredit the Bletchley Park Trust. The plan had been to deliver it to Bletchley Police Station on the day after the theft, with a note to say that 'that woman' − the same 'that woman' of the vicious letters − 'was incompetent to run Bletchley Park'. Journalists' pencils were skimming over shorthand notebooks. As Rodwell continued his measured explanations, late-arriving media representatives excused themselves past me to fill up the vacant places in the public gallery. Yates's account of 'the chain of events surrounding the theft and subsequent repatriation of Abwehr Enigma G312' was read out in court. It spoke of Yates's 'client who remains an innocent party throughout', and Yates claimed, 'I do not know the identity of the person at BP.' The press gallery pricked up its ears as the reading continued.

A certain disaffected party, who was not happy with the appointment of 'that woman' as director of the BP Trust, decided to try and undermine her position by arranging for the theft of G312. To this end he was prepared to invest £2000. He knew that this would be the last chance he had to embarrass her with the theft of the 'Jewel in the BP

Crown', because sophisticated infrared devices were being installed to protect the displays and any later attempt would be impossible. A local professional shoplifter was recruited to carry out the 'theft'. It was then to be 'dumped' outside Bletchley Police Station the next day with a note claiming how easy it had been to steal. It was hoped that CL (meaning Christine Large) would be held responsible, forced to resign, her plans for the redevelopment and changes at BP scrapped or put on hold, and the yearned-for days of 'how it used to be' would return once more.

A collective intake of breath rustled the hard-pressed notepads upstairs.

According to Yates, when the potential value of the stolen machine became known, whoever had stolen it to order decided that the payoff had been inadequate and had hung on to the Enigma. Almost immediately, news had appeared about G312's monetary value and, to the 'insider's' consternation, the thief had demanded £25 000, failing which he would 'shop' the person who had set up the theft. The insider, it was written, had started to look for a way to raise the money, which is how, Yates claimed, he and his client had become involved. Allegedly almost four months had elapsed before Yates had been approached by a person whose wont was to enquire about items of possible interest for purchase.

With the early scoop by 'Geordie' Fulton in having found Yates's account, the police had researched Yates's carefully strewn clues in the document. Fulton and Dickinson had not accepted Yates's feed at face value. They went back to his computer and extracted the edits and additions to the final text, revealing many inconsistencies and winnowing probable fact from likely fantasy. Yates's tale explained how very difficult it would have been for the client, whose agent had contacted Yates 'routinely', to have known that there had been an Enigma theft. The client 'lives in India, is of high office, is a very reclusive person' and was unaware of the theft (said the client's agent as 'quoted' by Yates), 'because of his lack of English and non-IT knowledge'. Reporters were intrigued to speculate about why a high-powered, non-Western gentleman with no particular interest in technology should have developed a taste for acquiring Enigma machines. Did the client exist or not? Investigation showed that Yates and a colleague had gone out to Calcutta and had stayed in a hotel there while, said Fulton, 'Dealers brought the gear to him'. The 'gear' in question was, as a general rule, watches but Yates also had a talent for selecting what looked like junk but increased in financial promise after restoration and passing through a chain of buyers and sellers. A rusty musical instrument picked up for £8000 found its final home after a £32 000-transaction.

Mick Jagger entered briefly into the investigation when he was rumoured by Yates to have been interested in buying an Enigma machine that Yates had his eye on at auction. Trevor Fulton got in touch with Victoria Pearman, Enigma's executive producer and the woman who made things happen for 'Mick' (as I discovered everyone called him). Most of my encounters with Victoria had been mobile; that is, she on the mobile phone being perfectly charming to me but distracted by the need to instruct companions in the room or the road at the time. While I waited for her to focus on Bletchley Park, I envisioned an elegant, long-haired child of the 1960s, clad in a mildly floral, floor-length print dress, wearing huge dark spectacles and marshalling unruly picnic baskets and perspiring champagne chillers with the point of a frilled umbrella. Victoria eluded Geordie Fulton in person, though he managed to establish that Mick Jagger had purchased 'not a four-wheel but a three-wheel and from Sotheby's, not Phillips, the auctioneers named by Yates'. The price had been 'a snip', £1400.

Fulton contacted Phillips. Yates had preened himself on having been 'filmed and actually seen on television buying it', but Phillips had computerised their records four and a half years before the Enigma investigation and the evidence trail faltered. Then the auction house produced a paper record of an

Enigma sold for a surprising value in April 1993. Jon Paul, whose California home is a temple to Enigma, invites very few visitors to his Crypto Museum of Marin. Paul is a regular and welcome visitor to Bletchley Park and keeps a gentle finger on Enigma traffic – information and artefacts – around the globe. When the Swiss Government released six or seven machines, Jon Paul was able both to augment his sublime collection and to trade one, in 1993, at Phillips. The £20 000-asking price was obtained. Dennis Yates went and paid £23 000 cash for the Enigma, a price, Jon Paul was led to understand, that the purchaser thought excessive (though Paul managed to sell another machine in July and again netted £20 000). Fulton discovered that Yates had been a bidder for the second machine, on which a purchaser had failed to complete. A stolen driving licence had been left to secure the lot at the auction house but it was never recovered, leading Fulton to conclude that Yates had driven up the price to justify the first Enigma's cost to the client. Yates's account states that this machine was bought for the same client as the G312, but Enigma expert Dr David Hamer was not maintaining a comprehensive purchasers' register then and cannot verify the claim.

'It was like going up and up a tree trunk,' says Trevor Fulton, 'along branches or small twigs and, for a time, we kept coming back to the core because the line of evidence petered out.'

Fondness for a jet-set lifestyle may have diminished Yates's profits from overseas trips – unless an amenable client was footing the bill. New York was the scene of another sojourn in Yates's high-rolling itinerary. Ever responsive to his client's needs, Yates had agreed to fly to New York because his client's agent told him that (or so his account said), his 'client was concerned about the machine having now heard about the theft of G312', and Yates had volunteered to go and check whether it was the authentic missing Enigma. 'He further indicated,' wrote Yates, 'that if it did turn out to be stolen, then he would seek to return it and get his money back, as he put it, "one way or the other". This I took to mean he would use it as a bargaining piece, which later proved to be the case.' Apparently, G312 was to be flown to New York in a diplomatic bag for the inspection. Mr and Mrs Yates flew to the Big Apple by Air India (an appropriately exotic touch), their passage 'mysteriously upgraded' to first-class, and stayed in Broadway's Holiday Inn. Yates kept a ballpoint pen from the room as 'evidence'.

FBI agent Larissa Mentzer was advised afterwards by, the bureau's attorney in London, 'not to comment on this case at the present time', but she and two fellow agents were Fulton's and Dickinson's nominated passports to a clean and above-board examination of the true Yates itinerary. Armed with correct visas from the US embassy in Grosvenor Square, London, the two intelligence specialists landed, wide-eyed as if from Ellis Island, in NYC's Times Square.

'The Federal Plaza was like going through a time lock,' remembers Fulton. 'We went through one door, then another. We were met at each by an agent and finally we came up in the FBI building's open forum.'

'Are you gents carrying?' asked Special Agent Mentzer.

She was referring to guns, of course, and after the merest pause, the two Brits chorused, 'No, ma'am.'

In the USA, the British officers had no jurisdiction and the agents were punctilious in ensuring that their evidence-gathering fell within the laws of the land.

It was a wildly different world from Geordie's north-east birthplace and adolescent images of coal staithes, bridges and docks were as remote as the Industrial Revolution. An ex-electrical engineer, he had joined the police fired up by a hunger for knowledge and who-dun-it. The Enigma case angles and dimensions were meat and drink to Fulton, whose experience of running an antiques stall on Sunderland's quayside had led to a passion for fine objects with a history. He was storing up this criminal curiosity along with other mysteries that maybe one day he would convert into detective novels.

Once the FBI had seen the two officers handle a couple of interviews, they relaxed and let them get on with burrowing through their Big Apple evidence-gathering. They were quartered in the Holiday Inn, a clean and pleasant modern hotel near Madison Avenue. The trail led not quite to 'an office on Madison Avenue', where Yates 'was shown the Enigma my client had purchased', but to a jeweller's gallery on Fifth Avenue. The glass door to the broker-jeweller's plush and hushed emporium opened up on a thickly carpeted hallway with cases lined either side like the rows on an airliner. A glamorous hostess whose collar and ears were afire with flamboyant gold and jewels greeted them with reserve. Fulton's suede shoes betrayed their custom but his direct northern charm soon won her over. She and the boss recalled an Ebay transaction with a watch being sold by two individuals and the shop had taken its usual commission for bringing buyer and seller together. A Rolex, naturally. Knowing, because of his telephone calls, that Yates had received a parcel at his hotel, Fulton and Dickinson tracked down Yates's contact with an individual who had seen a chronographic, £12 000-watch on the Ebay auction site and had wanted it for a client in Italy. While his wife was going to the airport, Yates collected the goods.

Word by word, line by line, fiction by fiction the detectives deconstructed the fanciful and self-serving account. Yates had used incidents from real life and warped them to his purpose of, as he believed, proving himself and his invisible client to be the honest and injured parties he made out. It must have been frustrating that, although

> The insider was asked to try and broker a deal with BP for its (G312's) return in exchange for the sum of £25 000 as paid by my client ... he refused, saying he would immediately be suspected of being involved in the theft because of his position

and despite overtures to persuade the insider that the only way for honour to be restored was to return the machine publicly, 'the person at BP refused to become further involved'.

The remaining text of TF1 is an approximate sequence of events leading up to the moment when Yates prepares to 'negotiate repayment for my client and the rotor's (sic) return with him'. Destroying the Enigma machine is a notion that elicits Yates's advice, 'not to act too hastily' and the document raises a few matters clearly irksome to their author. 'I must make it clear that at no time was the term 'the master' ever used by anyone other than CL, who appears to have had her own agenda for using it.' 'Master' appears in the second demand letter sent to Central News and Channel Four, one of the series produced on a wartime vintage typewriter. 'Dear Sirs,' it begins, 'I am instructed by my estemed, (sic) master to indicate this letter to your goodsel (sic) ...' and later on, 'There is no right of anyone from who (sic) the machine was got to say their right is more than my master ...' For good measure, a final appearance is made in the concluding line: 'not responding to this final offer will result in the machine to be destroyed as my master will not lose face by any means'. This missive went to television stations, not to me as Bletchley Park director, and its colourful language was a gift to journalists. Yates's reaction suggested to me that he was not the author of the first letter.

Yates's second gripe is accurate, in the sense that his facts are correct. It refers to the first call and states, adversarially, 'despite CL's claims to have been contacted by me at 4-30 in the morning after the midnight deadline it was in fact 4-15pm on the same day. I will leave you to decide her motives for this lapse of memory.'

Motives generally require forethought and what actually happened was that calling journalists the next day said to me, prompted by a rare slip of Simon Chesterman's tongue, that the call had been made at that time. Not having talked it through with Simon, I assumed he had a reason for letting the idea prevail and as I had anyway been working till way past 02.00 (a call of this nature tends to have a wide-awakening effect), I did not distract the callers by entering into a debate about it. The police had asked me not to mention Yates's afternoon call till they had had time to consider the implications and I had put down the phone and almost immediately taken another call from a journalist. The 'four-thirty a.m.' timing had inadvertently decreased the chance of mid-afternoon media enquiries to check whether there had been a repeat performance. It was quite lucky that the middleman had got through the barrage of other callers.

Finally, Yates's document questions whether 'his client's ... trust was misguided and that no ... "benefactor" ever existed.' Not long after the Abwehr Enigma disappeared, several individuals had offered amounts of up to £1000; in one case, to set up a fund to reward informants who might lead to the machine's recovery. Alan White, the British Telecom property chief who had a positive influence on Bletchley Park Trust's land negotiations, had got agreement for a £5000 'fighting fund', and I believe that BT's security arm could have made the money available in bona fide circumstances. They would certainly not have done so without a professional negotiator being in control.

Yates's document introduced an Indian client of high office and other notions, which had, for the best part, been checked out by the criminal investigators. However, there was no getting away from the red-handed demand phone call to Nick Fielding, nor from the evidence trail established by the police. Yates pleaded guilty. He would be sentenced on 19 October, pending which Mr Justice Rodwell followed the convention of calling for reports on Yates's character and background.

I turned sideways to facilitate the stampeding journalists' exit. 'Can I have a word with you afterwards?' 'Hi! Remember me? See you in a minute,' they went. The upper benches had cleared and down below, ushers were shooing out the court. The alcoves at the back of the gallery looked quietly inviting and I paced the short walk there, settling back into the dusk-filled recess. What did I feel? Mild shock, I think. A need for solitude. That the old files about my period of 'exile' from trust affairs had been reopened, releasing a rank stench of cowardice and spite.

A movement disturbed the shadows. 'Christine? I thought I saw you slip round here,' said Andrew Norfolk from *The Times*. 'Mind if we have a chat when you're done?' Fifteen minutes had passed and I started like an interloper caught unawares.

I mumbled I would be 'down in a minute', as I struggled to recover myself to the present.

The mood among the winning team downstairs was light. 'I'll carry your bags,' offered the police press officer as I congratulated Simon and Dave. A press conference had been confirmed for 11.00 on the next day, Thursday, at Bletchley Park. Yates and his entourage had swept out, circumscribed by an order for bail surrender of Yates's passport.

I took a deep breath and pushed open the outer door with both hands, arriving on the top step flanked by the Enigma case's two prime movers. There was a phalanx of cameras and microphones – journalists had frantically been telephoning their offices – but I was clear in my own mind what needed to be done. Tomorrow, there would be a bit of competition to take the credit, but here and now was time to define the news. I advanced, but not far, down towards the expectant media. 'This is a great day for history,' I said.

> The police have done an outstanding job. And I think you ought to talk to the people who have done all the work. There will be a news conference at Bletchley Park tomorrow at eleven a.m. Thank you.

Turning around on the spot, I left Chesterman and Buckenham and slipped back through the iron gates. They had seemed slightly surprised, but not displeased.

Fifteen interminable minutes later, Chesterman and Buckenham joined me in the cells, through whose yellow, gloss-coated corridors we passed to elude further questions. 'See you in the morning, then,' said Simon. 'Mind how you go!'

'You too,' I said.

Mental autopilot delivered me to Milton Keynes, possibly via a circuitous route. It had gone 18.00 and thankfully, the planning meeting had convened in a quiet bar.

For Trevor Fulton, the news that Yates's case had collapsed early signalled a new phase in the investigation, not its end. Fulton had followed Yates's map to Alice Fletcher's grave to its illogical conclusion. Yates fancied himself spy material, perhaps, but he was not the consummate undercover professional he portrayed himself to be. He made too many mistakes, like the inaccurate directions to the cemetery. The route Yates had specified, the long way, petered out where there should have been a sign. 'No way was it on the map,' thought Fulton, who had backtracked to a large roundabout, taken the third exit, gone a way up the road, before finding the missing direction panel.

'Like the bullshit about why Yates chose the cemetery, within sight of a farm and outbuildings, across open fields.' The document loftily implied some mystery behind the plenitude of 'Yates' graves in the location. 'As a matter of fact, "Large" was very popular among the occupants, but Yates didn't pick that up either,' Fulton ruminated.

He should know. The burly, persistent detective had checked the background to each and every tombstone in case it might yield intelligence. In reality, Yates had played football for the team from the nearby Ostrich pub and *that* explained his choice. When Fulton's police constable colleague had 'turned over' one of Yates's cars, a Ford Granada, it was filled with colourful products from the antiques trade: a Wm Younger monocled figure, a Gaymers 1911 painting and a Falstaff Ales pub sign. There were business cards too, 'Dennis Yates – Just call me.' Just call me.

'Well,' Fulton pondered, 'I haven't called "time" on this little affair yet.' There were inconsistencies, leads begging to be followed. There was just too much that didn't make sense.

CHAPTER THIRTY

White kid gloves

Michael Apted's film of the Enigma novel ended with panache, redolent of the pyrotechnic extravaganza in his James Bond film, *The World is not Enough*. The problem was that, unlike the novel, its logic was hard to follow. Tom Jericho, the reclusive codebreaking hero in Robert Harris's novel, enters the film having been recalled to Bletchley Park after suffering a nervous breakdown. We learn that the cause is not, as did happen in the real wartime Bletchley, the intense intellectual pressure of generating solutions to almost impossible problems. Jericho collapsed from unrequited love for Claire Romilly, a bright and mysterious femme fatale who, to paraphrase her roommate Hester, Romillies her way through the Park's susceptible males at a prodigious rate. Claire disappears from Bletchley at the same time as Bletchley's ability to read key German U-boat codes is lost, and there are suspicions of skulduggery. Jericho uses his return to the Park as a cover for the quest to protect Claire. By the end of the film, the miraculously restored and physically slight Jericho makes an astounding trip to Scotland, travelling without official sanction or apparent petrol coupons. His pièce de résistance is a daring chase across a channel where an absconding Pole is set to reveal Bletchley's secrets to the German enemy.

'The Polish Ambassador is on the phone for you,' said my PA. Instinctively, I stood to take the call. It had not been anticipated. The ambassador was exceedingly exercised by the treatment of Poland and the Polish contribution to breaking Enigma in the forthcoming film. His press attaché had briefed His Excellency on the preview screening. At that point, I had not seen the film, although the Trust's chairman, Sir Christopher Chataway, and his wife Carola had managed to squeeze in the screening at short notice. My principal recollection of their debrief had been Carola's delight at meeting Kate Winslet au naturel in the Ladies, where she had been unaffectedly feeding her young baby.

In his novel, Robert Harris is at pains to highlight the awful truth about Katyn, where Stalin, then an ally to Britain, massacred over 14 000 Jews. Katyn refers not to one but to three massacres. The first took place in a forest not far from Smolensk in Russia in 1940 when Stalin ordered the execution of 4500 Polish service personnel taken prisoner when the Soviet Union supported Hitler's 1939 invasion. A further 10 000 men imprisoned in two camps were murdered at around the same time. Aleksandr Solzhenitsyn wrote, in *Gulag Archipelago*,

> They took those who were too independent, too influential, too noteworthy; they took particularly many Poles from former polish provinces. (It was then that ill-fated Katyn was filled up; and then too that in the northern camps they stockpiled fodder for the future army of Sikorski and Anders.)

Understanding the Katyn massacre goes some way to explaining the strong official and unofficial Polish reaction to the Enigma film. When the Germans exhumed the Polish corpses in 1943, they claimed for propaganda purposes that 11 000 bodies had been uncovered and blamed the Soviets, though later admitting that the correct figure was 4254. At the Nuremberg trials for war crimes, the Soviets also used the figure of 11 000, knowing full well the true figure as they had carried out the massacre. Hermann Goering was blamed by the Soviets, who were trying to conceal the victims in the two camps at Starobiersk and Oshtanow. However, the Soviet accusation was eventually disregarded by the international community and it went unrecorded in the final judgement at Nuremberg. It was not until 1989, with the collapse of Soviet power, that President Mikhail Gorbachev admitted that the Soviets had killed the Poles and disclosed two other burial sites. Today, the debate about the exact number of Polish people massacred and the location of the graves still excites controversy.

Until the Bletchley Park Trust took the initiative of commemorating the Polish contribution to breaking Enigma, at a moving ceremony on the sixtieth anniversary of the Poles handing over Enigma secrets to the British and French, the Polish nation considered that Britain had not ostensibly recognised this outstanding feat. Official histories do record what the Poles achieved and Dilly Knox always made a point of paying tribute, as his entry in the *Dictionary of National Biography* shows. According to Bob Baker of Hut 6, a Pole had been billeted with chess champion Hugh Alexander, for, said Baker, 'They used to play all night and work on the day shift.' The two Polish mathematicians responsible for the inroads into Enigma and who escaped from Poland were not allowed anywhere near Bletchley. At the time, this made perfect sense because protecting Bletchley's secret was of paramount importance but of course to the Poles themselves and their fellow countrymen, it is something of a tragedy.

Thanks to Eugenia Maresch, archivist at the Polish Institute and Sikorski Museum in Great Britain, I am able to share extracts from Marian Rejewski's papers that disclose his state of mind.

A few comments on the present difficulties which the Polish section of German ciphers is encountering

During the French campaign the Polish analysts were assigned to the 'Bureau de Chiffres'. Instead of concentrating on research, they were dealing with ordinary traffic, a task

which could have been done by the general office staff ...
After the fall of France [June 1940], the cryptological work
was performed under conspiracy.

The background is that the British government was reluctant to
co-operate with the Bureau because of the ambiguous Vichy
Government. A memo, classified at the time, asks, 'We must ask
them [the Bureau]: Who are their masters (i.e.) If they are officially
paid by a government which may join the Nazis at any time, it is too
risky for us.' Too close a collaboration could have resulted in losing
the entire Ultra operation and, possibly, the Second World War.

When France was overrun, the *Biuro Szyfrow* had to be
liquidated and all materials, instructions and a replica of an
Enigma machine were hidden in a secure place. Some Polish
cryptanalysts were arrested and went to German prison camps.
Rejewski and Henryk Zygalski managed to reach England. They
resumed work at the Polish Research Centre in Stanmore and
Boxmoor – not at Bletchley Park.

The British recognised, in a secret memorandum that 'without
this liaison with the Poles, arranged by the French, we might not
have been able to break [Enigma] in 1939 and thereafter establish
daily contact'. On 9 January 1940, the then director of Bletchley
Park, Commander Denniston, wrote to his head of service
saying, in respect of the three Polish cryptanalysts,

If we are faced with a change [in Enigma] on the outbreak
of war (and we begin to suspect it), the experience of these
men may shorten our task by months. We possess certain
mechanical devices, which cannot be transferred to France.
These young men possess ten years' experience and a short
visit from them might prove of very great value.

Rejewski, writing in 1944, was of course unaware of the British
arguments and he found his isolation from top-level cryptanalysis
deeply painful.

It would be fitting to remind the English that they owe a
debt of gratitude to the Polish Cyphering Bureau ... it is

worth emphasising ... what precisely the Polish crypt-analysts expect from their English colleagues. First, they should be asked to return the Enigma machine which was given to them ... Subsequently one should enforce an agreement so that they would share their experience on German ciphers ... Lastly, one should try to persuade them to pass on the intercepted traffic material. This would be helpful as the Polish possibilities are very limited.

Rejewski was grateful for the 'exceptional hospitality on French soil' and referred to 'a personal bond of friendship' but he recognised that 'while the French co-operation would produce results at a later stage, the Anglo-Polish joint effort would show results almost instantly'.

Against this background, the Enigma film at one level portrays a Pole, Pukowski, as being prepared to divulge Bletchley's secret to the Nazis in retaliation for having discovered the Katyn massacres through Enigma decrypts. The fictional character Pukowski wants revenge on the British Establishment that, in the novel, seeks to prevent its Soviet allies' dark secret being discovered. Film rarely allows for the subtlety of plot in a full-length novel and it is not surprising that the Poles, an exuberant and passionate nation, reacted violently. The heroes of Enigma breaks portrayed as villains of the piece? 'Totally unacceptable,' said the Polish press attaché. 'The film has hijacked our history and we intend to make strong representations.'

Dr Stanislaw Komorowski, the Polish ambassador, was a model diplomat whose great discomfort at the misleading portrait in *Enigma – the film* was expressed in reasonable and controlled language. It nevertheless became clear to me that His Excellency would be declining the distributors' invitation to the London première, which had been intended as a peace offering, because he would not wish to embarrass His Royal Highness the Prince of Wales by making inappropriate representations. There had already been several intemperate radio interviews and a volley of pointed letters in the national press from aggrieved Polish organisations and individuals. I wondered whether Bletchley could pour oil on troubled waters and together with Aleksander Kropiwnicki, a counsellor in the embassy, we put together a conciliatory programme.

Our first move was to include an extended section on 'Polish Enigma' on the Trust's website. The Polish contribution was flagged up in a series of lectures entitled 'Action this Day' (there is a highly recommended book by the same title) and on the sixtieth anniversary of the letter to Churchill pleading for more resources dedicated to 'Ultra', 21 October, the Trust ran a special series of Enigma lectures at Bletchley Park in the presence of His Excellency the Polish Ambassador and in which an eminent panel – codebreakers Mavis and Keith Batey and Derek Taunt; Professor Czechanowski and Frank Carter – amply and ably expounded on the Polish wartime code- and cipher-breaking achievements.

Counsellor Kropiwnicki had been invited to say a few words on the subject at the Enigma preview held for Bletchley Park on the day after the London première, but his considerate words upset director Michael Apted. Although the film promoters had been warned about the Poles' presence and speech at the Bletchley dinner, Apted was like a man from under whom the ground has been cut. 'I've never been in a situation like it,' he fluttered.

'It will be fine,' Sir Christopher Chataway (who had become the Trust's chairman) attempted to reassure him. 'Just recognise the Poles' importance in all this and thank them for being here.'

But the film director was moved to an unpremeditated, emotional reply.

Dougray Scott, who plays the film's lead, brilliant codebreaker Tom Jericho, rose uncertainly to his feet afterwards and emoted, 'Bletchley Park, I want you to know that we love you all.'

At the 2001 Enigma Festival and exhibition opened by Robert Harris, he remarked, 'What a shame they didn't use the Bletchley Park mansion in the film.' I find it hard to dissent – there's still magic about the place.

CHAPTER THIRTY-ONE

Golden afternoon

'In Enigma, the factor is totally irrelevant,' said Art Levenson. The factor is the total number of possible combinations of all the machine's variables. 'The Germans thought a twenty-six-letter crib might do it, but who could get that? Well, in fact, we could do it on a much shorter crib, but we did get twenty-six letters via the message headings. For instance, "Daily report from this date" was frequently twenty-six letters!'

Levenson's comments define the nature of Bletchley Park codebreaking and the truth about Enigma – a brilliant concept whose near-perfect potential at that moment in time was undermined by the humans who used it. The human factor was decisive in Allied code and cipher war victory and Enigma was a fundamental component.

At first glance, realising the odds against reducing possible combinations of Enigma keys to discernible messages should have stopped any attempt to do so in its tracks. From discussions I have had with former codebreakers, the 'attack' on the problem starts with total intellectual immersion in it, the 'left brain' assembling disparate information. Then the mind starts to relax and lateral 'right brain' thinking kicks in, which is when solutions start to appear. At first, the problem can seem repellent, like an impenetrable crossword puzzle, but as the next clue emerges, it becomes obvious what the previous piece is. Codebreakers are looking for pattern recognition, something that the human brain is incredibly good at and computers are not. Breathtaking short cuts are ways of destroying randomness

by seeing patterns – linguistic, numerical, pictorial, spatial and combinations.

Being methodical is the worst possible approach. Compare the 'brute force' original bombe design, crunching through sequences to help determine whether cribs could be used to decipher Enigma messages. Welchman's insightful diagonal board made the bombes more efficient at a stroke by chopping down the number of combinations to be tested. Take Turing's approach to codebreaking, which he likened to finding a needle in a haystack. Method would suggest that the haystack should be divided into equal segments and searched. Turing would have thrown away each piece of straw until he found the needle. 'Which way round does a clock go?' asked Dilly Knox. Clockwise – the methodical answer – is wrong, if you are the clock.

It was fortunate that brilliant minds such as Dilly Knox's did not revere mathematics or probabilities and that talented intuitive codebreakers such as one of his assistants, Mavis Lever, reached their solutions without being inhibited by conventional processes and logic paths. Mathematicians' contribution was no less significant, though radically different in methodology and utterly suited to the exigencies of mechanised encipherment. Gordon Welchman's innovative diagonal board again comes to mind, for it substantially reduced the hunt for tell-tale 'stops' on the bombe machines developed with Turing, enabling teams to identify cribs that could be used to break keys and get out messages within a meaningful time. Engineers, and especially the electronics engineer Tommy Flowers (though his most groundbreaking work was not related to breaking Enigma) and Doc Keen who turned the bombe concept into a manufacturing reality, sit high in Bletchley Park's pantheon of pioneers. Losing sight of the total Enigma operation would, however, distort reality for it was not about half a dozen people in a wooden hut winning the war. The few were critical to success and it would not have happened without them; but the many were essential too. First, the people, eventually around 12 000, operating within Bletchley Park. To take examples, cryptographers depended quite heavily on the administrative staff logging radio traffic whose analysis and interpretation fuelled their daily Enigma breaks. Where too would the codebreakers have been without colleagues to translate their discoveries and assess the intelligence therein? Without the external 'Y' Service and the RSS units receiving and transmitting information, Bletchley would have been deaf and dumb. Worldwide, it was the centre of a vast wireless- and cable-encrypted communications network through which messages were pumped to the node most likely to produce a solution. As the true story here unfolded has shown, having timely information on the enemy's plans and situation was no guarantee that it could or would be used. Breaking Enigma to break the opposition involved acts of faith, hope and imagination before there could be results.

Indeed, the first Enigma results were not very exciting as they yielded mainly snippets of travel and recruitment administration. Not only was the intelligence culled less than thrilling; there was no frame of reference within which to evaluate it and the puzzles presented – such as a sheaf of decoded numbers that turned out to be map references for airfields – were unfamiliar and perplexing. It was the invasion of Norway in April 1940 that, in Bletchley veteran Peter Calvocoressi's opinion, first indicated Ultra's potential. Yellow Enigma cipher breaks came right at the beginning of the campaign and in contrast to the Green cipher's administrative content, breaking it revealed operational information, in this case on the Norway invasion. Enigma decrypts supplied the precise details that conventional sources – photo reconnaissance, observation and agents – had been unable to do. A breakthrough came between the time that Belgium capitulated to Hitler and he signed an armistice with the French: Red Luftwaffe Enigma yielded permanently to Bletchley codebreakers' techniques and it became a daily staple in the intelligence diet. Red Enigma revealed the Germans' massive strength in France and it may have prevented military resources being squandered on a hopeless quest, but the Luftwaffe Enigma's quality needs to be seen in an operational context for its challenge and use to be understood; the sources temporarily dried up after France fell and the German Air Force reverted to using land lines. Hitler's dominance in Europe severely impacted information through Allied diplomatic reporting and secret agents, increasing Enigma breaks' value.

During the Battle of Britain and Operation Sealion, the aborted invasion of Britain, Red Enigma intelligence showed the scale of the Luftwaffe effort to be directed against Britain. 'Red' dealt in significant issues and generalities rather than implementation and tactics but occasionally there was a jewel, as when the Allies found out that Hitler had disbanded the staff unit set up to control England's invasion, despite Hitler's attempt to maintain a deception that the staff was operational. Such material evidence proved invaluable in allocating troops and equipment to other arenas, the battles with Italy in Africa being an example.

The point at which Ultra revelations first had a major effect was during the blitz of winter 1940–41. Germany aimed to destroy Britain's morale, industries and ports by a sustained and terrible night-time bombing campaign. Three radio beams were used to guide the Luftwaffe to its targets and by understanding these aids used by German bombers, the British were able to foil the plan. There was an Enigma cipher called 'KGr100', which communicated with the German technical unit responsible for developing the beams. The pilots flew their craft along the beams and, at the intersections, bombs were automatically dropped. Two months before the blitz began, Bletchley had deciphered the first KGr100 message and later a single message pinpointed the existence of a beam transmission base on the Channel coast, confirming beyond doubt their existence. R. V. Jones, a young physicist, devised countermeasures to deflect the beams from their course and subvert the bombing plans. Intelligence about further beam bases, including details of one still at an experimental stage, was provided during the summer prior to the blitz and Enigma decrypts subsequently obliged with the beams' radio frequencies for each night's attacks and operational exchanges between German pilots coming on duty. Although enormous damage was perpetrated on British cities, Enigma Ultra prevented the crushing defeat that Hitler had wished to inflict.

Enigma breaks had allowed Britain to recover and stay in the war. Confidence in Ultra grew from early 1941, when the Allies were able to track operational moves in south-east Europe and to monitor transport movements through breaking infrastructure providers' Enigma. Hut 3's successes in army and air force Enigma had uncovered scientific traffic. They also disclosed shipping movements between Italian and Greek ports and North Africa and in Africa and, elsewhere, ground force preparations and manoeuvres. German ground and air forces operated as a coherent team, informed through Hitler's espousal of Basil Liddell-Hart's treatise on First World War warfare. Liddell-Hart had theorised that − but for lack of effective communications − tanks, backed up by infantry and aircraft, would be a formidable military force. With the advent of comprehensive, reliable air-to-ground communications in the Second World War, Hitler turned theory into practice. Mid-1941, Berlin was worried about its brilliant but unpredictable General Rommel and despatched a deputy to review the strategy in Africa. Strangely, the army general used the Luftwaffe cipher and dealt the Allies a telling insight into German plans and supply problems. Allied victory might have been assured ... had not the Germans been reading British battlefield ciphers. After sporadic successes in 1941, Bletchley finally sustained a flow of breaks into two rather difficult and time-consuming army Enigma ciphers, Chaffinch and Phoenix, in 1942. At a most critical point in the battle for Africa, Ultra revealed Rommel's intentions to Montgomery, enabling a rout that finally defeated the German general. Rommel knew he had been betrayed, but not how.

Enigma's undoing in the Battle of the Atlantic was the defeat that, while it did not win the Second World War for the Allies, prevented Hitler from doing so. By the end of 1941, the year in which first breaks into naval Enigma had been made, over

25 000 German naval messages had been read, an achievement that was almost tripled the following year. It has been estimated by Calvocoressi that about half a million naval Enigma messages had been read at Bletchley Park and in the Admiralty by the end of the war. Sinking the *Bismarck* in 1941 was a turning point, after which naval Enigma messages flowed till February 1942, when the Triton cipher halted Allied intelligence traffic from U-boats in the Atlantic until the triumphant break of December that year. The four-rotor Enigma's introduction in March 1943 was without a doubt the gravest threat to the naval Ultra source but even it was rapidly surmounted, signalling an end to major German U-boat victories in the Atlantic. Almost 8 millions tons of German shipping and 200 U-boats were at Dönitz's command in the Atlantic during 1942, where in November he exceeded his target of sinking 800 000 tons of shipping per month for the third – and last – time before Triton was broken. Enigma breaks allowed the Allies to engage in and win a deadly game of maritime safari, deflecting convoys away from prowling wolf packs and hunting down the hunters. Stemming the German tide in the Battle of the Atlantic prepared the way for Operation Overlord, the Allied landings in Normandy in June 1944, and other Ultra-supported campaigns in the war's final months.

Overlord's aim was to divert German troops and support away from Normandy, and the complex deception maintained through Operation Double Cross was shown by Abwehr Enigma decrypts to have been sensationally effective. One bogus German agent alone succeeded in diverting a whole German army away from the French front. In contrast, the lack of reliance placed on Ultra before the parachute operation in September 1944 at Arnhem resulted in complete underestimation of the German forces and tragic Allied losses.

Towards the Second World War's end, more political and personal messages infiltrated Enigma, highlighting attempts to jockey for Hitler's position. The successor eventually announced was the doyenne of the Atlantic and U-boat mastermind: Admiral Dönitz.

'A riddle wrapped in a mystery inside an enigma', said Churchill seven months before he became prime minister in October 1939. He was referring not to the Enigma machine or its ciphers, but to Russia, Britain's unfathomable ally and a fascinating, if unresolved, dimension to Enigma's legacy. Fearing a Russo-German pact to share the British Empire, Churchill imparted to Stalin the growing evidence of Hitler's intention to conquer 'Lebensraum' at Russia's expense. Ultra played a large part in the revelations, though Churchill did not declare his source. There was no question of doing so because German high-grade ciphers revealed that they could read much Russian traffic and would soon have known had the Enigma breaks been revealed. How the Russians interpreted this intelligence is guesswork, for Britain's ability to read Russian ciphers had disappeared when Baldwin unwittingly quoted a verbatim Russian decrypt while debating in 1926. The Russian resources committed to tank battles that devastated them suggest that insufficient credence was given to their British allies' confidences. After Germany invaded the USSR, Britain's need to work on Russian ciphers was marginal and the dearth of hard information about Russia's intelligence capability, given its fine mathematicians and technologists, leaves open the door to hypothesis.

When the cold war ended, logic suggested that there would be a diminishing need for British and American governments to maintain such a close partnership on intelligence and security matters. The memory of Second World War information imperatives had receded, as had the threat of a nuclear Armageddon. It costs a serious amount of money to maintain national security establishments and doing so when there is no apparent prevailing major antagonist is rather like financing an entire national health service for a trickle of patients. Yet the wartime cryptanalytic agreements were a marker for the future in several respects. They paved the way for sublimating the politics as rife in security and intelligence issues as anywhere else, to achieve a greater good (although one recognises the implicit value judgements therein). The Ultra-Magic agreements' effects carried on long after the war had finished, in my view a realistic recognition that this particular war set in train a series of changes with whose implications society today is still grappling and among which the policies and mechanics established in the wartime intelligence deals still have a valid role. Remote warfare, mass slaughter and imprisonment, new mass-production methods, new drugs to protect against and combat disease, modern communications technology such as radar, the first digital semi-programmable computer, ground-breaking inter-disciplinary solutions to problem-solving, the first electronic codebreaking, the first wireless encrypted communications network, arguably the Internet's forerunner, jet planes and rockets; these were all products of the 1939–45 conflict. On a political level, the Nazis' inexorable rise, the normalisation of genocide and the prevalence of racially motivated brutality (I hesitate to say 'inhumanity' because it is clearly a recurring feature of human behaviour) from the top echelons down, embracing all ages and walks of life, is a virulent example of nightmares made routine existence and ordinary. Ultra-Magic helped banish that spectre, but not indefinitely. Remember the Ceauşescu regime; think of Kosovo and Slobodan Milosovic's indictment for war crimes. The need for intelligent intelligence does not fade away. Its focus and locus merely changes.

Ironically, the communications technology spawned by Bletchley Park in the Second World War has led to a degree of connectivity and inter-operability that offers major opportunities to reveal ... and to conceal. While global positioning satellites can track individual phone users, Sir Francis Walsingham would doubtless have relished being able to extend his steganography techniques to hiding terrorist information in the pixels of images that appear on the Internet. Joined-up communications, especially the Internet, create the possibility of systemic information attacks, which could not have been carried out when technology was more primitive. For this reason, the US government has opted to build an intranet (an internal internet) dedicated to protecting key national functions from attack. Protected, that is, if the enemy is outside the gates.

Arguments rage on about the benefits of making strong encryption available to all, including consumers. As I write, these debates are largely contained within government policy-making circles, the academic community, security chiefs within banks and industries whose value would be destroyed by an encryption crisis, and the specialist information security companies who want to be poised with market-ready products having the right degree of protection. Consumers may not realise the meaning of the padlocks and other insignia designed to signify encryption comfort levels on their computer software, much as information security companies would like to build their brands. Knowing that the security on ordinary computers is very remote from the stronger 'commercial grades' and top-dollar, top-quality military encryption may not have been an issue. However, users who had ADSL lines installed to give them cost-effective Internet access and who were not advised to set up a 'firewall' – software that guards against intruders' attacks – would rightly be angry to discover their vulnerability to twenty-four-hour fishing in personal information from bank accounts to emails. Nubile and voracious email viruses beckon daily in seductive attacks variously motivated by boredom, mischief and revenge. Government computer servers have technological 'sentinels' that try to bar the gates to these intruders and they often, but not always, succeed, much to hackers' delight. Consumers tend to be 'open season' and emails are the thin end of the wedge.

Second World War descriptions and analysis frequently focus on the war's origins, national positions, key campaigns, battles and personalities, cutting off in September 1945. Studies published from the mid-1970s can inform their thinking with material drawn from the aspect of secret intelligence, 'Ultra', joining midway through the conflict with US 'Magic'. Yet aspects of the war that transcend national boundaries and preoccupations are those that exert the strongest, though sometimes unseen, influence on today's events and perceptions. Bletchley Park codebreakers on the whole were not preoccupied with the quality of their surroundings and it is doubtful whether some of them would have noticed buildings falling about their ears. In my experience, many of these modest great minds have forgotten that they solved very difficult problems and are surprised when they see others wrestling with expositions. Bletchley's occupants were obsessed with the urgent and seemingly impossible problems in hand. The codebreakers' enduring legacy lies in science and technology, it resides in their blueprint for innovation and ultimately, survival against the odds. In its clever, glossy recruitment brochure, the British Government Communications Headquarters publishes a full-page photograph showing the BBC's Jeremy Paxman with the Abwehr Enigma machine. The text reads,

> Enigma is a huge piece of history – not just in terms of the war, but also in terms of GCHQ and maths itself ... our work has similar ends today ... the maths is a little broader, covering everything from research into cryptography through to computer science.

A most important use of Enigma material happened in 1940–41, during the blitz, when Hitler was carpet-bombing urban targets in Britain. Communications were intercepted between the technicians who set frequencies for beams that allowed bombers to track to their targets. Bletchley intelligence told R. V. Jones where to deflect both the beams and the mission. Enigma's role in the D-day landings was even more crucial. Hitler did not move his troops from the Pas de Calais towards Normandy for ten days after the landings. Had he known about Ultra, he would have been aware that Operation Fortitude and the First US Army Group were a sham and he would not have taken the bait. The 'D' in D-day would have meant 'disaster', for US troops would have landed in the middle of a German division and the Allies would have been massacred on Normandy's beaches.

'Our work has similar ends today.' Perhaps the scale and bureaucracy of Allied intelligence gathering and analysis should have been more deliberately reassessed after the cold war dissolved. Perhaps the security services were slow to appreciate emerging forms of information warfare, with its asymmetric tactics. While giants slumbered, a new opposition, multi-headed like a hydra, competed for the hearts and minds of the brightest technologists and the hardiest fanatics. It secured the financial wherewithal to train its recruits ruthlessly. Nor can the adversary be found in a convenient back office, with traceable identity and a known 'background'. The human equivalent of 'one-time cipher pads' populates the ranks. The foot soldiers are self-selected, expendable assets ready to sacrifice themselves in what is promoted as a 'holy war'. And 11 September 2001 was a body blow to the American dream and the psyche of horrified onlookers everywhere.

'Nine-eleven' also reaffirmed the Ultra-Magic relationship. As US President George W. Bush engaged in his terrible new duties, UK Prime Minister Tony Blair joined him in drawing on the wartime agreements' historic benefits. At their heart was a partnership between two parallel agencies representing two sovereign governments. A coalition of interests was formed and extended, both by nations' request and by the leaders' invitation. New dimensions opened up in collaboration on international security issues. There have been the first stirrings of cyber-diplomacy. The speed and scale of the cross-boundary, counter-conventional intelligence gathering and analysis has its roots in Enigma at Bletchley Park.

In transformational times it is easy to neglect the aspects of our past that must be preserved to carry us into the future. NSA director, General Hayden, said at a meeting in 2002,

It is very difficult for us to talk about the today equivalent of what is going on at Bletchley Park, but by talking about Bletchley Park we build up the kind of confidence and put the human face on the agency that we need in the national debate about us and our tradecraft ... We need to be reminded what represents the best of us and to emphasise those things that do not much change.

General Hayden's then British counterpart in GCHQ was Francis Richards, a leader who has made great strides in modernising the agency while preserving its historic ethos. The two agency chiefs were reviewing what General Hayden called 'the rising global watershed of encryption' made inevitable by exported encryption products. Francis Richards's response went to the absolute roots of Ultra-Magic. He said, 'How many more mathematicians do you think we'll be needing?'

'It's the kind of mathematics and cryptanalysis that was done at Bletchley Park,' said General Hayden, 'and for any of you who think that was our past, I'm here to say that it's part of our future too.'

꧁ ꧂

CHAPTER THIRTY-TWO

Dead reckoning

Irst light tickled the ivory doves plumped around Bletchley's green copper cupola. Nourished by their ancestors' repu- tation as MI6 couriers to secret agents in Europe, the birds skittered lazily down a half-eave typical of Sir Herbert Leon's opportunistic building style and hovered on warming updrafts. Day rose over the autumn park, mellowing harsh contours on the wartime blocks and flattering faded wooden huts. A heady atmosphere infused the Trust's new dawn.

Jovial outbursts enlivened preparations for the mid-morning news conference. The mood was quite unlike the sober-suited briefing before the court case. I had been debarred from attending because the police were very concerned that the other side's lawyers would try to declare a mistrial or say it was impossible to have a fair trial given the media coverage. Sentence on Yates had not been passed and the judicious written statements from Bletchley Park Trust were thrice revised before we felt able to circulate them. In the ballroom at the front of the mansion, the Abwehr Enigma sat resplendent against deep blue panels. At my request, the machine was constantly guarded by a uniformed volunteer. Thames Valley Police press officers bustled around the spacious room. Sun and journalists streamed in. We were running late and, belying tradition, they had arrived early. Simon Chesterman opened up with a resumé of the case. I noticed Andrew Norfolk from *The Times* slip between the wooden wall panelling and people clustered by the door, and spotted Gary Grewal and Dave Barker in the full house. Tape recorders were committing the formal proceedings to the record and I clicked back into Simon's calm testimony on my right.

'There has been a lot of speculation about insider involvement and there had,' he emphasised, 'to be inside knowledge to allow the theft to take place. Someone out there must be very concerned right now – and they should be.'

'We will bring them to justice,' said DS Chesterman, his authority underlined by a recent promotion.

'We will bring them to justice, promise police,' composed tomorrow's headline authors.

'Ensure the disturbed ground is properly reinstated so as not to arouse suspicion,' urged one of the letters referred to by Simon in his review. Yates, he had said, was due to return for sentencing on 19 October.

'This was not a victimless crime,' said DS Chesterman. 'I want to pay tribute to Mrs Large.'

I glanced across to Simon and down at the felt-covered table. This was unscripted.

'Mrs Large was on the end of very menacing phone calls and letters – she is a very brave lady.'

I blushed. My priority was to thank the police and I picked out some of the lesser-known stalwarts in the audience. 'This closes one chapter of the Enigma case, but the book is not finished. People around the world rallied against this act of historic vandalism against the Park, the Trust and ultimately, against me.' I then previewed one of the Trust's next projects – a special exhibition at the Park featuring the prodigal Enigma machine. The opening day would be 1 April 2002, two years to the day that a thief snatched the historic machine and started one of the most fascinating crime stories of recent years. I had unexpressed hopes that Jeremy Paxman would do the honours at the opening.

Interviews and photographs criss-crossed like a cavalcade of popping champagne corks. Abwehr Enigma radiated centre stage. At one point, I sat down in the morning room with a group from the national newspapers.

'Christine,' hissed the police press office junior. 'You do realise there's someone from the *Sun* in there?' He was flapping like a turkey at Thanksgiving and insisted on mounting guard near the door. Enigma's popularity could only help Bletchley Park and the 'red top' newspapers had published some wonderful portraits of codebreakers following the Enigma Festival earlier in September.

Still later, I heard about Andrew Norfolk's devotion to duty. He had been involved in a car crash on the way to the conference, where he was too shaken up to keep pen to paper. The car was a write-off and he camped in my office upstairs by an ISDN connection, where disobliging technology eventually allowed his copy to squeak down the line just before it was overdue.

'"Enigma thieves stalked me," says director,' was emblazoned across the morning's *Independent*. Cahal Milmo had described me as 'no-nonsense', a characteristic that fitted *The Times's* 'spine of steel' tag from months earlier. 'Let me tell you something about Christine,' a source had told *The Times's* Moscow correspondent – presumably chosen for the task because of experience in labyrinthine situations. 'She's tiny. She's a Geordie. But she's got a spine of steel.' Underneath the rhino hide specified by Sir Philip Duncombe in the director's job description, it amounted to a charming physiognomy. Milmo noted that I 'had been forced to remain silent throughout the operation to recover the stolen machine', saying,

> I had to fight for what was right and not be cowed or give in to the kind of behaviour that was demonstrated by Mr Yates. In keeping with the traditions of Bletchley Park, I couldn't talk to my colleagues or the trustees. Except for a handful of police, I had to keep it to myself. It was an incredibly stressful time.

The Enigma story came to a pause although the exhibition continued to provoke mock-outrage comments like, 'talk about turning a problem into an opportunity!' from the BBC's Paul Meurice.

'Far from a simple theft' had been Peter Spindler's appraisal right from the outset. Spindler had a feminist streak and liked 'women who do'. His wife ran a highly successful book business that specialised in recherché texts for the medical profession. 'A woman had taken over Bletchley Park. Not a spy, not Oxbridge, not a civil servant or classic British establishment. I've been involved in other jobs with similarities but nothing ... ever ... quite like this.'

Trevor Fulton still nursed his 'Operation Verify'. Along with many others, he had enjoyed the case's vocabulary and extra dimension. Spindler had dubbed it, 'Operation Madison', and the naming of operations had historic roots. During the Second World War, the Americans and the British trawled dictionaries to extract thousands of potential code words – what else? – that were randomly applied to operations. Churchill carved out his own way, overriding the system and imposing his preferences. The Normandy invasion in which Enigma had played a fundamental part, had originally been called, 'Roundhammer'. Churchill produced the best campaign name of the war when he christened the operation, 'Overlord'. Such was the British Prime Minister's fascination with the subject that he issued instructions on the use of code names, which should not, he said, 'imply a boastful or overconfident sentiment', or conversely, have, 'an air of despondency'. A mistake to be avoided was choosing living people's names, or being frivolous. No mother, he stated, should have to say 'that her son was killed in an operation called ...' (for instance) '... Ballyhoo'. The Enigma theft would have avoided his strictures.

The Sunday following the news conference at Bletchley was special, for I met Charles Collins, a member of Captain Ridley's shooting party, who had long previously published just one short article about Bletchley in his college (Balliol) magazine. His daughter and son-in-law kept conversation flowing. Charles's natural modesty and grace forbore any reference to his accomplishments but it was obvious that he had felt intellectually at ease with the great Bletchley names, whose later eminence in no way affected his humorous and critical faculties. Daughter Madeline stayed in contact and after *The Times* magazine published a feature looking back over the Enigma saga, she wrote,

> It is truly a disgrace and an insult to the memory of all that was achieved at Bletchley Park for anyone associated with the Park to have behaved towards you in such an outrageous manner. My father – now in his ninetieth year!! – was very saddened to read the article. It can only detract from the achievement of those who originally worked at the Park and ensured the freedom we now enjoy, but which some clearly abuse.

On Friday 19 October I stayed away from the court where 'an antiques dealer alleged to have acted as a go-between for the thief who stole the Enigma encoding machine was jailed for ten months,' reported the *Daily Telegraph*. Mr Justice Rodwell said that Dennis Yates had adopted an 'extremely dishonest' course of action.

'You have admitted that you knew this machine was very valuable and that it was dishonest of you to receive it,' said Rodwell

> This was a premeditated dishonesty and one that went on for a long period of time. You had the expertise to know exactly what this machine was – an extremely rare example of a four-rotor Enigma, of which there are only two in the world, and an important and valuable part of our national heritage.

Judge Rodwell added that he accepted that other people had been involved in the theft.

Yates's lawyer John Causer said that Yates had become 'massively out of his depth' after becoming tangled with the Enigma machine plot, a statement condoned by the dealer, who admitted that he knew what he had done was wrong, but said that he had become trapped by circumstances. Dave

Buckenham, who had retired from being a detective superintendent by the time that Yates was sentenced, told Sam Lister
of *The Times* that Yates 'clearly had close relationships with
other people involved in this incident, yet he still refuses to
name them'. Judge Rodwell reinforced this when he said, 'You
were acting thoroughly dishonestly for two months to demand
£25 000. You had control of the machine and issued threats to
destroy it if the money was not forthcoming.' As the hour of
reckoning approached, Yates had unexpectedly changed his plea
to 'guilty' for the first charge, leaving the blackmail charge on his
record unproven.

Yates had a brief spell in Woodhill, Milton Keynes's high-
security jail, before being transferred to a 'white collar' prison
where the inmates were reckoned to be unlikely to attempt
escape or aggression. He was released, having served less than
four months of the sentence. Yates was ordered to report
regularly to a police station close to home and was fitted with an
electronic tag, a tough plastic ankle bracelet that transmitted the
paroled prisoner's position to a satellite, enabling police to keep
tabs on him. Interviewed on the jail doorstep by Simon Garrett,
his principal emotion was anger at the deception he laid at Simon
Chesterman's door. Detective Superintendent Chesterman had
said in October 2001 that police remained convinced it was
'an inside job', committed as part of a plot against me. The
hypotheses about the case boil down to a few plausible theories
and the available evidence is worth re-examining in parts.

No one disputes the 'revenge and disgrace' motive behind the
crime, but the time and nature of the theft raises doubts. Local
shoplifters, runs the argument, would have found the temptation
to brag quite irresistible and police should have been able to track
them down if they existed, especially given the reward incentive.
Second, what if the Enigma machine had been removed from its
case by an insider a while before the theft had been noticed?
Irrespective of the time, only an insider or an accomplice could
have moved the machine without raising suspicions. Yates's
account of his New York visit's purpose is not supported by the

evidence and not a shred of proof was turned up to suggest the existence of an Indian client. Why then, one might wonder, did the middleman decide to carry the can for other parties? At the hearing to sentence Yates, the court heard two recorded phone conversations in which Yates was told by an unidentified individual that he would 'end up in the ground' if the ransom transaction did not succeed. Could it be that Yates had been blackmailed into his financial demands, in which case Yates's behaviour might be less objectionable? The alleged 'blackmailer's blackmailer' was not named in court but the police had discovered his identity, one of Yates's friends who had used a false 'Brummie' (Birmingham) accent to disguise his voice. 'We could just imagine after he'd made the calls,' said a source, 'him getting on the phone again to Dennis Yates and asking, "Was that all right, Dennis?"'

After Yates's release, I was asked for interviews but only agreed to a couple. I assumed that he and his family had found prison a difficult experience, misaligned with his self-image and aspirations. Yates himself was not so coy and vented his spleen, generating some naïve comments by journalists and footage that suggested he would be enjoying a late but 'well-deserved' Christmas dinner.

Sandy McGovern had hoped to attend the press conference at Bletchley Park, under an assumed name of course. Unfortunately, business had intervened and here he was, parked in a mean little back street in some up-itself Home Counties village. The mellow autumn must have addled his middle-aged brain, he thought, because he'd left 'the wee 'un' with his girlfriend. They'd been going steady for a bit and though she was, well, gorgeous, he 'wasnae gonna let another female get her claws in', like his ex of three years ago. McGovern wasn't expecting the object of his attention back for a couple of hours, not unless the flights were delayed or the last lecture overran. He noted a climatologically confused winter flowering cherry, as he counted the petals pirouetting to earth in the soupy air. There wasn't any other action in sight or earshot. The suits had gone in for tea ('supper' in their parlance), those that bothered to come home during the week; and there were no kids around, all left home, or the occasional 'autumn crocus' turfed out to boarding-school. Uniform corporate vehicles, regulation blue or silver (sales reps. unwelcome) stretched up the road, each marking the end of an acceptable short front garden. Here and there, a runt car – second-hand, perhaps a disqualified director fallen on hard times – broke ranks. McGovern sat low in the seat, sipping black coffee from a poly cup. Ever since Dennis Yates's arrest, there had been an unchallenged assumption that the middleman had been pinpointed through a telephone tap on the *Sunday Times* line. 'Stupit bastard,' thought the detective. 'Fancy taking the rap for that worthless piece of shite who called himsel' the Master.' As a matter of fact, McGovern felt a bit sorry for Dennis Yates; he had been the fall guy for somebody else's ego trip.

McGovern and a select few knew that Yates had put the final nail in the investigative coffin when he clicked through to Alice Fletcher's message, buried in the Bletchley Park Trust's website. It was a case of 'When Alice shopped Dennis'. I, the Trust director (and McGovern had had some fun winding me up), had been the only other visitor there and I had straight afterwards faxed a secret number to advise the high-tech team. Otherwise, for sure 'the lads' would have come hammering down my door. An Internet service provider had supplied the team with details of the telephone line through which a second computer had clicked to the baited page on the Bletchley Park Trust website, leading the investigation to the middleman's home. When Yates left his house to telephone Nick Fielding, the field force was ready to move in. They got a fix on the telephone box, followed Dennis and, as he spoke to Fielding, recorded the call for evidence and claimed their 'strike'. 'Alice' was a looking glass, through which they had revealed Dennis Yates.

McGovern stretched his complaining spine and turned on the radio news, volume low. '... and DI, pardon, *DS* Chesterman, what is your last word on the Enigma theft, now that the machine has been returned to Bletchley Park?'

Chesterman's voice came on, 'There has been a lot of speculation about insider involvement and there had to be inside knowledge to allow the theft to take place. Someone out there must be very concerned right now – and they should be. We will bring them to justice.'

'Aye, another promotion in the offing, I dare say,' yawned McGovern. He himself wouldn't be closing in for the finale till they were good and ready. Patience, vigilance and a long memory, that's what it would take to secure a conclusive body of evidence. Hijacking Enigma? McGovern and co. were up for the job till the job was up. Earth extinguished sun and the sky blacked out. McGovern's eyelids fell, but he was still watching.

Epilogue

Yates's written account explained that his personal reason for sending the Enigma body to Jeremy Paxman had been 'so that it would get the maximum publicity for (Yates's) client'. I endeavoured to turn this tide to Bletchley Park's advantage. After Yates's conviction, Mavis and Keith Batey agreed to advise us on the historical and technical aspects of Abwehr Enigma for a new exhibition, 'Hide and Secret'. Jeremy Paxman nobly gave up a Bank Holiday so that he could help Bletchley Park to fulfil its anniversary promise and opened the exhibition, as I had hoped, on 1 April 2002. It was precisely two years from the date of a most notorious Enigma hijack.

Simon Chesterman was promoted to Detective Superintendent in headquarters and is pursuing a steady path towards an ever more influential career. Mr Justice Rodwell had taken the extremely rare step of issuing a judge's commendation to Chesterman for the manner in which he discharged his responsibilities. The video starring Chesterman, buried by Alice Fletcher's grave, still does the rounds at police parties, 'Just in case,' said a former colleague, 'he ever gets too up himself.' Dave Buckenham retired but is keeping his hand in with consultancy work. Detective Superintendent Peter Spindler has maintained his high profile in a string of successful investigations, not uncommonly paedophile crimes involving Internet use. Gerry McGowan, Trevor Fulton and Tim Dickinson disappeared into the woodwork, till their next mission. Dave Barker and Mark Smyth transferred to Milton Keynes's family protection unit. Along with Gary Grewal, their achievements were fêted at an in-house police awards ceremony in Oxfordshire.

Bletchley Park held a very private celebration for all those police and special services involved: the men and women of

Thames Valley Police, the National Crime Squad, the National Criminal Intelligence Service, and the National High Tech Crime Unit. The photographs went to a police museum at an undisclosed location.

Bletchley today is engaged in new battles for survival, for the means to dignify its place in history with a contribution to this century's challenges. Together with trustees, colleagues and volunteers at Bletchley Park, I am pursuing our mission to 'build on the work of the wartime pioneers and inspire a new generation of pathfinders'. The world needs them and it needs Bletchley's memory to reaffirm the significance of Enigma. 'We did not go to the reunion when we saw it announced in *The Times*,' wrote Mavis Batey, 'and we weren't enthused about a backward-looking museum but we were happier when the present aims of the Trust linked to the future were made clear; I think there are many others who would go along with that ...'

The Trust's plan is for Bletchley Park to become a vibrant centre for science education and technology innovation, using its historic legacy to stimulate progress in engineering, mathematics, computing science and languages. Will it work? There are encouraging signs, but the trust's 28-acre site has much outdated infrastructure and capital investment is needed to realise the full plan. The Trust's strategic plan is based on four domains: history, learning, conference and knowledge. From 2002, we opened for visitors every weekend and weekdays too (apart from closure for refurbishment during the winter) and visits were 25 per cent up on the previous year. There should be at least one new exhibition annually and there are many exciting events, including the Enigma Festival, the Churchill Festival and the Polish Festival. An American festival is planned. Millions of pounds still separate us from the compelling major exhibition that tells Bletchley's story.

The Trust's business model shows that visitors alone will not make the Park sustainable in the long term, even at double or triple the number. Conferences, such as 'Action This Day' (2001) and 'Enigma and the Intelligence War' with Christ Church,

Oxford, are important for the future. In the pipeline are a Churchill conference in Washington DC, day schools at Bletchley Park and a symposium on the history of mathematics.

The British chancellor, speaking in April 2002 after talks with the US treasury secretary, urged a new generation coming up through the universities to take up the challenge of becoming codebreakers to track down the secret flow of international terrorist funds. Codebreakers are unlikely to start dropping off the end of a conveyor belt from universities. In wartime, when lives depended on it, there were no government-imposed education targets or sponsored centres of excellence. There was a need and the leadership made resources available. As one irate Bletchley veteran asked, 'Can anyone these days get on with it, flat out, without giving the game away?'

This millennium's generations face, among many questions and problems, grave security issues, related to shifts in the global balance of population and power. Bletchley does not pretend to offer a panacea, but it still has a contribution to make. Codebreaking is neither the province of one particular discipline, such as mathematics (though mathematicians tend to be good at it), nor is it a homogeneous body of knowledge. Often, the breaks happen through inspired guesswork and 'thinking outside the box', for which Bletchley's special history and inter-disciplinary approach to problem-solving provide an ideal environment. The Trust has received a significant grant from the Gatsby Foundation for a mathematics and technology education programme and Bletchley Park is becoming established as a science learning centre. For example, we have held events with hundreds of children, friends and families who brought along their robots to compete in football, robot rescue, ballroom dancing and other activities inspired by Alan Turing's legacy.

Bletchley Park is positioned at the centre of a triangle between Oxford, Cambridge and London. We have been awarded government funds for a technology incubator, due to open across from the codebreakers' lake. Inventors have already established a foothold in the Park's mansion and we aim to accommodate some of the expanding enterprises within the grounds, enabling the innovators to capitalise on their ideas.

My daughter Sofy (then aged sixteen) had been press-ganged by me into appearing for duty at Bletchley Park's first Enigma Festival, in autumn 2001. On the late drive home, I asked what she had thought of the event, anticipating the usual teenage put-down. 'Do you know,' she began, 'I never understood what you saw in *that dump* (meaning Bletchley). Until today. It felt alive. I even think that young people *like me* would be interested.' I knew better than to invite her to elaborate, but she volunteered to give a hand at the opening of 'Hide and Secret' on April Fool's Day 2002, when we had the busiest bank holiday in the Park's post-war history.

Charles Collins wrote, in 2001, about giving:

> deserved praise to the spirit that prevailed at wartime Bletchley Park ... We were naturally all keen to respond to the challenges of the war, a sharpening, an expansion, and an enhanced justification of our peacetime work. Of course as numbers increased it became harder to maintain the informal 'family' atmosphere and enthusiasm, but it *was* maintained to a remarkable degree.

I dream of seeing a renaissance at Bletchley, whose wartime ethos and organisation hold contemporary messages, rich with learning and brimful of potential. Bletchley Park is recovering its family atmosphere, its sense of adventure and youthful exuberance. There is still a distant shadow in the shape of a cuckoo, a graceless bird that lays its eggs in the family nest, stealing its nourishment. Hijacking Enigma G312 put Bletchley Park's existence at risk for 'the Master's' selfish motives. Churchill was prescient: we must be alert and we must 'Never give up'.

Bibliography and Sources

HUMINT

Bletchley Park veterans

Robert Baker
David Balme
The Hon. Sarah Baring
Mavis and Keith Batey
Morag Beattie
Marie Bennett
Robert Button
Charles Collins
Barbara and Joe Eachus
John Herivel
Lady Bobby Hooper
Sheila and Oliver Lawn
Art Levenson
Reg Parker
Alan Stripp
Jean Valentine
Bob Watson

Bletchley Park

Frank Carter
John Gallehawk
GCHQ
David Hamer
Mac Hobley
Merryl Jenkins
Peter Wescombe
Dave Whitchurch

Other interviewees

Dave Barker
Elizabeth and Libby Buchanan
Dave Buckenham
Simon Chesterman
Claire Dean
Tim Dickinson
Nick Fielding
Trevor Fulton
Gerry McGowan
Robert Harris
Oliver Knox
Eugenia Maresch
Major General John Morrison
Mark Smyth
Ron Southey
Peter Spindler
Darren Wray

SIGINT

NO such book

Simon Adams, *Code Breakers*, Dorling Kindersley, 2002
Ralph Bennett, *Behind the Battle*, Pimlico, 1999
Patrick Beesly, *Very Special Intelligence*, Greenhill Books, 2000
Frank Carter and John Gallehawk, *The Enigma Machine and the Bombe*, Bletchley Park Trust, 1999
Peter Calvocoressi, *Top Secret Ultra*, Cassell, 1980
Curt Dalton, *Keeping the Secret*, Curt Dalton, 1997
Jozef Garlinski, *The Enigma War*, Scribner, 1979
Stephen Harper, *Capturing Enigma*, Sutton Publishing, 1999
Robert Harris, *Enigma*, Arrow Books, 1996
F. H. Hinsley and Alan Stripp, *Code Breakers*, Oxford University Press, 1994
R. V. Jones, *Most Secret War*, Hamish Hamilton, 1978
David Kahn, *The Code Breakers*, Scribner, 1996
David Kahn, *Seizing the Enigma*, Souvenir Press, 1991
Wladyslaw Kozaczuk, *Enigma: How the German Machine Cipher Was Broken*, University Publications of America, 1984
Karl de Leeuw, 'The Dutch Invention of the Rotor Machine,' *Cryptologia*, Vol. 27, Number 1, 2003.
Ronald Lewin, *Ultra Goes to War*, Hutchinson, 1978

Dr A. Ray Miller, *The Cryptologic Mathematics of Enigma*, Center for Cryptologic History, National Security Archive, n.d.

S. W. Roskill, *The Secret Capture*, Collins, 1959

Simon Singh, *The Code Book*, Fourth Estate, 1999

Bradley F. Smith, *The Ultra-Magic Deals*, Airlife Publishing, 1993

Michael Smith, *Station X*, Channel 4 Books, 1998

Michael Smith and Ralph Erskine, *Action This Day*, Bantam Press, 2001

Gordon Welchman, *The Hut Six Story*, Allen Lane, 1982

Jennifer Wilcox, *Solving the Enigma*, Center for Cryptologic History, National Security Archive, 2001

F. W. Winterbotham, *The Ultra Secret*, Orion Books, 2001

Richard Woytak, 'A Conversation with Marian Rejewski', *Cryptologia*, Vol. 6, Number 1, January 1982

INDEX

2 for 1 entry to Bletchley Park!

Simply keep your proof of purchase when you buy this book and take it to Bletchley Park to obtain free entry for one person when visiting with a paying guest.

Bletchley Park Competition

Enter the Bletchley Park annual prize draw to win fantastic prizes!

The first 312 correct* entries will receive a year's free membership of Bletchley Park Friends and an Enigma range souvenir. All correct entries will also be entered into a prize draw, which will take place on April 1st every year. The lucky winner will receive a special, behind the scenes tour of Bletchley Park with Christine Large, two years family membership of Bletchley Park Friends and a range of Enigma merchandise.

Simply answer the three questions below and send your solutions to:

> The Hijacking Enigma Challenge
> The Director's Office
> The Mansion
> Bletchley Park
> Milton Keynes
> MK3 6EB

along with **your name and address** (only one entry per household).

Question 1: What is the common factor in the chapter headings?

Question 2: How do the chapter headings relate to Dilly Knox?

Question 3: What is the significance of the annual grand prize draw date of April 1st?

Good luck!

---

* Prizes will be awarded at the discretion of Bletchley Park. Where insufficient correct answers have been received prizes may be offered to the entries which, in the opinion of the judges, are closest to correct.

Bletchley Park Trust

Bletchley Park Trust, a registered charity, aims to secure the historic site's future by building on the wartime codebreakers' pioneering work, celebrating their achievements and using them to inspire scientific progress. Bletchley Park initiated the world's first automated codebreaking and the first large-scale programmable computer – a legacy that the Trust seeks to protect.

Winston Churchill championed Bletchley Park, which was the foundation of the Anglo-American special relationship. Though times and circumstances have changed, Bletchley Park can make a unique contribution to resolving challenges faced by the world today. The Trust runs education programmes, technology incubation, special events, and exhibitions. It is preserving the extraordinary site, which enables us to learn organisational lessons and to gain an understanding of modern day intelligence operations.

Although Bletchley Park receives no public subsidies, the Trust has raised a substantial amount towards the cost of running and revitalising the site where 12,000 people worked in total secrecy at the heart of a global communications network.

Now *you* can be part of this great monument to human endeavour and ingenuity, by becoming a Bletchley Park Friend or making a financial contribution that will help save the codebreaking heritage and inspire visitors and young scientists.

Every amount, large or small, will help preserve and regenerate Bletchley Park, as will every visit, and each purchase made at the Park or through the online Enigma shop. Any bequest made to the Trust is wholly exempt from UK tax. If you or your advisor would like to know more about the Bletchley Park Trust and how a legacy would help, please contact us on +44 1908 640404 or write to us at the Park. To enrol as a Friend, either telephone +44 1908 640404, fax +44 1908 274381, write to us, or visit www.bletchleypark.org.uk

Thank you for thinking about how to make a difference.

Bletchley Park Trust, The Mansion, Bletchley Park, Milton Keynes MK3 6EB
Registered Charity No. 1012743